SHE SHOOTS . . .
SHE SCORES!

Sports are here to stay. And before you think becoming a Sports Goddess is easier said than done, here's a sample of Jean M. McCormick's fellow Sports Goddesses who will give you insider advice from the world of sports:

- Robin Roberts, host of ABC's *Wide World of Sports*
- Julie Moran, host and reporter of *Entertainment Tonight*
- Willow Bay, anchor of CNN NewsStand programs on business and entertainment and former anchor of the NBA's *Inside Stuff*
- Lesley Visser, sideline reporter, ABC's *Monday Night Football*
- Linda Cohn, ESPN *SportsCenter* anchor
- Serena Altschul, MTV anchor
- Jackie MacMullan, *Sports Illustrated*
- Lyn St. James, Indy car driver and automotive expert

and influential women from all walks of the sporting life!

TALK

Sports

LIKE A PRO

99 Secrets to Becoming a Sports Goddess

JEAN M. McCORMICK

A Perigee Book

For my family: my parents, my siblings, and my aunt Helen

and

For #4: Bobby Orr

His dignity, class, and awesome talent inspired my lifelong love of sports.

A Perigee Book
Published by The Berkley Publishing Group
A division of Penguin Putnam Inc.
375 Hudson Street
New York, New York 10014

Copyright © 1999 by Jean M. McCormick
Book design by Tiffany Kukec
Cover art Venus figure from *The Birth of Venus* by Botticelli/Granger collection
Cover design by Charles Björklund

First edition: September 1999

Published simultaneously in Canada.

The Penguin Putnam Inc. World Wide Web site address is
http://www.penguinputnam.com

Library of Congress Cataloging-in-Publication Data

McCormick, Jean M.
    Talk sports like a pro : 99 secrets to becoming a sports
goddess / Jean M. McCormick.—1st ed.
        p.   cm.
"A Perigee book."
    Includes bibliographical references and index.
    ISBN 0-399-52534-3
    1. Sports Miscellanea.   2. Sports Terminology.   I. Title.
GV707.M394   1999
796—dc21   99-34873
                                                              CIP

Printed in the United States of America

10   9   8   7   6   5   4   3   2   1

Sports Goddess \'gä-dəs\ *n.* (1999) 1: a female sports deity 2: an adored woman who knows about sports 3: a sports-savvy siren who has read this book

CONTENTS

viii　　　　　　　　　　　　　　　　　　　　CONTENTS

FOREWORD

NOTE ABOUT THE *author: Goddesses, if you remember the name Chris Fowler, you will immediately connect to the sports world. Chris was the original host of Scholastic Sports America, a critically acclaimed program on high school sports. Today, he anchors most of ESPN's college football and basketball coverage. He also hosts the Summer and Winter X Games, the Olympics for Extreme Sports.*

The first Sports Goddess in my life was my grandmother. Each summer afternoon she sat in a lawn chair behind her apartment building, listening to the Chicago Cubs' broadcasts on her transistor radio. Hits, runs, and errors were all carefully recorded in her spiral-bound scorebook. She could recite everyone's batting average and deliver a passionate monologue on the skills of Ernie Banks.

That those Cubs teams were usually awful, and the games played after June were mostly meaningless didn't matter. She was a fan. And she taught me how to be one. I can't think of a more wonderful and lasting gift.

I thought of my grandmother on a sticky September afternoon in St. Louis' Busch Stadium, wedged together with 50,000 other sweaty souls who shared a common wish for Mark McGwire to provide dramatic punctuation to baseball's best home run race ever. But mostly we came just to salute the slugger. It seemed greedy to expect further heroics.

But McGwire delivered on his second at-bat. His 69th homer soared into the left field stands and the thunderous curtain call lasted forever. Gone was the collective tension. When Big Mac smacked home run number 70, delirium reigned. Strangers hugged or high-fived. I admit it: I got choked up.

I walked out of the ballpark with my voice hoarse from cheering, still smiling and shaking my head. The jaded journalists . . . even the players on the victimized Montreal Expos . . . all of us felt amazed at our good fortune. We had shared in something special.

That McGwire wore the uniform of the baseball rival I'd been raised to hate hardly mattered. I know my grandmother would have understood.

Jean McCormick shares that passion for sport, and a keen appreciation of its power. At the Atlanta Olympics, she and I witnessed it together. Walking to the exit of the wrestling venue, we were suddenly engulfed by an impromptu pep rally of Iranian-Americans. There was no avoiding a sweaty mass of jubilant singers and fervent flag-wavers. It was a sight. Neither of us have a drop of Iranian blood, but you couldn't help getting a little caught up in their nationalistic joy. So, for maybe ten hilarious minutes, we stood trapped—smiling and snapping pictures with our new Middle Eastern friends. Diplomacy on the edge of a wrestling mat!

Jean's credentials speak for themselves. Her journalistic leadership produced a pile of Emmys for ESPN. She has been a friend, colleague, mentor (or all three) to almost every woman working in sports television. But Jean also knows how to cut to the chase and keep it fun. There is no one more qualified to shepherd your passage into Sports Goddess–hood. In case you didn't have a sports-mad grandma, this book will help make up for it.

Chris Fowler
Sportscaster
ESPN

PREFACE

I LOVE SPORTS. I was not a talented athlete as a child. However, I found that following professional teams provided me with a conduit to the athletic arena. I lived in Boston, a wonderful sports town, during the era of the Big Bad Bruins, the Celtics dynasties, and the Impossible Dream Red Sox. In fact, in 1967, I tried to sneak into my father's car when he was going to the Red Sox pennant game. It's one of my first memories.

My parents encouraged my love of sports. My father had season tickets to the Bruins and box seats to the Red Sox. He never hesitated to take his girls along. For my thirteenth birthday, I received a subscription to *Sports Illustrated*. Later that year, I received the Bobby Orr Award from my eighth grade class, for being the hockey star's biggest fan. When I was fifteen, I attended game 6 of the World Series, perhaps the greatest postseason game ever. For years, whenever I sensed a lull in the conversation with a man at a party, I simply said, "I attended game 6 in '75." I never had to say much after that remark.

While my interest in sports never decreased, my interest in many other activities increased. I stopped talking about sports on a regular basis. I attended Wellesley College, an all-women's institution, and I found few opportunities to discuss professional sports with my classmates. However, I made many lasting friendships through my sports participation (my athletic ability had improved by this time). I played junior varsity lacrosse, rowed intramural crew, sailed, and spent a lot of time on the tennis courts.

After college, I moved to New York, enemy territory for a Boston fan, and was the chief researcher at ABC News *Nightline*.

My ability to memorize statistics and standings facilitated my career in research. Occasionally, my sports knowledge revealed itself in conversations with colleagues. They were very surprised. Yet, once they knew of my interest in sports, they sought me out for conversations. I found it an easy way to build relationships.

Then the Red Sox came back into my life. In the fall of 1986, I was a first-year student at Harvard Business School. The Red Sox were competitive again. During the week of my first exam, I read my "case studies" at Fenway Park while the Red Sox clinched the AL pennant. I started talking baseball with my classmates. Of course, the Red Sox humiliated themselves in the World Series, but it didn't matter. I was hooked on sports again.

After Harvard, I returned to my former employer (then Capital Cities/ABC, Inc.) in a very different capacity. I became the first female studio producer and, eventually, coordinating producer, at ESPN, the cable sports network in Bristol, CT. Many, many friends and former colleagues thought I had lost my mind. Who leaves news? Who chooses to work in Bristol, CT, rather than New York City or Boston?

I spent six and a half years at ESPN. I worked for a gracious, gifted man named John Walsh. For John, I helped develop, produce, and supervise the series *Sunday SportsDay* and *Outside the Lines*. I reported on substantive, serious issues in sports and thus never left the world of news. On *Outside the Lines*, I collaborated with Bob Ley, one of the finest journalists (and I'm not qualifying it with "sports") in television. The series tackled such issues as racism, sexism, sexual assault, violence, gambling, drug use, and AIDS in sports. *Outside the Lines* received seven Emmy Awards during my time at ESPN. I eventually left to help set up CNN/Sports Illustrated, a Time Warner Turner network prior to its launch. Once again, I collaborated with some thoughtful newsmen and -women, including, Jim Walton, the president of CNN/SI.

During my career in sports broadcasting, most men and women reacted very differently to my chosen profession. Many of my male friends thought I had the coolest job. Many of my female friends had never watched one moment of ESPN. My male friends initiated conversations with me that would not have occurred without my sports affiliation. My female friends, particularly those in the business world, began asking me for "suggestions" to start talking sports.

In the fall of 1997, I began a two-year appointment as a Visiting Scholar at the Wellesley College Center for Research on Women. I conducted a series of surveys with children, college students (at Wellesley and the University of Michigan), and Harvard Business School male and female graduates. I interviewed male and female patrons of sports bars. I audited two courses in gender studies. I ran research groups with Wellesley student volunteers who tested many of the suggestions in this book.

My studies with Harvard Business School graduates yielded the most interesting results. In my first wave of more than 400 respondents, 99 percent said that the men in their offices talked about sports and 83 percent stated that those conversations were held mostly with men. Moreover, 85 percent said that men in their offices talked about sports with some frequency while only 34 percent of the women did so at the same rate. Most important, 88 percent said that knowing about sports mattered in the business world. Now, my sample size was small and my survey was primarily qualitative. However, these numbers were so overwhelming (even with a wide margin of error) that I included them in reports.

Many respondents wrote comments that yielded crucial insights. Many men viewed a woman who knew about sports positively. Women who did know about sports felt empowered professionally and socially. While most felt that knowing about sports helped, many stressed that "a little goes a long way." Finally, a significant number of men apologized that they might "skew" my survey because they were not big sports fans. However, many noted that even if they didn't follow sports closely, they still were included in conversations because of their gender.

Beyond my surveys lies an obvious truth. Sports play a major role in our society. Many newspapers dedicate one fourth of their content to sports. Most major networks program a significant number of their weekend hours with sports. Many large corporations hire motivational speakers from the mostly male sports world. Sports speak has crept into our social and professional jargon. Yet, the media still portray women in many cases as excluded from or stupid about sports. I counted three different instances on one night of NBC's "Must See" TV. For example, on the hit show *Friends*, Monica asks Chandler, "What should I wear to the Knicks game?" He replies, "A T-shirt that says 'I Don't Belong.'"

Women *do* belong. While I have written a fun and spirited book, I also hope to get across a serious message: women should feel part of the sports culture in this country. *Talk Sports Like a Pro: 99 Secrets to Becoming a Sports Goddess* offers easy and playful suggestions that can help women to understand, follow, and connect with the sports culture in this country. This handbook encourages women to build professional, social, and familial relationships with their newfound sports knowledge.

I hope that *Talk Sports Like a Pro: 99 Secrets to Becoming a Sports Goddess* helps you find the Sports Goddess in yourself!

Jean M. McCormick
Wellesley, MA
March 1999

SUPER SPORTS GODDESSES

THROUGHOUT THIS BOOK, I have included bonus secrets from the following talented women in the sports industry. You could learn a lot by reading only their contributions, which appear in boxes labeled Bonus Secret. I thank all of them very much for their participation in this project.

Val Ackerman, WNBA commissioner

Serena Altschul, MTV anchor

Julie Anderson, HBO Sports producer

Willow Bay, CNN *NewsStand* anchor

Bonnie Bernstein, CBS Sports, NFL studio reporter

Charlsie Cantey, ABC Sport reporter and horse trainer

Linda Cohn, ESPN *SportsCenter* anchor

Emilie Deutsch, ABC Sports coordinating producer

Inga Hammond, CNN/Sports Illustrated anchor

Mary Ann Grabavoy Heaven, former ESPN reporter and lawyer

Sally Jenkins, senior writer, Condé Nast's *Women's Sports & Fitness*

Andrea Joyce, former CBS Sports anchor, cohost of Winter Olympics during the daytime

Deb Kaufman, MSG Network anchor

Suzy Kolber, FOX Sports anchor

Andrea Kremer, ESPN reporter

Sara Levinson, President of NFL Properties

Jackie MacMullan, *Sports Illustrated* senior writer and CNN/SI correspondent

Julie Moran, host and reporter, *Entertainment Tonight*

Robin Roberts, host of ABC's *Wide World of Sports*

Lyn St. James, Indy car driver and former automotive expert

Summer Sanders, host of NBA's *Inside Stuff* on NBC and 1992 Barcelona gold medal winner

Shelley Smith, ESPN reporter

Michele Tafoya, CBS Sports and Lifetime anchor and reporter

Lesley Visser, sideline reporter, ABC's *Monday Night Football*

SUPER SPORTS GODS

WHILE I INTENDED this book to celebrate and promote the many gifted women in the sports industry, I realized that I had to include at least a few prominent men. After all, you do eventually run into them in the sports world! The following eight super sports gentlemen graciously agreed to share a secret or two with neophyte Sports Goddesses.

Chris Berman, anchor of ABC's *Monday Night Football* half-time show and ESPN'S *NFL Countdown*

James Brown, anchor of FOX Sports and reporter for HBO *Real Sports*

Bob Costas, anchor and reporter for NBC Sports, NBC News, and MSNBC

Jeff Greenfield, anchor and political analyst for CNN

Stephen Greyser, professor, Harvard Business School

Fred Hickman, senior anchor for CNN Sports and CNN/Sports Illustrated

Jim Nantz, anchor and reporter, CBS Sports

Charley Steiner, anchor, ESPN

ABBREVIATIONS & TERMS...
for the fledgling Sports Goddess

BS method. How to get out of watching or going to a game like a Goddess. Always **B**e **S**avvy!

G & Gs (Gods & Goddesses). The powers that be in certain sports.

SG (Sports Goddess). What you will be when you finish this book.

SGIT (Sports-Goddess-in-Training). What you are right now.

Sports Goddess Book Review. Summarizes certain beloved sports books for the Goddess. She can read the book or she can skim the summary.

Sports Goddess Experience. What you will have when you start using the suggestions in this book. Dr. Suzanne Moranian, a fellow Visiting Scholar at Wellesley College, came up with this term during her SGIT phase to describe the phenomenon.

Sports Goddess Movie Review. Tells a Sports Goddess what she can learn about a sport from a certain movie. Highlights famous quotes. Summarizes plot from the vantage point of the Sports Goddess.

Sports Goddess Power Talk. Defines popular sports terms and shows how they can be used in a professional context.

Sports Goddess Profile. What a Sports Goddess must know about certain athletes or coaches. The Sports Goddess Profile skips the boring statistics and gives you the most crucial ones, as well as what a Sports Goddess wants to know about an athlete or coach. That's right, the good stuff.

Sports Goddess Tip. A useful suggestion that the SGIT should tuck under her wing.

FIVE INSIDER TIPS & THE GOLDEN RULE

ANY WOMAN CAN become a Sports Goddess. Any woman can become a sports-savvy siren who can hold her own with a guy in a conversation about any professional team or player. I promise. The only person holding her back is herself.

Over the years, I have talked with many women who wanted to know more about professional and big-time college sports. But something stopped them. They didn't have the time. They found the action too confusing. They didn't think that they could "get it."

Whenever I have shared the following five insider tips with women, I have sensed relief. Gratitude. A sense of hope. In addition, women are amazed at the ease with which they can initiate a sports conversation. And how much fun they can have with it! They love the reaction from both sexes. You will, too.

5 INSIDER TIPS

INSIDER TIP #1 You never have to watch a game.

INSIDER TIP #2 Let others do the homework for you.

INSIDER TIP #3 Learn the names of just one or two players at first.

INSIDER TIP #4   **No matter where you live, you can become the fan of a winning team.**

INSIDER TIP #5   **Pick one team in one sport to follow at first.**

GOLDEN RULE   **Think of yourself as a Sports Goddess, and you will become one.**

I developed these insider tips in response to the most commonly heard complaints from women learning about sports.

COMPLAINT #1. "I just don't have the time."

INSIDER TIP #1.   You don't need it. You never have to watch a game.

When you are a full-fledged Sports Goddess, your life may well revolve around your favorite team or sport. However, for now, you are an SGIT (Sports-Goddess-in-Training). So, instead of watching the game, think THIN (**T**V, **H**eadline News, **I**nternet, **N**ewspaper). If you think THIN, it will take you five minutes to find out how any team did, as well as something you can say about the game.

For example, on a beautiful autumn Sunday, your favorite team, the Green Bay Packers, plays the San Francisco 49ers. Now, you can

T Spend three minutes watching on TV the recap on ESPN's *SportsCenter* or *NFL PrimeTime*; you will be told who won, who lost, and the two or three key plays.

H Surf to CNN's *Headline News* or ESPN2 at any point in the evening and wait for the score to flash at the bottom of the screen.

I Zoom to a sports Internet site (e.g., *www.sportsline.com*) and find the score and a recap of the game.

N Read the first two or three paragraphs of the Newspaper summary in *USA Today* or your local paper on Monday morning.

or

Spend nearly four hours watching the game and do nothing else.

Throughout this book, I will offer suggestions on how to watch various sports. These hints will help if you choose to tune in to an event. **However, you still can be a Sports Goddess without watching a game!**

SG TIP. *USA Today* lists every major score from the night or weekend before on the front page of the sports section. If you're heading into a meeting, fold the sports section in quarters. You will find the scores in the upper left quarter. Keep them in front of you at all times.

COMPLAINT #2. "There's too much to learn."

INSIDER TIP #2. Let others do the homework for you.

Sportswriters, sports newscasters, and sports game announcers are very knowledgeable. Almost all of them do their research and know their subject matter better than their audience. They have no alternative. Because it is their job and because sports fans keep track of records and details, they have to be on target.

When I researched for ABC News *Nightline*, I took pride in providing precise and accurate information to the anchor, reporters, and producers. Still, no one ever challenged me on the number of nuclear missile silos in Cheyenne, Wyoming, or the electoral vote in the 1932 presidential election. However, fanatic sports viewers pay close attention to the obscure facts and records. A sports fan might not be able to name the Secretary of Defense, but he can tell you how many home runs Hank Aaron hit during his career. *And* where he hit his last one. *And* who caught the ball in the bullpen when he broke Babe Ruth's record.

Sports reporters have to know their stuff. So you can use their knowledge and make it your own.

Therefore, if Bob Costas (NBC's distinguished sports announcer) says during the World Series, "Hershiser seems to have lost some heat from his fastball," you, too, can say the next day, "Hershiser seemed to have lost some heat from his fastball last night." If Dan Patrick on ESPN's *SportsCenter* tells you that "Shaq was cold from the free throw line," you, too, can assert the next day, "Shaq was cold from the free throw line last night."

I encourage all SGITs to listen to and study these Super Sports Gods and Goddesses. You can see them on NBC Sports and ABC Sports and CBS Sports on the weekends. You can watch them before you go to work or after you come home from work on ESPN and CNN/Sports Illustrated and FOX Sports. You can catch them on your local newscasts or read them in your local newspapers. You can learn so much from them: vocabulary, pronunciation, syntax, and jargon. They are walking, talking sports encyclopedias and dictionaries. Use them to learn more about sports. Men do it all the time.

> I find knowledge of sports to be a very valuable asset. Like knowledge of pop-culture, popular music or contemporary TV, sports knowledge gives you the ability to adapt to more situations. I may not always use it, but when I have, it has helped me to gain respect among some colleagues. Since most of my professional experience is in male-dominated industries (investment banking and high technology), sports knowledge has helped me forge many professional friendships.
>
> —female technology executive

COMPLAINT #3. "There are too many positions and too many players—it's too confusing!"

INSIDER TIP #3. Learn the names of just one or two players at first.

In each sport, there are two or three key players who impact the game more than any of the other players. Find out their names and follow them throughout the game. In football, for example, determine the quarterback's name and pay attention to him (and perhaps only him) during the game. If he has a good game, the team usually will have a good game. If he doesn't, either someone else on the team will step up and perform well or the team will lose. Either way, you'll learn the story of the football game by following the quarterback.

Try it. Keep track of the following players the next time you watch any of these games.

Football	Quarterback, one wide receiver, and/or one running back
Basketball	High scorer and high rebounder
Baseball	Pitcher and hitter with highest batting average or most home runs
Hockey	Goalie and highest scorer

How do you know which player is the highest rebounder or highest scorer? Go back to Insider Tip #2: **Let others do the homework for you.** If you listen, you will be told.

I'll give you more information about each of these positions and each of these sports. For now, just know to pay attention to them.

COMPLAINT #4. "All the teams in my town lose. What's the point?"

INSIDER TIP #4. No matter where you live, you can become the fan of a winning team.

Twenty years ago, most sports fans obsessed about their local teams—win or lose—and paid attention to other national teams only when they came into town or won championships.

Cable television changed that. Suddenly, the number of games on television increased dramatically and national newscasts on sports (e.g., ESPN's *SportsCenter* or CNN's *Sports To-*

night) became popular. If you lived in Detroit, your favorite baseball team didn't have to be the Tigers and your favorite sports newscaster didn't have to hail from Motown. Today, Sports Goddesses can track their favorite teams over the Internet (e.g., *www.cnnsi.com*, *www.espn.com*).

So don't worry. You can be a Cowboys fan in Minneapolis. You can be a Vikings fan in San Francisco. You can even be a fan of your home team!

COMPLAINT #5. "There are too many leagues, too many divisions, and too many teams in sports."

INSIDER TIP #5. Pick one team in one sport to follow at first.

This way, you will learn about the sport, its players, and its conferences from the vantage point of your team. For example: you pick the Miami Heat basketball team of the NBA. After a game or two, you'll realize that they are in the Eastern Conference of the NBA. And that when they play the teams above them in the standings, the games matter more. And that their coach is Pat Riley, a basketball icon who coached the Los Angeles Lakers in the 1980s. Remember, you don't have to watch games, just use the think THIN approach.

The more focused you are on one or two players, one or two teams, and one or two leagues, the more you will learn about all sports. And the more you will care. And the more passionate a Sports Goddess you will become.

The Golden Rule: Think of yourself as a Sports Goddess, and you will become one.

In the movie *There's Something About Mary*, Cameron Diaz portrays a beautiful and brilliant surgeon. She cracks golf balls far on the driving range. She talks about professional sports with potential dates. She watches ESPN's *SportsCenter*. She roots for the San Francisco 49ers even though she lives in Miami. Men adore her. Women bond with her. Patients flock to her. She is the ultimate Sports Goddess!

You may never be a super Sports Goddess like Mary. How-

Robin Roberts's
Bonus Insider Tip—

"You don't have to know anything about sports to appreciate its great drama."

A Sports God or Goddess drops the names of sports television hosts all the time. For the SGIT, it can be confusing. Too many hosts. Too many similar names. Too many personalities who appear for a few days and then disappear for a year. Where does the SGIT begin?

That's easy. Start with Robin Roberts. Watch Robin Roberts. She is very easy to find. She hosts ABC's *Wide World of Sports*, anchors ESPN's *SportsCenter*, calls WNBA games, reports from the Olympics, and assumes many other responsibilities for her employer, ABC/ESPN. (Check your local listings for show times.)

Robin achieved scholastically and athletically at an early age. A star tennis and basketball player, she attended Southeast Louisiana University with a scholarship for both sports. After she graduated with honors, she moved quickly in her chosen profession. She was anchoring for ESPN in her twenties. In 1995, she was tapped to host ABC's *Wide World of Sports*, the show that created modern sports television. She won an Emmy for a hard-hitting documentary on racism and numerous other journalism accolades for her thoughtful, insightful reporting. She inspires her colleagues and friends with her extensive work in charitable endeavors and her dignified demeanor. Each week, this distinguished reporter carves her own legacy in broadcast journalism with her class, composure, character, and considerable knowledge of sports.

Robin's insider tip for Sports Goddesses emphasizes the spirit of sports. "It's great drama! You don't need to know the rules to appreciate the drama in front of you in real time. You don't even need to root for one team or the other. You don't have to wait. The action unfolds in front of your eyes. Different story lines happen every game. You will see and hear wonderful stories and feats just by watching an event. No other form of entertainment offers this type of drama on a regular basis!"

Watch Robin. Quote Robin. Learn from Robin.

Sydney Mandelbaum

Sydney Mandelbaum epitomizes the Sports Goddess spirit. A petite and poised New Yorker, Sydney attends Knicks games. She roots for New York teams. She poses for photographs with a tennis racket. She gives the hand signal for touchdown when her team scores.

Sydney is three.

Her father, Jay, a top Wall Street executive, has shared his love of sports with his daughter since her birth. She has responded enthusiastically. No one has told her, yet, that she may be defying a gender stereotype. Hopefully, no one ever will!

ever, you, too, can use sports to build professional and social relationships. Sports can be fun. Sports can empower women. Whether you are talking about mountain biking in the Colorado Rockies or the chances of the Colorado Rockies in the play-offs, you become part of a special, shared community. Start thinking of yourself as a Sports Goddess today!

1

A SPORTS GODDESS
STARTS TALKING

It's actually exciting for me to talk about sports—somewhat like entering forbidden territory. Caring about and talking about sports seemed like a male birthright. So I feel empowered as a woman to seize control of this type of conversation: for example, when I talked with another mother at a birthday party about Coach Bill Parcells leaving the New England Patriots for the New York Jets, or when I chatted with my van driver at a conference about the stinginess of the Boston Red Sox management causing the loss of Roger Clemens and Mo Vaughn. I consider each conversation a new Sports Goddess experience. I feel as if I can now participate in an important part of life that had been closed off to me, when in fact it hadn't been.

*—Dr. Suzanne Moranian, Visiting Scholar,
Center for Research on Women, Wellesley College*

So you want to talk about sports. Today. Right now. But you're not about to memorize every rule of football or basketball. OK. Here are ten simple secrets to get you started right now! Try one or two this week. Before you know it, you will start having Sports Goddess Experiences like my colleague at Wellesley, Dr. Suzanne Moranian.

Secret #1. Find out who is on the cover of *Sports Illustrated*. Then understand that he or she is jinxed.

That's it. Just the cover. Most likely, you will be told why this athlete or this team made it there (e.g., "We're CRAZY about Duke," accompanied by a photo of a Duke University player).

You can look at the cover at your local newsstand. You can borrow your significant other's or your child's copy of the magazine. You can surf to *www.cnnsi.com*, the CNN/Sports Illustrated web site. The magazine releases its cover each week on the Internet.

Then mention it in a conversation. "So, Duke made the cover of SI." (**SG Tip**: Most times, refer to *Sports Illustrated* as "SI," pronounced as if you are saying the letters individually.) Sports fans don't need much else to start a conversation.

EXTRA CREDIT Be aware of the *SI* cover jinx. Sports fans love to talk about the *SI* jinx. Winning teams who make the cover start losing. Star players on the cover fall fast. Of course, most winning teams eventually lose. Most athletes (and individuals, for that matter) suffer setbacks. It doesn't matter if the *SI* jinx is true or not. It just matters that you, as a Sports Goddess, know about it!

So when you mention that you saw Duke on the cover of *SI* you can follow it up with the comment "Great. All they need is the *SI* jinx this season!"

Of course, when you are a full-fledged Sports Goddess, you will devour *SI*. You will be moved by its powerful prose, compelling stories, and award-winning photographs. However, for now, just know who's on the cover and that they're jinxed.

Secret #2   **Watch the first ten minutes of ESPN's**
                    ***SportsCenter*. Then refer to the 11 P.M. ET**
                    edition as "The Big Show."

ESPN's *SportsCenter* has become part of American pop culture. Its commercials are cool. Its anchors are young. Its sports highlights are fun.

SportsCenter follows an easy format. It gives you that night's games and sports news in order of importance. So if you watch the first ten minutes and you see a series of highlights on the New York Jets, the Green Bay Packers, the Chicago Bulls, and the Utah Jazz, those games were probably the most significant of the day. And the ones most likely to be discussed tomorrow.

It's hard to miss *SportsCenter*. It's on most of the time. (M–F 6 A.M.–Noon ET; M–F 6:30 P.M. ET; M–Su 11:00 P.M. ET; M–Su 1 A.M. ET & 2 A.M. ET) You can watch it before you go to bed. You can watch it before you go to work. You can even watch it at work.

When you watch, learn the names of the sportscasters. Then, when you drop "I caught the Knicks highlights on *SportsCenter*," you will receive extra points for adding, "**Kenny Mayne** said they went scoreless for the last three minutes."

Most *SportsCenter*s run one hour. Most *SportsCenter*s contain a mixture of highlights, news, and human interest stories. The one-hour version at 11 P.M. ET refers to itself as "The Big Show."

Dan Patrick and Keith Olbermann (former ESPN anchor now with FOX Sports) hosted this edition for many years. It became very popular because of the wit and camaraderie of these two anchors. They wrote a book together called *The Big Show*. It sold well.

So if you say, "The Bulls highlights on *SportsCenter*'s 'The Big Show' were great," you will receive bonus Sports Goddess points for knowing it was "The Big Show."

SG TIP. Never refer to any of the other *SportsCenter*s as "The Little Show"! No *SportsCenter* is little to a fan.

Finally, some SGITs have found that they can't watch ESPN in the early stages of their training. It's a little overwhelming: the stats, the pace, the inside jokes. It's like trying to break through the sound barrier. They try. But they bounce back.

Don't worry! Other options exist. An SGIT can watch CNN *Sports Tonight*, which airs at 11 P.M. ET every night of the week. It's safe. She's watching a *news* channel and not a *sports* channel. An added bonus: she will catch *Sports Illustrated* reporters on many editions. *Or*, she can watch popular sportscaster Keith Ol-

Charley Steiner's Bonus Secret—

"Know the SportsCenter lingo!"

Charley Steiner knows sports and he knows news. He can tell you when the two intersect and when they don't. A veteran newsman with a distinguished baritone voice, he was a leading news and sports radio broadcaster for many years at several top stations in New York City. In 1988, he joined ESPN and quickly became one of the signature hosts of *SportsCenter*, the number one boxing reporter, and eventually, a play-by-play announcer for baseball, football, and basketball on television and radio. His tough, factual reporting on the Tyson rape trial in 1992 brought him acclaim and journalistic accolades. Yet, despite his often serious demeanor, Charley can have fun. He has starred in several of the funniest ESPN commercials including one in which he swapped places with Andrew Shue of *Melrose Place* and portrayed "pool boy" at the Melrose apartment complex.

Charley suggests that when an SGIT watches *SportsCenter,* she should know that "There are no tulips in Madison Square *Garden.* You both *blow up* and *sew up* a football. When one is *en fuego* he is not conducting a political protest in Southeast Asia, but rather, a player who can't miss his target, no matter what he does. That *Bruce Arena* is a soccer coach and not the home of an expansion basketball team. That *boo-yeah* is not a negative response to an inept play, but rather a term of exclamation, akin to 'gee-wilickers wasn't that an impressive athletic endeavor?' And ultimately, when an athlete is listed as *day-to-day* it is not that big a deal. Because after all, athlete or not, aren't we all day to day?"

berman on FOX Sports Net. *Or* an SGIT can promise herself that when she watches her local newscast, **she will not get up during sports!** If she learns the name of *one* sportscaster in her town and a few of his or her favorite phrases, she'll start connecting. Most likely, she'll get hooked. And then she will be ready for "The Big Show" on ESPN!

Willow Bay's Bonus Secret—

"Focus on the human interest stories."

Willow Bay can analyze stock market fluctuations or basketball shooting droughts with equal precision. She speaks both languages fluently. Throughout her career, she has journeyed between the worlds of sports, business, politics, and entertainment. She has mastered all.

Perhaps Willow couldn't avoid sports. Her mother watched a Giants football game soon after her birth. She grew up in New York in a sports-mad family with tickets to Knicks, Rangers, and Giants games. She started running marathons in her teens. During her undergraduate years at the University of Pennsylvania, she began her career in the highly competitive business of modeling. She served as the spokesperson and exclusive model for Estee Lauder. After her graduation from Penn cum laude, she modeled, began her career in television, and studied for an MBA at the NYU School of Business at the same time.

In 1991, she began anchoring and reporting for the ultra hip NBA show *Inside Stuff,* which airs on NBC. Her business training served her well. Early in her career at the NBA, she was quoted as saying that many NBA players are "excellent businessmen." A few years later, she began cohosting ABC's *Good Morning America Sunday* as well. In 1998, she consolidated all her reportorial duties under the umbrella of one network when she joined CNN to host its prestigious *NewsStand* shows on business and entertainment.

While Willow enjoys the athletic arena, she describes herself as "not a classic sports person." She suggests, "Forget about statistics. Forget about scores. **Focus on the people!** Sports coverage is so broad these days. You always can find a great story loaded with fun facts that gets you into the game. The stories are fascinating. Be the one in the meeting telling them!"

Secret #3. **Build a relationship with a sports columnist in your local newspaper.**

Dan Shaughnessy, the *Boston Globe* sports columnist (*www.bostonglobe.com*), has noted that "No one who is a citizen of this country should throw out *any* section of his or her paper—international, national, local, business, living, *and* sports—without at least a cursory glance. Some individuals consider it a badge of honor not to read the sports section. Well, they shouldn't. They're missing out on a part of the world they live in."

You may not be ready to read the entire sports section. So read *one* of the sports columns. Learn the name of the columnist. Find out which days his or her column appears. Follow him or her for a few weeks.

You'll be surprised. Most likely, you will be reading more than a series of complaints about one or two of your local teams. You will be learning some of the more compelling stories of players, following debates on such serious issues as sexual assault, and understanding the team's strategy and importance in your town. These men and women columnists often challenge conventional fan thinking. Jim Cohen, the former deputy sports editor for the *Philadelphia Inquirer*, captures their spirit and sensibilities when he says, "In many papers, some of the best writing is by the sports columnists. Not surprising, given all the spicy issues supplied by modern-day jocks, who are raised to scorn reasonable conduct."

Cynical Sports Goddesses embrace columnists because so many point out the negative side of sports. More positive ones gravitate toward the many moving human interest stories told by columnists, such as the foundation for research on autism set up by Doug Flutie of the NFL and his wife.

Through the Internet, an SGIT can peruse some of the finest columnists in the country. The following chart lists a few female scribes. Visit their sites. Browse through their archived columns.

Columnist	Newspaper	Internet Address
Christine Brennan	*USA Today*	www.usatoday.com/sports
Jennifer Frey	*The Washington Post*	www.washingtonpost.com/sports
Melissa Isaacson	*Chicago Tribune*	www.chicagotribune.com/sports
Gwen Knapp	*San Francisco Examiner*	www.examiner.com/sports
Vicki Michaelis	*The Denver Post*	www.denverpost.com
Diane Pucin	*Los Angeles Times*	www.latimes.com/sports
Claire Smith	*The New York Times*	www.nytimes.com/sports

As you become more and more of a Sports Goddess, you will be able to agree or disagree with their opinions and gain new perspectives on how to watch, and talk about, sports.

My perception is that sports is a very safe nonbusiness topic in social situations (as opposed to politics or religion). You can be passionate, disagree with someone else's view, or even openly hate someone else's favorite team with very little risk of offending or being viewed negatively.

—male manager

Secret #4. **When you discuss a game, know three things. Who won. Who lost. One key play or fact.**

Remember those insider tips. Think THIN (**T**V, **H**eadline News, **I**nternet, **N**ewspaper) and let others do the homework for you.

For example, your boss begins every meeting with a comment on the L.A. Lakers. You want to contribute to the conversation. But every time you try, you lose yourself. Keep it simple. Watch a highlight on ESPN or CNN. Note three things: (1) the Lakers won the game; (2) the Warriors lost; (3) Shaquille O'Neal of the Lakers had a big night with twenty-seven points.

Or, if you don't want to wait around for a highlight, you can pick up *USA Today*. Find the score on the front page of the sports section. Turn to the game recap inside and find one key fact. Usually it will be in the first paragraph.

> **EXTRA CREDIT**   Determine the impact of the game. The outcome of every game in sports impacts something. The standings. The playoffs. An individual's chances for winning an award. Once again, let others do the homework for you. You will be told the significance of the game by the sportscaster or sportswriter.

For example, let's say that Lakers-Warriors game occurred early in the season. It shouldn't matter much in the overall picture. Still, it means something. Every game does. That's why so many people care so much about sports. You will almost always find the impact in the first paragraph or two of the game recap or the televised highlight (e.g., The Lakers remain undefeated this season at 4 and 0).

> **SG TIP.**   A Sports Goddess will say 4 and oh, not 4 and zero.

So after you, in your best Sports Goddess manner, say "The Lakers blew out the Warriors and Shaq had a great night," you can add, "and they're still undefeated this season at 4 and oh." Most likely, this will trigger a discussion of the Lakers' prospects for the season. A Sports Goddess Experience will take place.

Secret #5.   Know one superstar from each major sport and one fact about him or her.

Sports stars stand side by side alongside other figures of popular culture. Harrison Ford acts. Mick Jagger sings. Mark McGwire plays baseball.

A Sports Goddess should at the very least know one star from each of the major sports. So learn these names (if you don't know them already) and understand one reason (only one) for their fame.

Troy Aikman
(football, Dallas Cowboys quarterback)

Led Cowboys to three Super Bowl victories.

Cynthia Cooper
(basketball, Houston Comets)

In the first two seasons of the WNBA, won back-to-back Most Valuable Player awards.

Wayne Gretzky
(hockey, New York Rangers)

He scored more goals and points than any other player *ever* in the history of the NHL prior to his retirement in 1999.

Martina Hingis
(tennis)

At the age of sixteen, Hingis was the youngest player ever ranked #1 in tennis.

Michael Jordan
(basketball, Chicago Bulls)

In ten different seasons, he scored the most points in the NBA. Though he retired in early 1999, he is still the one NBA player to know and talk about with fellow Goddesses.

Mark McGwire
(baseball, St. Louis Cardinals)

Hit seventy home runs in one season.

Se Ri Pak
(ladies golf)

Won back-to-back "major" golf tournaments at the age of twenty.

Pete Sampras
(tennis)

Won U.S. Open at the age of nineteen.

Tiger Woods
(golf)

Won Masters Tournament at the age of twenty-one.

In the following chapters, I will give you a few more facts about each of these stars, and a few more stars for each of these sports. For now, just focus on these superathletes.

Secret #6. **Listen to a few minutes of sports radio each day.**

When you get up in the morning. When you drive to work. When you come home from work. Most major metropolitan areas have either one radio station with an all-sports format or one with several hours of sports programming. Or both. You can become attuned to the athletic culture of your hometown by listening to a few minutes of sports radio. Note, Goddesses, that I said "a few minutes." Some Goddesses can listen for hours (or at least for their entire commute) to sports radio. Some can't. Start small so you won't get overloaded or discouraged.

On sports radio, an SGIT will hear a summary of her local teams' performances. She then will hear analysis. Plenty of it. Local fans call in with their comments. Local commentators add their thoughts. While a Sports Goddess may not agree with everything, she can learn pronunciation and syntax from these radio Gods and Goddesses. She also will realize (quickly) that they tend to be far less objective than most TV, newspaper, or magazine reporters. However, she can pick up differing viewpoints on the major sports players in her town. When she becomes a Super Sports Goddess, she can call in and voice her own views.

Secret #7.   Buy a sports cap or T-shirt. Then wear it.

Sports fans love to bond with each other. But they need visual cues to know who supports which teams. So they send out signals. For example, they wear caps and T-shirts with team logos. Try it. Wear a cap or T-shirt during a jog. Or a workout at your health club. Or a barbecue. Most likely, you will strike up a conversation with someone. Maybe it will be an interesting conversation, maybe not. However, it's an easy way to feel part of the sports culture.

At one time, you could buy only your local team's merchandise in your hometown. Now you can buy a Seattle Mariners cap at a mall in Dallas. And a Texas Rangers cap in Seattle. You can purchase NHL caps in malls in cities with no hockey team. I spotted Green Bay Packers T-shirts in a booth at an international festival in Kiel, Germany!

Now, the best news for many Goddesses: **You can purchase a cap or a team T-shirt simply because you like the color or logo**. That's right. If silver and black appeal to you, go ahead and buy that Oakland Raiders hat. Sports Gods and Goddess will approve. These days, teams spend a lot of money on consultants to help them select the most popular colors and the most fashionable logos. For example, in March 1993, the Florida Marlins baseball team had not played one game. (They debuted one month later.) Yet their merchandise ranked fourth in sales out of twenty-eight teams in Major League Baseball. Why? The team had selected its teal, black, and gray color scheme and its fish logo on the basis of sophisticated market research. They designed their product to meet market demand. And it did.

Make sure that you are purchasing a licensed piece of merchandise (most items carry a tag with the league's logo on it.) If you have access to the Internet, you can purchase these products from each league's or each team's web site. It's very easy.

League	Web Site	Click on
Major League Baseball	www.majorleaguebaseball.com	MLB store
National Basketball Association	www.nba.com	NBA store
National Football League	www.nfl.com	NFL store
National Hockey League	www.nhl.com	NHL store

Of course, the multitude of clothing options can confuse a Sports Goddess in Training. So here are four suggestions, one for each sport!

	Team	Colors	A Sports Goddess Purchases This Because
NBA	Chicago Bulls	Red/White/Black	When Michael Jordan played for them, the Bulls won. A lot.

	Team	Colors	A Sports Goddess Purchases This Because
MLB	Florida Marlins	Teal/Black/Gray	Great fish logo. In addition, the Marlins won the World Series just five years after joining the league.
NFL	Dallas Cowboys	Royal Blue/Metallic Blue/White	Cool star logo. Plus, the Cowboys refer to themselves as "America's Team."
NHL	Colorado Avalanche	Purple/White/Blue	It's purple. Also, the Avalanche won the Stanley Cup in 1996.

EXTRA CREDIT   If you want, buy clothing you know will ignite discussion. For example, if you live in Arizona, purchase a Montreal Canadiens cap. Or wear a Chicago Cubs T-shirt because they never win the big one. I know a popular Sports God who wears a Texas Prairie View cap because they had the longest losing streak in college football!

Secret #8.   Rent a sports movie.

OK, maybe live sports dramas rival the movies. You don't care. You opt for Hollywood productions. Good news—over the years, Hollywood has produced many wonderful movies with sports themes. Better news—Sports G & Gs revere many of these movies. These films also provide insights into the culture of many professional and collegiate games. Thus, a Sports Goddess should rent a sports movie or two. Tonight. And then talk about them tomorrow.

The following list names one great movie for each sport. Throughout the book, I summarize the plots of many other movies. For now, focus on this list. Go rent at least one of them tonight!

James Brown's Bonus Secret—

"Learn the Game of Life from the Games of Sports."

James Brown presently hosts FOX's NFL studio programming and reports for HBO's documentary unit, *Real Sports*. His Harvard degree has led to a Renaissance man career. He has reported from the Olympics and the Final Four for CBS Sports, worked in sales and marketing management for such Fortune 500 companies as Xerox and Eastman Kodak, moderated a debate on the documentary *Hoop Dreams* on PBS, and even hosted a special on the musician Yanni, on PBS.

"JB" notes that "Sports is not just about the biggest, strongest, swiftest. It can be about anyone who brings a unique capability to the game." In basketball "It is the little man who controls the ball most of the time. If you have perfected a skill or two in basketball or in any other sport, you can achieve." Presently, he is working with his daughter, a star on her high school track team, to help her compete successfully in her sport and in her future career.

JB draws on his own experiences to explain the role of sports in life. He was a star player at DeMatha High School in Maryland, which has one of the finest basketball programs in the country. He majored in American government at Harvard, where he also earned all-Ivy honors in basketball. After Harvard, he was drafted by the Atlanta Hawks in the NBA. When he didn't make the team permanently, he felt that despite his success, he had not worked as hard as he could have on his basketball skills during his collegiate career. He then vowed no one would ever outwork him in the Game of Life. And no one has. As JB put it, "Sports teaches you lessons for the game of life. If you're not working hard enough on your skills, you will fail."

Sport	Movie

Auto Racing   *Days of Thunder* (1990). *Stars*: Tom Cruise, Nicole Kidman, Robert Duvall. *SG summary*: Nicole Kidman plays a Sports Goddess/neurosurgeon who falls in love with a race car driver (Tom Cruise). *SG note:* Pay attention to crew chief Robert Duvall. You can learn about the sport from his dialogue. *SG fun fact:* The Kidman-Cruise romance began on this movie set!

Baseball   *Bull Durham* (1988). *Stars*: Tim Robbins, Kevin Costner, Susan Sarandon. *SG summary*: Susan Sarandon plays the number one fan of the Bulls, a minor league baseball team. She sees poetry, religion, beauty, and mysticism in baseball. She becomes involved with the rookie pitcher (Tim Robbins) and the aging catcher (Kevin Costner). *SG fun fact:* The Sarandon-Robbins romance began on this set. *SG should remember the line*: "Never been a player who I slept with who didn't have the best year of his career."

Basketball   *White Men Can't Jump* (1992). *Stars*: Woody Harrelson, Wesley Snipes, Rosie Perez. *SG summary*: basketball hustlers on the courts in Los Angeles. Humorous subplot involves Rosie Perez studying for the quiz show *Jeopardy*.

Boxing   *Rocky* (1976). *Stars*: Sylvester Stallone, Talia Shire, Burgess Meredith. *SG summary*: Small-time boxer goes up against the champ. Has the feel and spirit of an independent, low-budget movie (differs from its sequels in this respect). *Rocky* won the Academy Award for Best Picture. *SG should remember:* the sequence of shots where Rocky trains for the big fight.

Football   *North Dallas Forty* (1979). *Stars*: Nick Nolte, Charles Durning. *SG summary*: depicts eight days in the life of a professional football player in Dallas. *A Sports Goddess will see:* a lot of sex, drugs, and rock 'n roll.

Golf	*Tin Cup* (1996). *Stars*: Kevin Costner, Don Johnson, Rene Russo. *SG summary*: Rene Russo plays a Sports Goddess/psychologist. She takes lessons from "Tin Cup" (Kevin Costner), a down-on-his-luck golf pro. He attempts to qualify for the U.S. Open, one of golf's four major tournaments, to impress her. *An SG will learn*: a lot about golf if she pays attention. She should note the scenes where the pro and caddy talk. She should listen when Costner describes different swings. She should pay attention to discussions of "shanking." She will learn that any golf professional can attempt to play in the U.S. Open.
Hockey	*Slap Shot* (1977). *Star*: Paul Newman. *SG summary*: Minor league hockey team plays dirty and starts winning. *SG note*: Hockey Gods and Goddesses sometimes refer to characters in this movie as if they had actually played in the NHL. In particular, the movie featured the "Hanson Brothers," three goofy-looking brothers who played on one shift together.

Secret #9.   Read a sports book.

When I joined ESPN, Executive Editor John A. Walsh handed me a reading list. I looked at it, and it reminded me of my summer book lists in grammar school. I quietly questioned the reasoning behind his suggestions at such a busy time in my life. In John's view, "The best of sports writing has originality, creativity, and nuances which gives a way of seeing the many possibilities of the English language."

He was right. I learned a tremendous amount about the culture of sports from these books. But before you pick up any old sports book, be aware that sports books vary. An SGIT can engross herself in a sports mystery novel by Dick Francis. She can be stunned by the brutal beauty of Joyce Carol Oates's essays on boxing. She can acclimate herself to the importance of base-

Julie Moran's Bonus Secret—

"Entertain a Sports God with your football definitions!"

Julie Moran has played sports, talked sports, broadcast sports, and been around sports her entire life. The granddaughter of Sterling Dupree, a legendary Georgia football player and coach, she inherited his athletic ability. In high school, she excelled in basketball (Georgia all-state player), track (a state finalist in the 100 meters), and tennis (a regional champion). She graduated from the University of Georgia magna cum laude and segued into a successful career in sports and entertainment broadcasting. As host of the NBA show *Inside Stuff*, she talked hoops with the pros like a pro. She pioneered new ground for women when she became the first female host of ABC's *Wide World of Sports*. She anchored and reported segments of ABC's prestigious documentary series *Passion to Play*.

In 1995, Julie moved on to a reporting and hosting role on the very popular *Entertainment Tonight*. Yet, she hasn't left sports behind entirely. In 1996, she reported from the Olympics in Atlanta for *ET*. In her present career on the entertainment beat, she notes the constant synergy between the entertainment and sports worlds. Julie says, "Going from *Wide World of Sports* to *Entertainment Tonight* didn't really change my job description when it comes to interviewing. The megawatt star power of a Michael Jordan or a Mel Gibson is interchangeable."

Julie suggests that if you are involved with a Football God, even if you don't want to watch a game, entertain him and your friends with her alternative definitions: **Kickoff**—the last time he speaks to you for three hours. **Fumble**—remember the first time you made love. **Time Out**—stand clear, he's going to the bathroom. **Tight End**—no definition needed! The best reason for Julie and every other woman to love football!

ball in the life of a young girl in Brooklyn during the 1950s in *Wait Till Next Year*.

Here is my list of books, one for each major sport. They can be found in bookstores or libraries or on bookstore Web sites. On the following pages, I will summarize the plots of many other books. For now, focus on this list!

Baseball   *Wait Till Next Year.*   **Author:** Doris Kearns Goodwin.   **SG summary:** Kearns describes the role the Brooklyn Dodgers played in her neighborhood and her childhood.   **An SG will learn:** a lot about the legendary Brooklyn Dodgers.

Basketball   *Best Seat in the House.*   **Author:** Spike Lee. *SG summary:* Spike, the ultimate fan, speaks out on the sport. He tells you why he loves it. He mentions what he doesn't like about it. He talks about its importance in his childhood.   **An SG will realize:** why so many fans consider basketball the hippest sport.

Boxing   *On Boxing.*   **Author:** Joyce Carol Oates.   **SG summary:** Joyce Carol Oates, a renowned writer, details her fascination with the beauty and brutality of boxing.   **An SG should absorb:** the many paradoxes of the sport of boxing.

Football   *Dark Side of the Game: My Life in the NFL.*   **Author:** Tim Green, an NFL player-turned-National-Public-Radio reporter.   **SG summary:** a literary, thoughtful, and realistic look at a player's life in the NFL.   **An SG will learn:** what really goes on in the NFL.

Golf   *Golf in the Kingdom.*   **Author:** Michael Murphy.   **SG summary:** captures the mysticism and magical qualities of the game of golf. It's set in the golf kingdom of Scotland.

Hockey   *Hockey sur Glace*.   **Author:** Peter LaSalle.   **SG summary:** series of beautifully crafted short stories and poems about hockey and its meaning in life. **An SG can have fun with**: the poem "Goalies Are Weird"

Horse Racing   *The Danger*.   **Author:** Dick Francis.   **SG summary:** a series of kidnappings hits the international horse racing community.   **SG note:** Dick Francis, the former steeplechase jockey, has written many mysteries with racing themes.   **SG fun fact:** The Queen Mother of England loves them.

EXTRA CREDIT   Browse in a library or a bookstore in the sports section. Look at the numerous books by coaches that preach winning techniques in business. Check out the inspirational biographies of female and male athletes. Learn some history from the many books available on most sports.

*Secret #*10.   **Learn one name of one team today. When you visit a city, know something about its sports culture. When you meet someone, determine the name of a team in his or her town.**

It's February. You have a business trip to Indianapolis. You want to relate in some way to the individuals on the other side of the table. An easy way to do that is by creating a Sports Goddess Experience. To do that, use this guide to determine which teams play in this city or state at this time. In Indianapolis, college basketball is huge. Before the meeting, check the local paper for the Hoosiers (Indiana University) score. Be honest. Say "I don't know that much about college basketball. But I saw that the Hoosiers won last night, so I hope you're in a good mood." (Or "I saw that they lost, so I hope you're not in too bad a mood.") If the team didn't play the night before the meeting, "I don't have to worry about your mood because I know the Hoosiers didn't play last night!"

Even if you don't want to bring up the team in conversation, try to learn about one team in a city you're visiting. Walk through the airport and note the team uniforms in a store. Recognize the name of the team on the highlights of the local news. Read the headline of last night's game. By doing this, you'll connect to the city and to the people.

Or perhaps you'll meet someone you like and you want to connect with him. Use this guide to determine the teams in his cities. Pick one. Be honest. You can say "I don't know that much about baseball, but I do know the Diamondbacks play in Phoenix. Are you a fan? What should I know about them?"

Do not try to memorize every team in every sport. You'll never relate well to sports if you try to learn by rote. **Do** pick one team from this list for any reason. (Even if you're not going there.) You like the name. You always wanted to visit the city. You want to impress a guy from there. Then think THIN. Start watching for the highlights on *SportsCenter*. Look for the score on CNN's *Headline News* or ESPN2 or in *USA Today*. Read a columnist (via the Internet) from that city. Make them *your* team. (Note: MLB-Major League Baseball; NBA-National Basketball Association, WNBA-Women's National Basketball Association; NFL-National Football League; NHL-National Hockey League; NL-National League; AL-American League.)

ALABAMA

Birmingham

College   U Alabama *Crimson Tide*, Auburn *Tigers*

Note: In Alabama, you are either a Crimson Tide or a Tigers fan. Never both! The state splits into two camps when the teams play one another in football in November.

ARIZONA

Phoenix

MLB   Arizona Diamondbacks (NL)
NBA/WNBA   Suns/Mercury

NFL	Arizona Cardinals
NHL	Coyotes
College	U Arizona *Wildcats*, Arizona State *Sun Devils*

ARKANSAS

Little Rock
| College | Arkansas *Razorbacks* |

CALIFORNIA

Anaheim
| MLB | Angels (AL) |
| NHL | Mighty Ducks |

Los Angeles
MLB	Dodgers (NL)
NBA/WNBA	Lakers & Clippers/Sparks
NHL	Kings
College	UCLA *Bruins*, USC *Trojans*

Oakland
MLB	Athletics (AL)
NBA	Golden State Warriors
NFL	Raiders
College	U Cal Berkeley *Golden Bears*

Sacramento
| NBA/WNBA | Kings/Monarchs |

San Diego
MLB	Padres (NL)
NFL	Chargers
College	San Diego State *Aztecs*

San Francisco
MLB	Giants (NL)
NFL	49ers
College	Stanford *Cardinal* (**SG note:** Stanford always refers to the Cardinal in the singular. It is never "the Cardinals.")

San Jose

NHL	Sharks
College	Stanford *Cardinal*

CANADA

Calgary

NHL	Flames

Edmonton

NHL	Oilers

Montreal

MLB	Expos (NL)
NHL	Canadiens

Note: The Montreal Canadiens have a very distinguished history in their league. The Expos do not.

Ottawa

NHL	Senators

Toronto

MLB	Blue Jays (AL)
NBA	Raptors
NHL	Maple Leafs

Vancouver

NBA	Grizzlies
NHL	Canucks

COLORADO

Denver

MLB	Colorado Rockies (NL)
NBA	Nuggets
NFL	Broncos
NHL	Colorado Avalanche
College	U Colorado *Buffaloes*

CONNECTICUT

Hartford
College   U Conn. *Huskies*

DISTRICT OF COLUMBIA

NBA/WNBA   Wizards/Mystics
NHL   Capitals
NFL   Redskins
College   Georgetown *Hoyas*

FLORIDA

Jacksonville
NFL   Jaguars
College   U Florida *Gators*, Florida State *Seminoles*

Miami
MLB   Florida Marlins (NL)
NBA   Heat
NFL   Dolphins
NHL   Florida Panthers
College   U Miami *Hurricanes*, U Florida *Gators*, Florida
                       State *Seminoles*

Orlando
NBA/WNBA   Magic/Miracle

Tampa/St. Petersburg
MLB   Devil Rays (AL)
NFL   Buccaneers
NHL   Lightning
College   U Florida *Gators*, Florida State *Seminoles*

GEORGIA

Atlanta
MLB   Braves (NL)
NFL   Falcons
NBA   Hawks

| NHL | Thrashers |
| College | U *Georgia Bulldogs*, Georgia Tech *Yellow Jackets* |

*Note: In Atlanta (and the South for that matter), college football is very big. Even if the Braves make the World Series, talk **still** might center on the Bulldogs!*

ILLINOIS

Chicago

MLB	Cubs (NL), White Sox (AL)
NBA	Bulls
NFL	Bears
NHL	Black Hawks
College	Northwestern *Wildcats*

Note: If it's summer, see secret #51 about the curses on the Cubs and the White Sox.

INDIANA

Indianapolis

NBA	Indiana Pacers
NFL	Colts
College	Indiana U *Hoosiers*, Notre Dame *Fighting Irish*, Purdue *Boilermakers*

KENTUCKY

Lexington

| College/Other Sports | U Kentucky *Wildcats*/Kentucky Derby (held at Louisville in May) |

Note: Cincinnati is near Lexington, so learn about its teams!

LOUISIANA

New Orleans

| NFL | Saints |
| College | Tulane *Green Wave*, LSU *Fighting Tigers* |

MARYLAND

Baltimore

NFL	Ravens
MLB	Orioles (AL)
College/Other Sports	U Maryland *Terrapins*/Preakness (held in Baltimore in May)

MASSACHUSETTS

Boston

MLB	Red Sox (AL)
NBA	Celtics
NFL	New England Patriots
NHL	Bruins
College	Boston College *Eagles* (primarily football)

MICHIGAN

Detroit

MLB	Tigers (AL)
NBA/WNBA	Pistons/Shock
NFL	Lions
NHL	Red Wings
College	U Michigan *Wolverines*, Michigan State *Spartans*

Note: The Detroit Red Wings won back-to-back Stanley Cups in 1997 and 1998 after a forty-five-year drought. Motowners love their Wings.

MINNESOTA

Minneapolis/St.Paul

MLB	Minnesota Twins (AL)
NBA/WNBA	Minnesota Timberwolves/Lynx
NFL	Minnesota Vikings
NHL	Minnesota Wild
College	Minnesota *Golden Gophers*

MISSOURI

Kansas City
MLB	Royals (AL)
NFL	Chiefs

St. Louis
MLB	Cardinals (NL)
NFL	Rams
NHL	Blues
College	U Missouri *Tigers*

NEBRASKA

Omaha
College/Other Sports	Nebraska *Cornhuskers*/College World Series (held in June)

Note: College football is very big in Nebraska. 'Huskers shared the National Championship in the 1997–1998 season.

NEW JERSEY

Newark
NBA	New Jersey Nets
NFL	New York Giants
NHL	New Jersey Devils

Note: All three of these teams play their home games at the Meadowlands in East Rutherford, NJ.

NEW YORK

Buffalo
NFL	Bills
NHL	Sabres

Long Island
NHL	Islanders
College/Other Sports	Belmont Stakes (held at Elmont in June)

New York City

MLB	Yankees (AL), Mets (NL)
NBA/WNBA	Knicks/Liberty
NFL	Jets (AFC), Giants (NFC)
NHL	Rangers

NORTH CAROLINA

Charlotte

NFL	Carolina Panthers
NBA/WNBA	Hornets/Sting
College	U North Carolina *Tar Heels*, NC State *Wolfpack*, Duke *Blue Devils*

Raleigh

| NHL | Carolina Hurricanes |

OHIO

Cincinnati

MLB	Reds (NL)
NFL	Bengals
College	Ohio State *Buckeyes*, U Cincinnati *Bearcats*

Note: Cincinnati Bearcats have been a college basketball powerhouse in the 1990s.

Cleveland

NFL	Browns
NBA/WNBA	Cavaliers/Rockers
MLB	Indians (AL)
College	Ohio State *Buckeyes*

Note: At the end of the 1995 football season, the much beloved Cleveland Browns moved to Baltimore (and became the Ravens). Drew Carey and all other Cleveland fans were heartbroken. In the fall of 1999, an expansion franchise, the Browns, starts its first season in Cleveland. So the city has Browns football again, though it's a different team). "How do you feel about the new Browns?" will ignite conversation in any setting.

Columbus

NHL	Blue Jackets (in 2000)
College	Ohio State *Buckeyes*

OKLAHOMA

Oklahoma City

College	Oklahoma State *Cowboys*
	U Oklahoma *Sooners*

Tulsa

College	Oklahoma State *Cowboys*
	U Oklahoma *Sooners*

Note: Sooners football and basketball are very big throughout the state.

OREGON

Portland

NBA	Trail Blazers
College	U Oregon *Ducks*, Oregon State *Beavers*

PENNSYLVANIA

Philadelphia

MLB	Phillies (NL)
NBA	76ers
NFL	Eagles
NHL	Flyers
College	Temple *Owls*

Pittsburgh

MLB	Pirates (NL)
NFL	Steelers
NHL	Penguins
College	Penn State *Nittany Lions*, Pittsburgh *Panthers*

Note: Penn State football is very big throughout the region. Coach Joe Paterno (Joe Pa) is revered.

TENNESSEE

Nashville
NFL   Tennessee Oilers
NHL   Predators
College   U Tenn. *Volunteers*, Vanderbilt *Commodores*

*Note: The U Tennessee **women's** basketball team is very, very successful.*

TEXAS

Austin
College   U Texas *Longhorns*

Dallas
MLB   Texas Rangers (AL)
NBA   Mavericks
NFL   Cowboys
NHL   Stars
College   U Texas *Longhorns*, Southern Methodist University *Mustangs*

Houston
MLB   Astros (NL)
NBA/WNBA   Rockets/Comets
College   U Texas *Longhorns*, U Houston *Cougars*

San Antonio
NBA   Spurs

Note: College and high school football are very big in Texas.

UTAH

Salt Lake City
NBA/WNBA   Utah Jazz/Starzz
College   Brigham Young *Cougars*, U Utah *Utes*

WASHINGTON

Seattle
MLB	Mariners (AL)
NBA	SuperSonics
NFL	Seahawks
College	U Washington *Huskies*

WISCONSIN

Green Bay
NFL	Packers

Milwaukee
MLB	Brewers (NL)
NBA	Bucks
College	U Wisconsin *Badgers*

EXTRA CREDIT Make sure you know which sports are in season!

It seems easy. Hockey is played in the winter. Baseball in the summer. Football in the fall. However, hockey starts in October and ends in June. Baseball begins in April with low temperatures in northern climes and finishes in October with equally chilly weather in most venues. The Super Bowl takes place in the middle of winter. Again and again, I have been asked such questions as "Has college basketball started yet?" by an SGIT who needed to appear savvy for an evening.

This calendar guides the SGIT through the major sports and events during the year. Once again, **do not try and memorize it! Do** look at this month. **Do** check which sports are in season. Then choose one. See when it begins. See when it ends. Then pick your team (if you haven't already) in that sport. Think THIN. Check the score tonight. You're getting closer and closer to becoming a Sports Goddess. (Note: LPGA = Ladies Professional Golfers Association; PGA = Professional Golfers Association.)

A SPORTS GODDESS'S CALENDAR

January

MLB	Off season
NBA	Regular season
NFL	Play-offs/Super Bowl
NHL	Regular season/All Star Game
College Baskeball	Regular season
College Football	Bowls (first week)
Extreme	Winter X Games
Tennis	Australian Open

February

MLB	Off season/spring training begins at the end of the month
NBA	Regular season/All Star Game
NFL	Pro Bowl/off season
NHL	Regular season
College Basketball	Regular season/ tournaments begin at the end of the month
Auto Racing	Daytona 500

March

MLB	Spring training
NBA	Regular season
NFL	Off season
NHL	Regular season
College Basketball	NCAA Tournament
Golf	Dinah Shore Tournament (LPGA)

April

MLB	Regular season
NBA	Regular season/play-offs
NFL	Off season/NFL draft
NHL	Regular season/play-offs
College Basketball	Final Four (usually first weekend)
Golf	The Masters Tournament (PGA), The Tradition (Sr. PGA), PGA Seniors (Sr. PGA)

May

MLB	Regular season
NBA	Play-offs
NFL	Off season
NHL	Play-offs
Auto Racing	Indy 500
Golf	LPGA Championship
Horse Racing	Kentucky Derby, Preakness
Tennis	French Open begins

June

MLB	Regular season
NBA	Play-offs/finals/NBA draft
NFL	Off season
NHL	Play-offs/finals
College Baseball	College World Series
Extreme	Summer X Games
Golf	U.S. Open (Men)
Horse Racing	Belmont Stakes
Tennis	French Open ends/ Wimbledon begins

July

MLB	Regular season/All Star Game
NBA	Off season
NFL	Training camp
NHL	Off season
Extreme	Gravity Games
Golf	British Open (PGA), Senior Players (Sr. PGA), U.S. Senior Open (Sr. PGA)
Golf	U.S. Women's Open (LPGA)
Tennis	Wimbledon ends

August

MLB	Regular season
NBA	Off season
NFL	Exhibition season
NHL	Off season
Golf	PGA Championship (PGA), du Maurier Classic (LPGA)
Tennis	U.S. Open begins

September

MLB	Regular season
NBA	Off season
NFL	Regular season
NHL	Exhibition season
College Football	Regular season
Tennis	U.S. Open ends

October

MLB	Play-offs/World Series
NBA	Training camp/exhibition season
NFL	Regular season
NHL	Regular season
College Football	Regular season

November

MLB	Off season
NBA	Regular season
NFL	Regular season
NHL	Regular season
College Football	Regular season
College Basketball	Regular season

December

MLB	Off season
NBA	Regular season
NFL	Regular season
NHL	Regular season
College Football	Regular season/bowls
College Basketball	Regular season/holiday tournaments

Go ahead. Try one or two of these secrets. Sneak a look at the cover of *Sports Illustrated* at the newsstand. Try to figure out which channel belongs to ESPN on your remote. At the very least, find out the name of a popular columnist from your local newspaper. Once you've started, you'll want to learn more about all sports. Then you'll want to know more about *each* sport. And, if you're like many other women, you'll really want to understand football first.

2

A Sports Goddess Talks
PROFESSIONAL FOOTBALL

A Sports Goddess knows:

The league's name—National Football League (NFL).

The NFL is divided into—the National Football Conference (NFC; 15 teams in '99) and the American Football Conference (AFC; 16 teams in '99).

The NFC and the AFC each are divided into—the Eastern, Central, and Western divisions.

The number of games in the regular season is—16.

The game is divided into—four 15-minute quarters. Teams break at halftime.

The regular season runs from—September to December
The play-offs are held in—January.

The championship game is called—the Super Bowl.

The number of players on the field for each team is—11.

The object of the game—Each team wants to get the football into its opponent's *end zone*, a 10-yard area at the end of the 100-yard-long football field.

Game summary—Each team has 50 yards, half of the field, assigned to it. Each team makes a series of *plays*. A play begins when the team's center snaps the ball back to the quarterback and usually ends when the player with the ball is tackled to the

ground, falls, runs out of bounds, scores, or a player misses a
ball thrown to him.

IN MY SURVEYS, no sport ignited greater emotion among men or
women than football. Many women resented that I asked them
football questions. "Women don't PLAY the game!!!" they wrote.
Yet, invariably, the football questions were the ones that received
the highest number of correct responses **among the women.**

Football can appear chaotic and confusing. There are more
players than in other sports. There are more rules. There are
more complex plays. In the beginning, a Sports Goddess
shouldn't worry about all the players. Or all the rules. She
should simply learn the names of two or three positions (you
already know to watch the quarterback, a wide receiver, and/
or a running back). And one or two rules. And one or two pieces
of strategy.

Bob Rauscher, the ESPN executive who developed the network's NFL studio programming, offers this insight into football: "To the casual observer, it may look like chaos and
confusion! However, it is the intricate balance between grace
and brutality which attracts people to this sport."

Gravitate toward the grace (e.g., the diving catches, the well-
orchestrated plays) in the sport. See how it coexists with brutality. You will feel the powerful pull of the game.

Secret #11.   Refer to each week of the regular season
by its number.

The regular NFL season lasts 17 weeks. That's it. Each team
plays 16 games, one per week. Every team gets one week off.
Nearly every game (with the notable exception of *Monday Night
Football* and a few games on Thursday and Saturday at the end of
the season) is played on Sunday. Thus, Football Gods and Goddesses can keep track of their sport in terms of weeks. And they do.

No tricks exist in this secret. In the days before the first Sunday of the NFL season, you will start hearing talk about Week

1. Week 1 ends after the first *MNF (Monday Night Football)* game. Conversations about Week 2 will start before the second Sunday. Week 2 ends after the second *MNF* game. And so on. When sports commentators look back on the season, they often refer to "the John Elway injury in Week 4" or "the New England-New Orleans game in Week 5."

So how do you know which week you are in? Once again, think THIN. If you open up *USA Today* on a Friday during the NFL season, **you will be told.** If you surf to any of the popular pregame television shows (e.g., CBS's *The NFL Today*, ESPN's *NFL Countdown*, FOX's *FOX NFL Sunday*), **you will be told.** If you surf to an Internet site, **you will be told.** Or, on a Friday, simply ask a Football God or Goddess, "Which week are we in?"

Now, here's the bad news for the lazier Sports Goddess. **Each week in the NFL counts.** After all, each team plays only 16 games. Baseball teams play that many in two and a half weeks. In addition, only **12 teams** (40%) make it to the playoffs. More than half of the basketball and hockey teams play in the post-season. Very few Basketball Gods and Goddesses watch all 82 games of their favorite teams. Fewer Baseball Gods and Goddesses see all 162 games of their teams. However, many Football Gods and Goddesses watch every minute of every game during every season.

However, if you think THIN, you still can be a Football Goddess. It's only 17 weeks! Tune in to the highlights of your city's teams on your local news or on ESPN's *NFL PrimeTime* (7:30 P.M. ET; it recaps all the games). Check scores on *Headline News* or ESPN2 on Sunday night. Visit a sports web site (*www.sportsline.com, www.espn.com, www.cnnsi.com*) before you go to bed on Sunday. On Monday morning, buy *USA Today* and look in the upper left-hand corner on the front page of the sports section for the scores. They will be waiting there for you.

Secret #12 Know that each Super Bowl has a Roman Numeral in its title. You see Super Bowl XX or Super Bowl XXX. However, you say "Super Bowl Twenty" or "Super Bowl

Sara Levinson's Bonus Secret—

"Sports is an equalizer."

Music and sports intersect in our society. Rock songs blare at most sports events. Shaquille O'Neal records rap albums. Hootie and the Blowfish headline NFL pregame shows. And Pat Boone, the wholesome singing star from the early 1960s, drives race cars!

In 1994, the NFL hired MTV's co-President, Sara Levinson, as President of NFL Properties, the league's marketing arm. She immediately became the highest-ranked woman in any of the professional sports leagues.

Sara's marketing savvy manifests itself in the numerous projects under her supervision. During her tenure, she has tackled new terrain for the NFL. She has shrewdly recognized the need to sell the game to today's children, who possess many more entertainment options than their parents. She has pitched the game to current and future female fans. The league now holds seminars to help women understand football better; offers a clothing line for women; sells an NFL cookbook; promotes flag football programs in schools; and places its products in such hit movies as *Jerry Maguire*.

Sara also uses sports to connect with her son, stepson, and others. She stresses, "Sports is a great unifier and equalizer—people from all different walks of life can enjoy each other's company with it. The more women can understand—the better!"

Thirty" and not "Super Bowl double XX" or "Super Bowl triple XXX"!

The Super Bowl occurs each year at the end of January. The AFC champion plays the NFC champion at a "neutral" site. The first Super Bowl took place in January 1967, in Los Angeles. It was not called the Super Bowl at the time. It simply was the AFL-NFL Championship Game. Then Lamar Hunt, the owner of the Kansas City Chiefs, came up with the name "Super

Bowl," after "Super Ball," one of his child's favorite toys. Commissioner Pete Rozelle added the **Roman numerals.** Super Bowl III was the first championship game to use the moniker. It stuck. The NFL changed the names of the first two championship games to Super Bowls I and II in the record books.

Today, Football Gods and Goddesses use the Roman numerals when they talk about each Super Bowl. While a Sports God or Goddess might refer to the '49 World Series or the '99 Stanley Cup, they usually will say, "Joe Namath took the Jets to Super Bowl III" or "Green Bay won Super Bowl XXXI." In part, the Roman numerals lend dignity and a certain weighty importance to a game named after a toy. In part, they solve a tough situation for the Sports God or Goddess. The Super Bowl takes place at the end of January in a calendar year different from the regular season. For example, the Super Bowl in January 2000 is actually the championship for the 1999 season. So you can't really call it the 2000 Super Bowl. And it doesn't sound right to refer to it as the 1999 Super Bowl. Thus, the Roman numerals solve a messy problem for Football G & Gs.

EXTRA CREDIT Know that the Super Bowl usually is not a very good game. According to the National Football League, more women watch the Super Bowl than the Academy Awards. At times, more than 50 million Sports Goddesses have watched. You may have been one of them. It may have been the only football game you have ever seen, which is too bad. The regular season games are usually much more exciting and interesting and dramatic than the Super Bowl.

A few exceptions exist to this rule. Super Bowl XXXII (January 1998) surpassed expectations. Finally, John Elway's Broncos won their first championship after four attempts. Football Gods and Goddesses cheered his win and the caliber of the game.

However, if you have watched a particularly poor Super Bowl, do not judge the sport by this one experience. Watch one game (or a little bit of one) between two top teams during the regular season or watch a Conference Championship game. Most likely, you will see a better contest than the Super Bowl!

Chris Berman's Bonus Secret—

"Sports is the last great melting pot in this country."

During the 1998 football season, Chris Berman hosted all of ESPN's NFL studio programming on Sunday from Bristol, CT, and ABC's on Monday from Baltimore. He also, among his many other responsibilities for ABC/ESPN, calls play-by-play for the baseball play-offs. He is considered the leading sports presence on both networks. He mixes a powerful, pleasant personality with intelligent, insightful commentary. He links sports to society with his thoughtful references to history, music, politics, and pop culture. He concocts clever nicknames that Sports G & Gs constantly quote.

A history major at Brown University, Chris offers this perspective on sports: "The United States has always prided itself on being a melting pot of all cultures. Sports connects everyone. Man or woman. Black or white. Old or young. Rich or poor. Everyone can speak the language. A millionaire and someone on welfare can carry on a conversation and have the same opinion. Sports captures the spirit and soul of Ellis Island. It is about the last place where we can say we have the melting pot." Chris then adds, "If a woman can talk about sports with a dash of interest and excitement, it will connect her not only to men but to everyone."

I married my wife after she took me to a 49ers game!

—*male executive*

Secret #13.   **Listen to the Hank Williams, Jr., song that opens *Monday Night Football*. Then watch the first few minutes of the broadcast.**

Monday Night Football usually offers a good game. After all, ABC programs entertainment in this time slot. *Monday Night*

Football teams are selected on the basis of their records and rivalries from previous years.

A Sports Goddess will be entertained by the first few minutes of *MNF*. Tune in to ABC at 9 P.M. ET. (As always, check your local listings in case the time has changed since the writing of this book.) Singer Hank Williams, Jr., opens the show with a song about the two teams.

In the first few minutes of a game, the SGIT can learn a lot from ABC's broadcasters who will announce and analyze the game. These announcers pack in a lot of information: each team's record, each team's strengths and weaknesses, who hates whom. The good stuff. In addition, Lesley Visser will report on something "newsy" related to the game.

Some popular "women's shows"—*Murphy Brown, Ally McBeal*—have gone up against *MNF*. For years, network executives have been subtly telling women that football doesn't belong to them. Challenge their programming logic, SGITs! At least for a few minutes. During the evening, switch back to *MNF* for the score. The next day, mention that you saw the Hank Williams, Jr., song and "The last time I checked, Denver was ahead of New England. Then I went to bed." You'll get a conversation started.

Secret #14. Football=one team's offensive unit versus the other team's defensive unit.

Each team has **11** players on the field at a time. One team has **11 offensive players** (those trying to score) out there and the other team has **11 defensive players** (those trying to stop the offense from scoring). When the offense's "turn" ends, they go to the sidelines and 11 of their defensive players take the field. (Usually, in between "turns," a kicking unit will come out. More on that later.)

Football differs from other team sports. It is far more specialized. Each basketball team has five athletes on the court who master both offense and defense. Each hockey team sends out three offensive players and three defensive players (two defensemen and a goalie) on the ice *at the same time*. Each base-

Lesley Visser's Bonus Secret—

"Turn down the sound and watch the plays unfold."

You can't miss Lesley Visser on ABC's *Monday Night Football*. Her sideline reports place her in the center of the network's football coverage. She often breaks news on that night's matchup before, during, and after the game.

Lesley's career in sports journalism sets the standard for aspiring reporters of both sexes. In 1976, at the very beginning of her career with the *Boston Globe*, she became the first female reporter to cover the NFL beat. She attributes her drive and her success to her family's positive attitude. No one ever told her, "You can't do that."

Vince Doria, the former sports editor of the *Boston Globe*, told her that she could do anything in sports. Then and now, Vince praises Lesley's tremendous ability to coax comments out of the most taciturn player.

In the 1980s, Lesley gradually moved into broadcast journalism. Since 1988, first for CBS Sports and now for ABC/ESPN, she has covered the NBA, the NCAA tournament, Major League Baseball, the Olympics, and Triple Crown races. In 1992, she hosted the postgame presentation ceremonies at the Super Bowl. She was the first woman ever to assume this role. In 1998, she became the first woman to join the *Monday Night Football* team.

Lesley excelled at sports at a young age. In her sophomore year of high school, she was named the best athlete in her class. She captained her field hockey and basketball teams. In addition, sports helped build other relationships in her life. She met her husband, the sportscaster Dick Stockton, at game 6 of the 1975 World Series, one of the most thrilling postseason games ever.

Lesley thinks of sports as a "great passport" to connecting with other people.

She suggests that when you are watching a football game, "Turn the sound down" for a while. Watch the plays unfold. Draw your own conclusions.

She reminds women that "men were not born with a genetic blueprint" for sports. "They learned it! So can you."

ball player assumes the role of offense for half an inning and defense for the other half. Not in football. An offensive team member plays offense. And only offense. A defensive team member plays defense. And only defense.

When you first start watching football, don't worry too much about the defensive players. Just know that every defensive player is trying to stop the "play." The defensive player may **tackle** (bring a player with the ball down to the ground), **intercept** (catch the ball when it is being thrown by the quarterback to another offensive player), or try to **sack** (pull down to the ground) the quarterback when he has the ball. The more sacks a player makes in one season, the more money he will earn the next year. In addition, a defensive player may simply take hits from opposing offensive linemen in an attempt to distract them from protecting the quarterback.

As for the offense, focus on two or three players: the quarterback, a running back, and/or a wide receiver. I'll give you more tips on each of these players in the following pages. **The following explanation may be too simple for some SGITs. If so, skip it. However, if you don't know anything about football, start here.**

The offense will either *throw the ball* or *run with the ball*. In most games and plays they will do a little bit of both.

Throwing the ball. If the quarterback throws the ball, he will aim for a wide receiver, a tight end, or a runningback. The player who catches the ball will run with it until he scores or is tackled, falls, or runs out of bounds. He can't throw it or hand it off to another player. **Remember: every step of the way, defensive players are trying to stop the quarterback from throwing the ball and the wide receiver or tight end from catching it.** And if a player does catch the ball, they don't want him to go far with it. If a Sports Goddess knows this, it increases the excitement. Will the player catch it? How far will he run with it?

Running the ball. The quarterback will run as far as he can with the ball or will hand it off to another player (usually a **running back**). That player then will rush as far as he can with the ball until he falls or is tackled. **Once again, defensive play-**

ers are trying to stop these players every step of the way. When a Sports Goddess knows this, she should cheer either for the player to keep running (if it's her team) or for the defensive player to bring him down (if it's not her team).

Secret #15.   Understand one football rule: *Four downs.*

Football has a lot of rules. It has a lot of plays. It has a lot of diagrams.

However, understanding one rule, and just one rule, can make it much easier to understand the entire game: **when a team has the ball, they have four chances (four "downs") to move the ball 10 yards.** If they do manage to advance the ball 10 yards, then they have four more chances (four more "downs") to move the ball another 10 yards.

Thus, when you hear "first and 10," a team has its first chance to make 10 yards. If you hear "second and 7," a team is on its second down and now has 7 yards to make before they can start over.

Many SGITs have told me about situations in which a business colleague has said "we're at first and 10" or "fourth and 1." The men in the room know exactly where "we are" and the women don't have a clue. When you hear "We're at first and something," *"we" are at the beginning of a project. When you are told "We're at fourth and anything," "we" are at the end of a project and most likely in a tense situation!*

When you're listening to a game, you also might hear a phrase like "first and 10, Miami 30." A football field is 100 yards long. One half, 50 yards, belongs to each team. For example, Miami. The other half belongs to the other team. For example, Buffalo. Miami wants to get the ball into Buffalo's end zone. When Miami controls the ball and they are on the 30-yard line in their half of the field, you will hear "first and 10, Miami 30." They have **seventy yards to go to score a touchdown.** When Miami is on the 30-yard line in Buffalo's half, you will hear "first and 10, Buffalo 30." **In this case, Miami has only 30 yards to go to score a touchdown.**

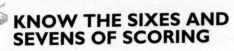

KNOW THE SIXES AND SEVENS OF SCORING

Name of Score	How You Get It	How Much It Is Worth
Touchdown	An offensive player **catches** the ball in the end zone or an offensive player **runs** with ball into the end zone.	6 points
Extra Point	After scoring a touchdown, a kicker usually comes onto the field and attempts to kick the ball above the crossbar and between the poles of the goalpost, which is at the back of the end zone.	1 point. Thus, you can score 7 points from a touchdown.
Field Goal	Instead of a fourth down (more on this later), the team attempts a field goal. A kicker tries to kick the ball between the poles of the goalpost from the field of play.	3 points
Two-Point Conversion	Instead of going for the extra point after a touchdown, a team tries for a two-point conversion. They begin their play at the 2-yard line and try to have a team member run or catch the ball in the end zone.	2 points

| Safety | When a member of the offense is holding the ball and is tackled, falls, commits a penalty, or runs out of bounds *in his own end zone, the defense scores.* | 2 points |

SG TIP. Do not try to memorize each type of point. Do listen for the different points when you watch a game. Keep this list by your side. It's a simplified version of scoring. But it's all you need to know.

SG TIP. It's easy to spot an excellent play in football. Football players tell you. They dance. They run around. They celebrate. **However, watch out.** Offensive players celebrate after **making** a great catch, a first down, or a touchdown. Defensive players dance after **stopping** a great catch, a first down, or a touchdown. Make sure you know which team just made the big play!

Secret #16. **Understand one strategic concept. *Teams usually don't go for a fourth down.* Also, know what's happening when you see a kicking unit come out on the field.**

Unless the team is very close to the end zone or in desperate need of a touchdown, they usually don't go for the fourth down. Instead, they do one of two things:

(1) Attempt a field goal. They bring out a kicker, who attempts to kick the ball over the crossbar of the goalposts. If he is successful, the team receives three points.

or

(2) Punt. If they are too far away to attempt a field goal (usually 55 yards or more), the punter (i.e., kicker) will "punt" (kick) the ball as far as he can to the opponent's end zone. The other

team will attempt to pick up the ball and move it toward the kicking team's goal as fast as they can.

Whenever a team punts, they have not scored. Thus, the term "punting" can be used in a derisive tone in professional or social jargon. *You had to punt that one; or He punted.*

If the team does go for the fourth down and does not achieve 10 yards, then they must turn the ball over to the other team at that spot. Thus, the opposition may be closer to scoring a touchdown than if the team had punted.

> **EXTRA CREDIT**   Kicking units will come out on the field on two other occasions.
>
> (1) *Extra Point.* When a team has scored a touchdown, they usually bring out a kicker to score an extra point. The kicker must kick the ball over the crossbar of the goalposts to get the point.
>
> (2) *Kickoff.* At the start of a game, the beginning of the second half, or after a team has scored, there is a kickoff. The ball is placed on a tee. The kicker kicks the ball off the tee. He is flanked by 11 teammates who run alongside him. He attempts to kick the ball as far down field (toward the opposing team's goal line) as possible.

SPORTS GODDESS MOVIE REVIEWS— FOOTBALL

Black Sunday (1977).

Stars: Bruce Dern, Robert Shaw.   **SG summary:** Terrorists try to blow up the Super Bowl. For many, a pre–Sports Goddess fantasy.   **A Sports Goddess should note:** In 1991, at the height of the Gulf War, many worried that terrorists would try to blow up Super Bowl.

Brian's Song (1970; TV movie).

Stars: James Caan, Billy Dee Williams.   **SG summary:** SG tearjerker. True story of friendship between two Chicago Bears' players, Gale Sayers and Brian Piccolo, during the latter's terminal illness.   **A Sports Goddess should listen for:** sappy theme music. Sports Gods and Goddesses hummed it for years.

Diner (1982).

Stars: Kevin Bacon, Ellen Barkin, Steve Guttenberg, Paul Reiser.
SG summary: Six friends talk about life and sports in a Baltimore diner.
Crucial SG subplot: The fiancée of one of the friends must take a football test prior to the wedding. Her marriage hinges on her performance. Sports fans love the "quiz" scene.

Jerry Maguire (1996).

Stars: Tom Cruise, Cuba Gooding, Jr., Renee Zellweger.   **SG summary:** Fired agent fights the system with his one remaining client, a football player.   **An SG should note:** the NFL draft scene in New York City. This event happens every April.   **An SG should quote:** "Show me the money!"

The Longest Yard (1974).

Stars: Burt Reynolds, Bernadette Peters, Eddie Albert.   **SG summary:** Former football player lands in jail. He ends up organizing a team of cons that plays a team of guards.   **SG fun fact:** A young Bernadette Peters plays the warden's secretary who delivers the game tapes and herself to Burt Reynolds.   **An SG should listen to:** discussions on point spreads. She might learn about them.

Secret #17.   Pay attention to the quarterback. Know a few famous ones.

The quarterback directs the game on the field. He runs, he throws, he chooses whether to run or throw. He decides whom to throw the ball to and when. (Actually, many of his decisions have been mapped out in a playbook that he memorizes. Still, he executes these plays.) So if you watch the quarterback, you will not be disappointed. When he's off the field, and his team's defensive players are on the field, you can watch the quarterback on the other team.

Even if you never watch a game, you still should learn the name of the quarterback of your city's team and the names of one or two others. Remember to think THIN to get info on the QBs. Quarterbacks are considered the leaders of teams. They also are seen as the thinkers and the decision makers. Thus, if your boss compares you to a certain quarterback, you will want to know his most recent performance and his general reputation!

SG TIP. Football Gods and Goddesses talk about a quarterback's skills in terms of his "weapons." And so should you.

SPORTS GODDESS PROFILES: CURRENT QUARTERBACKS

Troy Aikman

SG fun fact: According to *People Online*, Troy had a "flirtation" with actress Sandra Bullock. *'98 team:* Dallas Cowboys. *One reason he's a star:* He led his team to three Super Bowl victories. (I know I told you this in Chapter 1. However, it's impressive enough to mention again.) *His weapons:* He's an accurate thrower. Reads the other team's defenses well.

Drew Bledsoe

SG fun fact: He ran into some trouble during the '97 season when he jumped from the stage into the mosh pit at an Everclear concert. The New England media did not view this incident well. *'98 team:* New England Patriots. *One reason he's a star:* He led his team to Super Bowl XXXI during '96 season. *His weapons:* can throw a lot. In one game, he threw the ball **70** times. It's a record. The ball was caught—or in football lingo, the pass was completed—45 of those 70 times.

John Elway

SG fun fact: Elway was an outstanding **baseball** as well as football player at Stanford University. He was drafted by the New York Yankees and played minor league ball for a summer. *'98 team:* Denver Broncos. *A few reasons he's a star:* Elway led his team to five Super Bowls. They lost the first three. They won the fourth and fifth (Super Bowl XXXII and XXXIII). When you have had several setbacks in pursuit of a goal, think of Elway. *His weapons:* Elway is known for his fourth quarter comeback performances. *SG additional note:* Elway retired in 1999. However, his ability to rally his team in the fourth quarter and his victory in his fourth and fifth Super Bowls will be talked about by Sports Gods and Goddesses for a long time.

Brett Favre

Nickname: "Country" (hails from rural Mississippi).   *SG fun fact:* Favre appeared in the hit movie *There's Something About Mary* with Cameron Diaz.   *'98 team:* Green Bay Packers.   *One reason he's a star:* He led his team to two back-to-back Super Bowls (Super Bowl XXXI and Super Bowl XXXII). Won the first one. Lost the second. The first player to be named the Most Valuable Player three years in a row.   *His weapons:* He has a laser arm and quick feet.   *SG additional notes*: Favre possesses tremendous determination. He suffered injuries in a car crash the summer before his senior year of college (at Southern Mississippi). He came back that season. He was **not** selected in the first round of the NFL draft. He has gone on to a Hall of Fame career. In the summer of 1996, he underwent treatment for an addiction to painkillers. The next January, the Packers won the Super Bowl.

Steve Young

SG fun fact: He is a direct descendant of Brigham Young, the early leader of the Mormon church.   *'98 Team:* San Francisco 49ers.   *One reason he's a star:* He holds the highest rating for passing in the history of the NFL. What does that mean to a Sports Goddess? He's a very good thrower. And his passes get caught.   *His weapon:* He knows how to throw to his targets.

SPORTS GODDESS PROFILE:
PAST QUARTERBACKS

Terry Bradshaw

SG fun fact: He was formerly married to ice skater Jo Jo Starbuck.   *Played for:* Pittsburgh Steelers (1970–1983).   *One reason he was a star:* He played on four winning Super Bowl teams.   *His weapons:* He had a very strong arm. Could throw far.   *Can now be seen on:* FOX *NFL Sunday* on the FOX network.

Joe Montana

SG fun fact: During the football season, the town of Ismay, Montana, changes its name to Joe, Montana. The town's name reverts to Ismay after the Super Bowl. *Played for:* San Francisco 49ers (1979–1992) and Kansas City Chiefs (1993–1994). *One reason he was a star:* He played on four winning Super Bowl teams. Was MVP in three of those games. *His weapons:* He could throw accurately while running. Very mobile.

Joe Namath

Nickname: "Broadway Joe." *SG fun fact:* He epitomized the "swinging bachelor" of the late 1960s. Wore pantyhose in a commercial. *Played for:* New York Jets (1965–1976) and the L.A. Rams (1977). *One reason he was a star:* On the eve of Super Bowl III, he boldly "guaranteed" that the New York Jets, the underdogs, would win the game. He was right. *His weapons:* Like other star quarterbacks, Namath could throw accurately. However, his persona—brash, sexy, confident—may have been his greatest weapon on and off the field.

Think of yourself as a quarterback. Are you more of a comeback kid like John Elway? Someone who throws everything out there like Drew Bledsoe? Or someone who doesn't throw as much but usually hits the target like Joe Montana? When you personalize sports, you start to feel the fun.

SPORTS GODDESS TV GUIDE

Many SGITs enjoy the pregame shows. They preview the key games, show moving features on athletes' lives (e.g., Broncos QB John Elway talking about his relationship with his wife), and tackle troubling issues in the sport (e.g., the drug addiction of former NFL great Lawrence Taylor). Many SGITs also like to tune in at halftime or catch a postgame recap show. They can find the scores and highlights in a few minutes. Scott Ackerson, the Executive Producer of FOX's NFL studio shows, offers this advice: "When you are watching sports television shows, be it live game action or studio shows, *look to get the big picture.* Who's good and who's not. Pay particular attention to teaching segments, because all you need is just a little knowledge to make it appear that you're very knowledgeable. Every male believes he comes out of the womb with this inherent knowledge of sports, when in fact, he's just as clueless as you are; he just fakes it better."

NFL Studio Show Guide

CBS. *The NFL Today* (Sunday, noon ET)

CNN. *NFL Preview* (Sunday, 10 A.M. ET)

ESPN. *NFL CountDown* (Sunday, 11 A.M. ET), pregame. *NFL PrimeTime* (Sunday, 7:30 P.M. ET), postgame highlights

FOX. *FOX NFL Sunday* (Sunday, noon ET), pregame

As always, check local listings for times in your area.

*Secret #*18.   **Know what OJ Simpson did. In football.**

Once upon a time, OJ Simpson played professional football. He spent most of his career with the Buffalo Bills. He was very, very good. He was a running back, the player who runs or "rushes" the ball down the field. (Sometimes they catch the ball. But don't worry about that right now.) If you tire of looking at the quarterback, you can watch the running back throughout a play.

> **SG TIP.**   Running back=OJ's football position. Football G & Gs measure running backs by *how many yards they "rush for"* (run) *and by how many touchdowns they score.* In a game. In a season. In a career.

SPORTS GODDESS PROFILE: PRESENT RUNNING BACKS

Barry Sanders

SG fun facts: Barry Sanders is one of 11 children of a roofer in Kansas. All the children graduated from college. Sanders is known for his dignified demeanor in an era of showier, louder athletes.   *'98 team:* Detroit Lions.   *One reason he's a star:* He won the Heisman Trophy (given to the most outstanding college football player) in 1988 and NFL Rookie of the Year in 1989.   *Watch for these moves:* He darts. Weaves. Runs forward and backward and sideways. Fast.

Emmitt Smith

SG fun facts: In 1990, he left the University of Florida after his junior year to play in the NFL. However, he promised his mother that he would earn his degree. He took courses in the off-season. In 1996, he donned a cap and gown, received his degree, and fulfilled his promise.   *'98 team:* Dallas Cowboys.   *One reason he's a star:* Along with Troy Aikman, he helped lead the Cowboys to three Super Bowl victories.   *Watch for these moves:* He runs very, very fast.

SPORTS GODDESS PROFILE: PAST RUNNING BACKS

Jim Brown

SG fun facts: A superb athlete and a powerful personality, he dominated football in the 1960s. He retired at the **top of his game** and became (for a while) an actor. He starred in the movie *The Dirty Dozen.* He has been very active in civil rights causes.   *Played for:* Cleveland Browns (1957–1965).   *One reason he was a star:* Brown holds records for most years leading the league in yards gained (eight) and most consecutive years leading the league in yards gained (five). If he had kept playing, he probably would hold many other records. However, he left without compromising his dignity.   *SG additional fact:* Brown excelled in lacrosse at Syracuse University.

Frank Gifford

Nickname: "Giff."   *SG story:* Yes, Kathy Lee's husband and the former "Mr. Monday Night Football" played the game very well. He's in the Hall of Fame. In the late 1950s and early 1960s, Frank Gifford was a major star with the New York Giants. In 1960, his career almost ended when he was the recipient of the "hit of the decade." Late in a game with the Philadelphia

Eagles, Gifford was hit by Eagles linebacker Chuck Bednarik. He fell on the back of his head and was knocked unconscious. When he recovered the next day, he couldn't remember the game. After surviving that hit and missing one year of football, he moved to the position of wide receiver. *Played for:* New York Giants (1952–1960, 1962–1964). *One reason he was a star:* He was the NFL's MVP in 1956. Led New York Giants to three NFL Championship Games. *An SG should read*—*A Fan's Notes* by Frederick Exley, which talks about his hero worship of Frank Gifford and his reaction to Gifford's injury.

Walter Payton

Nickname: "Sweetness." *SG fun facts:* His teammates bestowed his nickname on him because of his disposition. *Played for:* Chicago Bears (1975–1987). *One reason he was a star:* He holds the record for most yards gained in a career (16,726 yards). Basically, that statistic tells you that he has run farther than any other running back in his career.

Orenthal James Simpson

Nicknames: "OJ," "Juice." *SG fun facts:* OJ won the Heisman Trophy (given to the best college player) and went on to a very distinguished professional career. Very few Heisman Trophy winners have accomplished that feat. In addition, he became the first Heisman Trophy winner to be elected to the Professional Football Hall of Fame. *Played for:* Buffalo Bills (1969–1977) and San Francisco 49ers (1978–1979). *One reason he was a star:* OJ still holds the record for most games with 200 yards or more gained (six). In addition, he played for some very bad teams yet managed to achieve Hall of Fame numbers.

SPORTS GODDESS BOOK REVIEWS

North Dallas Forty

Author: Peter Gent, a former professional football player. *SG note:* It's out of print. Many libraries and used bookstores carry it. *SG summary:* It recounts eight days in the life of a professional football player in Dallas during the 1970s. Lots of sex, drugs, and rock 'n' roll.

Green Bay Replay: The Packers Return to Glory

Author: Dick Schaap (sports journalist). **SG summary:** It chronicles Green Bay Packers during their triumphant return to the Super Bowl during the 1996–1997 season. Previously, Schaap had written a bestseller on the Packers of the 1960s, *Instant Replay*. Many libraries and used bookstores carry it.

Shark Among Dolphins

Author: Steve Hubbard. **SG summary:** It documents one season with Jimmy Johnson, the Miami Dolphins coach and the former Dallas Cowboys coach. Intense.

Rude Behavior

Author: Dan Jenkins, a former writer for *Sports Illustrated*. **SG summary:** Billy Clyde, a fun-loving former professional football player, tries to buy a team. Jenkins introduced the character of Billy Clyde in his novel *Semi-Tough*, which can be found in libraries.

> **Secret #19.** If a Football God talks about a player having "beautiful hands," he's referring to the wide receiver.

If the quarterback is not handing the ball off to a running back or running himself, then he is throwing to a **wide receiver** or the **tight end** (basically, a wide receiver who lines up next to the offensive line). A wide receiver receives the pass. Hence, the name.

Football Gods and Goddesses evaluate wide receivers *by the number of receptions (passes) they catch, and the number of touchdowns they score*. In a game. In a season. In a career. Football G & Gs also talk about wide receivers in terms of their "hands." Thus, when you hear a Football God say "he has beautiful hands," he's not talking about them aesthetically.

The greatest wide receiver of all time, Jerry Rice, still plays the game. (Or at least he did during the '98 season. A Sports Goddess never knows when a player will quit.) If an SGIT wants to watch just a few moments of football this season, make it a

49ers game (she probably can see it on her FOX affiliate or by going to a sports bar on a Sunday afternoon and asking for the 49ers game). Someday she can tell her little Sports Gods and Goddesses that she saw Jerry Rice's beautiful hands.

SPORTS GODDESS PROFILE: ONE GREAT PAST & PRESENT WIDE RECEIVER

Jerry Rice

SG fun fact: In 1995, *People* magazine named him to the Top 10 list of "Best Bods." *'98 team:* San Francisco 49ers. *One reason he's a star:* Through the '98 season, Jerry Rice led all NFL receivers in the number of career receptions, the number of career yards, and the number of career touchdowns. What does this mean for the Sports Goddess? Jerry Rice catches, runs, and scores a lot. Rice can run very far, very fast after receiving the ball. *SG additional note:* Rice has a tremendous work ethic. He keeps that great bod in shape with a lot of hard work.

> *A few years ago, I lived in Green Bay, Wisconsin—a very small town (under 100k population) and home of the renowned Green Bay Packers. There, EVERYONE talked about professional sports frequently—and women were as involved as men. Though many of the Monday conversations occurred among the (mostly male) senior execs, my secretary (a woman) was also anxious to discuss the previous Sunday's action every week during the football season.*
>
> *—male retailing executive*

Secret #20.   Know where to find "Titletown" on the U.S. map.

Titletown is Green Bay, Wisconsin, the home of the Packers. Green Bay is the smallest city to have a professional franchise. The town takes tremendous pride in the "Pack." Fans refer to themselves as "Cheeseheads." Some even wear plastic wedges of cheese on their heads when they go to games. The Green Bay Packers have contributed much to the lore of football. If you know a few things about the past and the present of the Packers, you will be connecting not only to the team but also to the history of football.

1. Green Bay is called "Titletown" because the Packers have won so many titles (12 through the '98 season).

2. The Green Bay Packers are community owned. Actually, today they are globally owned. However, Football Gods and Goddesses still like to talk about the community ownership. In 1923, at the height of the Jazz Age, the Packers were in financial trouble. Residents of Green Bay raised money for the team and received shares of stock in the Packers. Several stock offerings later, the Packers are the only publicly owned team in the NFL. The descendants of those residents have now scattered across the globe. Later investors hailed from other communities. However, when a Sports Goddess talks about the ownership of the Packers, she should note enthusiastically that they belong "to the community."

Today, when a Sports God or Goddess buys a share of stock in the Packers, he or she receives a certificate. That's it. It can't be traded on any exchange. (The Packers are publicly owned, not publicly traded.) It can't be sold back. It never increases in value. (A share of stock purchased for $25 in the 1950s is still worth $25 today.) The owner will not receive the annual report for the Packers unless he or she asks for it. However, he or she can say that he or she owns a piece of the Packers.

SG TIP. If you can purchase a share of Packers stock, it makes a great gift for a Sports God or Goddess.

3. Vince Lombardi coached the Green Bay Packers. Football Gods and Goddesses revere Vince Lombardi, the legendary coach of the Packers. The NFL even named the Super Bowl trophy after him.

A deeply religious, disciplined individual, Lombardi began coaching the Packers in 1959. He didn't innovate many fancy plays. He didn't create many complex schemes. Instead, he emphasized the fundamental skills of football. He drove his players very, very hard. He demanded perfect execution of each play. He won. A lot. Five titles in seven years, including the first two Super Bowls.

A Sports Goddess may never have heard of Lombardi. However, she is probably familiar with one of his sayings. Lombardi phrased many things well about sports, competition, and football. Today, his catchy phrases would be called sound bites. When he first said them, they were known as quotes. Many coaches and executives have incorporated Lombardi's words into their own philosophies.

Winning isn't everything, it's the only thing is considered the most controversial of Lombardi's quotes. Some defenders now insist he originally said *Winning isn't everything, the will to win is*. According to them, Lombardi went along with the misquote for a while. Then he worried that he would be misinterpreted as advocating that one should win at all costs. Other biographers have written that that is exactly what he said in private, though he did later say to a sportswriter, "I wish to hell I'd never said the damn thing . . . I meant the effort . . . I meant having a goal . . . I sure as hell didn't mean for people to crush human values and morality."

However, don't worry too much about what he really meant. Just know the saying is attributed to him.

Other famous Lombardi quotes:

"The harder you work, the harder it is to surrender."

"Fatigue makes cowards of us all."

"Anything is ours providing, we are willing to pay the price."

Remember one. Throw it out at work. Drop it on a friend. Make Lombardi's slogans your slogans.

Recently, Mike Holmgren coached the Pack. He showed a softer, gentler side to his players. He counseled them on investments and where to find soul food in Wisconsin. He sang Beach Boys songs and rode a motorcycle. He met his wife for coffee each day during the season. He encouraged innovative plays and offenses. However, he shared one key trait with Lombardi. He won. He led the Packers to two Super Bowls. At the end of the 1998 season, he left the Packers to coach the Seattle Seahawks. And his replacement, veteran coach Ray Rhodes, now had to live up to Lombardi's *and* Holmgren's legacies.

4. The Ice Bowl. When an SGIT starts reading about or watching the Pack, she sees or hears references to the "Ice Bowl" or to "the frozen tundra of Lambeau Field." The Ice Bowl was the 1967 NFL (now the NFC) Championship game. The temperature was −19 degrees. The ground froze into ice. Players slipped. Lombardi shivered. Sixteen seconds were left in the game. The Cowboys led the Packers by three points. Then Packer guard Jerry Kramer blocked a Cowboy player. Packer quarterback Bart Starr snuck behind him. The Packers won the game, went on to victory in the Super Bowl, and achieved immortality in football.

Know the Ice Bowl happened. It wasn't a Super Bowl. It was a Conference Championship game. It involved the Packers and Lombardi. And it was very, very cold.

SG TIP.   Visit a sports bar.

An SGIT may want to watch a game. She just doesn't want to view any of the games available to her at home. In these days of satellite dishes, she has options. She can visit a sports bar (with friends) that can downlink a game of her choice. (Most sports bars list, on a blackboard outside, the games they will be showing that afternoon. Some take requests.)

Many sports bars do not resemble other drinking holes. They're bright. They offer meals. (Of course, their clients stay for hours.) They erupt in cheers or groans every few minutes.

If you ever wondered where guys hang out, check out a sports bar.

Of course, they may be too engrossed in whatever game they are watching to notice you. Then again, maybe not.

Secret #21. Make "America's Team" your team. Or at least know something about the Dallas Cowboys.

Although the Cowboys lost the legendary Ice Bowl, they went on to a distinguished career in the 1970s. They played in five Super Bowls in that decade and won two of them. Football G & Gs nicknamed them "America's Team." Their logo—a Lone Star—symbolized winning. Like the Packers, the Cowboys again achieved greatness in the 1990s with three more Super Bowl victories. While their image may not have been as wholesome as that of the Packers, the Cowboys have contributed to the legend and lore of professional football.

1. The Dallas Cowboys Cheerleaders are one of the oldest professional dance squads in sports. They may repulse you. They may amuse you. But they are worth knowing about. The Dallas Cowboys Cheerleaders represent a sexy slice of American popular culture. They have been depicted in made-for-TV movies. They have appeared on everything from *The Love Boat* to *Geraldo*. They have toured with USO troupes. They have survived for nearly 30 years.

More than a thousand women try out each year for the squad. No one is assured of a position the next year. An incumbent cheerleader must audition again the next year. And they do.

2. The Dallas Cowboys are not community owned. The city of Dallas may worship the Cowboys, but it does not own them.

Over the years, two legendary owners have etched their personalities on the team and on the game of football. **Clint Murchinson, Jr.,** made history in the 1960s when he gave a **10-year** contract to Coach Tom Landry. Think of that the next time you negotiate with your boss. ("Listen, I'm not looking for a 10-year deal like Tom Landry.") **Jerry Jones,** the present owner, hails from Arkansas. In 1989, soon after he purchased the Cowboys, he fired Tom Landry, the only man ever to coach the team. It was not a popular move. However, he propelled the Cowboys to a new era of winning in the 1990s with a series of shrewd decisions.

3. Tom Landry coached the Dallas Cowboys for many years. Then Jimmy Johnson and Barry Switzer coached for a much shorter time.

Tom Landry coached Dallas for 29 years. He had 20 straight winning seasons. He took the "Boys" to five Super Bowls and won two. He possessed a low-key, humble personality. He was better known for his sartorial sensibilities (he always wore a fedora on the sidelines) than for any quotes. He managed well for a long time. When he was fired, he took it with grace.

Jimmy Johnson took over the team in 1989. While in many ways he symbolizes the antithesis of Lombardi, **he epitomizes the attitude "winning isn't everything, it's the only thing."** Soon after Johnson assumed the coaching position with Dallas, he divorced his wife. Dallas newspapers reported that he had said he no longer needed the "social prop" of a spouse. He admitted in a biography that he forgot his family's birthdays and didn't have much time for Christmas. However, he brought the "Boys" back to the Super Bowl twice and won both times. He was known for the slogan "Win or else." And he did. (Still does.) Eventually, his relationship with Jerry Jones became troubled. He resigned. He now coaches the Miami Dolphins.

Barry Switzer took over the Cowboys in 1994. His autobiography was titled *Bootlegger's Boy*. He had coached at the University of Oklahoma, where some of his players ran into a lot of trouble with the law. Things didn't change much in Dallas.

Barry Switzer brought the Cowboys to another Super Bowl, which they won. However, during his tenure, some of the "Boys" were involved in heavy partying, arrests, and drug rumors. In August 1997, police arrested Switzer at the Dallas airport for carrying a gun. He left the Cowboys at the end of that season.

Chan Gailey now coaches Dallas. Like Landry, Gailey belongs to the Fellowship of Christian Athletes. He lives by the motto "Do everything the right way." Unlike Johnson and Switzer, he remains married to his first and only wife, a former star athlete in high school. In fact, she often questions him on his plays!

Thus, America's Team presents four very different coaching models for a Sports Goddess. Is she a long-term manager like Landry? Does she sacrifice her personal life to win at all costs in the manner of Johnson? Is she a bit of an outlaw like Switzer? Or is she a by-the-rules executive in the mold of Chan Gailey?

> I have always been into sports (it's actually my mom's fault), but now I am even more hooked (especially on football, since that's where the fun pools are). In fact, I beat out 47 other folks (only about 6 women) to win the football pool this last season. The $550 certainly helped at Christmastime!
>
> —female computer executive

Secret #22. **Understand the spread. Know how to fill out a pool sheet. Even if you don't want to wager money.**

When a Sports Goddess picks the winner of a game before it starts, she usually cares about the outcome. She doesn't have to wager money. She can play for pride.

But first, she has to understand the spread.

Prior to a game, football oddsmakers *set the line*. The line basically predicts by how many points one team will beat the other. The winning margin is called the *point spread*. For example, if Green Bay is favored to win over San Francisco by seven points, the point spread is 7. If Green Bay wins by more than seven, they *cover the spread*. If Green Bay wins by less than seven or loses, then San Francisco *beats the spread*. Sometimes, you may hear a cheer erupting in the stadium near the end of the game when a losing team scores a few points (but not enough to win the game). Most likely, that team just beat the spread and won money for some fans.

The NFL does not approve of gambling. Players cannot place bets. However, betting does occur every week in small and large ways across the country. Most likely, at some point, you will be offered a chance to join a football pool. Whether you throw in your last dollar or simply ante up your pride, **your first question should be, "What's the spread on these games?"**

> *Ironically, as a female, one of my biggest "bonding" activities with a male direct report of mine is to talk sports. We both follow the same professional teams and rehash games/trades the day after big events, and in fact, for most of the pro football season, kept track and compared our "picks" against the spread (I beat him by two games cumulative!).*
>
> *—female technology executive*

SPORTS GODDESS POWER TALK:

Know your Xs from your Os. Talk the talk of football.

I've slipped a lot of popular football terms and lingo into these secrets. However, I'll give you a few more here. Once again, skim through the list. See which ones sound familiar ("Oh, so, that's what it means!"). Pick two or three. Incorporate them into your sports, social, and professional vocabularies. Then select one or two more. Very soon, you will be a football-talking Sports Goddess.

Jeff Greenfield's Bonus Secret on Politics & Sports—

"Know Why So Many Politicians and Journalists Embrace Sports"

Sports jargon seeps through the language of politics. Politicians "run races." At the end of campaigns, they talk about being in the "last inning" or the "final stretch." During the final days of the Clinton impeachment trial in the Senate, the *New York Times* pontificated in an article on the need for both Senate Republicans and Ken Starr to throw "Hail Mary" passes.

Many politicians have embraced sports and its accompanying photo opportunities. Presidents invite winning teams to the Rose Garden. Teddy Roosevelt boxed; Dwight D. Eisenhower golfed; John F. Kennedy sailed (and actually was a better golfer than Eisenhower); and Bill Clinton jogs. Presidents, First Ladies, and other political types are always on hand to throw out the first baseball of the season. Richard Nixon even designed a play or two for Redskins coach George Allen and talked college sports with antiwar protesters on the Washington Mall. Conversely, Bill Bradley (former New York Knicks star) and Jack Kemp (former Buffalo Bills quarterback) are two former professional athletes who have achieved success in the political "arena."

Jeff Greenfield, the CNN anchor and senior analyst, understands both worlds. He is one of the top political analysts in the country and has written nine books. A lifelong sports fan, in 1994 he wrote a memorable essay for *USA Weekend* on "Why I Love Baseball" alongside an essay on "Why I Hate Baseball" by David Greenfield, his eleven-year-old son. Jeff shares this insight into understanding the confluence of the worlds of sports and politics: "The late Chief Justice Earl Warren used to say that he read the front page of the newspaper to read of mankind's failures—and the sports pages to read of mankind's triumphs.

"In this age of lawsuits, strikes and lockouts, physical assaults and criminal misdeeds, and the relentless pursuit of ever-more-astonishing amounts of dollars, this may seem quaint; but it still embodies a fundamental truth. One of the reasons so many political players and political journalists are fascinated by sports is that there is, at the core, an absolutely objective measure of success and failure. You can't "spin" a fifteen-game losing streak; you can't argue about who won the last World Series. (Yes, you can argue that Ted Williams was better than Dimaggio, or that Mays had them both beat, but that's another matter.) And whatever dark deeds happen in front offices, everything about the game happens in full view—unlike the world of politics. And there is also the endless opportunity for optimism, the hope that a ninth-inning rally or "Hail Mary" pass will produce a last-minute victory.

"False optimism? Not always; that son of mine who hated baseball five years ago is now an enthusiastic Yankee fan with a steel-trap mind for stats."

Basic Jargon

Xs and Os   **Football definition:** X stands for defense. O represents offense. A coach will diagram plays using "Xs and Os."
If your boss says, "Show me the Xs and Os"—Use the Xs to represent the defensive moves and the Os to chart the aggressive, offensive plays.

Drive   **Football definition:** A drive is the series of plays that will, hopefully, lead to a touchdown.
If your boss says, "We're driving down the field"—You're on the offensive. And, most likely, there's a defensive player ready, every step of the way, to knock you down!

Line of Scrimmage	**Football definition:** It's not a real line on the field. Players line up on either side of the LOS after play has stopped at that point on the field.

Defense

Football has **man-to-man coverage** (one man defending one man) and **zone coverage** (players defend an area and not a person).

Quarterback Jargon

Audible	**Football definition:** When the play changes, a quarterback (QB) calls an "audible" (code word for play change) on the field.
Dummy Audible	**Football definition:** When the play does not change, but the QB wants to confuse the defense, he calls a "dummy audible."
Blitz	**Football definition:** Several defensive players "swarm" the quarterback in an effort to sack him. Meanwhile, the QB tries to hand off the ball or throw it to an unguarded player! **If your boss says, "We're going to blitz the opposition on this"**—Identify the recipient of the blitz. Prepare a backup plan in case he or she "hands it off" to someone else.
Huddle	**Football definition:** The offense gathers in a circular group to discuss the upcoming play. The quarterback receives radio communication (in his helmet!) from the offensive coordinator. **If your boss says, "Let's huddle"**—Know who calls the plays. And how much you can say.

Offense

Prior to a play, the offense and defense stand on opposite sides of the line of scrimmage. Football bestows names on the different patterns of lining up. Once again, if you listen, you usually will be told.

Shotgun	**Football definition:** The QB stands five yards behind the center. The center snaps the ball into the air (or "shoots") to the QB.
	If your boss says, "We'll use a shotgun formation"—Know whether you are shooting or receiving.

I formation **Football definition:** The QB and the running backs form a straight line behind the center. It looks like the letter I.

If your boss says, "We're using an I formation here"—Know where you are standing on the I. (O=Offensive player.)

O (C)   C=Center
O (QB) QB=Quarterback
O (RB) RB=Running Back
O (RB)

Split T **Football definition:** The running backs stand on either side of, and behind, the QB.

If your boss says, "We're using the split T"—Know whether you are standing to the left, the right, or in the center. And where you go, once the action starts.

O (C)
O (QB)
O (RB)   O (RB)

One Throw to Know

Hail Mary **Football definition:** The quarterback throws a desperation pass down the field. It's usually thrown high in the air and often very far (for example, attempting 80 yards). It tends to occur at the end of a half or at the end of the game.

If your boss asks you to throw a Hail Mary—Know how far you must throw. And how desperate you are.

SGITs, start connecting to the NFL. If you're reading this in the fall, figure out by thinking THIN which NFL week it is or which teams are scheduled for the next *Monday Night Football*. If you're reading this in another season, learn about one or two players (e.g., Barry Sanders and Drew Bledsoe). Look up their biographies on the NFL's Internet site (*www.nfl.com*). Learn more about the Green Bay Packers and Titletown through one of Dick Schaap's books on the team. Or start a group of fellow NFL SGITs and talk about the sport with each other!

Andrea Kremer's Bonus Secret—

"Pick a team and root for them!"

Andrea Kremer not only talks sports. She speaks the language with such fluency and ease that few men or women can keep up with her.

Andrea danced her way through her childhood in Philadelphia. A gifted ballerina, she graduated from the University of Pennsylvania cum laude. Then she moved from the theatrics of the dance world to those of the professional sports arena. Early in her sports career, she produced and reported for *This Is the NFL*, a nationally syndicated show of NFL films.

In 1989, she joined ESPN. She quickly established herself on the NFL beat and just about every other beat she covered. She generated the idea for an ESPN documentary on the impact of sexism in the world of sports. For this broadcast, she interviewed Nigel Clay, a former Oklahoma football player who had been convicted of rape and sentenced to prison. Several years later, she updated her story with an uplifting twist: after his release, Clay moved to Ohio and was attending college again, in a far less pressured setting. Andrea's initial work inspired my gender research project at Wellesley and, ultimately, this book. In 1997, Andrea was cited as Best Female sportscaster in *P.O.V.* magazine. In January 1999, she was featured on an NFL special on Lifetime, *Women and the NFL*.

Her boss, ESPN's Managing Editor Bob Eaton, boasts: "Her contacts range from star players to guys that are barely on the depth charts, from owners to secretaries, from coaches to clubhouse personnel. What's more, she genuinely likes these people and cares about them as more than people who can give her a story." Bob recalls an evening when he attended the annual Commissioner's party with Andrea at the Super Bowl. "It took us two hours to make a circuit of the room as Andrea greeted people that she knew—exchanging greetings but picking up information that she would use the next day. She never quits!"

Andrea reinforces the think THIN theory: "You don't have to know every rule or memorize each roster, but a daily perusal of the sports headlines or a glance at the weekly *Sports Illustrated* can't hurt." She offers comforting advice to the SGIT: "Remember that love of, and knowledge about, sports is not genetically predisposed or gender specific! Sometimes we're intimidated by the unknown—so become familiar with the world of sports. It's very inviting and fascinating." Finally, she suggests that if you're watching football, "Don't worry about the rules or the analysis or the play calling—**root for a team to win and your interest will grow because the game will actually have meaning.**"

3

A Sports Goddess Talks
PROFESSIONAL BASKETBALL

MEN'S PROFESSIONAL BASKETBALL

A Sports Goddess knows:

The league's name—National Basketball Association (NBA).

The NBA is divided into—the Eastern Conference (15 teams) and the Western Conference (14 teams).

The number of games in the regular season is—82.

The game is divided into—four 12-minute quarters. Teams break at "half-time."

The regular season runs from—November to April.

The championship series is called—the NBA Finals (four out of seven games).

The number of players on each team on the court is—5.

The object of the game—Each team wants to get the basketball through its opponent's basket.

Game summary—A basketball court is 94 feet long and 50 feet wide. A basketball game begins with a **tipoff**; a referee throws the ball up between each team's center (usually the tallest player on each team). The team that gains possession of the ball has 24 seconds to shoot it at the opponent's basketball net. After a successful shot, the other team takes possession of the ball. After an unsuccessful shot, the team that gets the ball on the rebound takes possession of the ball.

MANY BASKETBALL GODS and Goddesses refer to the sport as "the hottest game on the planet." It's true. You can be a Sports Goddess of pro basketball anywhere on earth. For example, in Russia, nested wooden dolls (one large doll filled with a series of successively smaller dolls) can be found in most bazaars in most cities. At several stands in St. Petersburg, I spotted Michael Jordan and Alonzo Mourning nested dolls side by side with the more traditional figurines.

Why is the NBA so popular? Basketball has been played nearly everywhere for a long time. It's easy to follow. The NBA also has a strong, marketing-oriented commissioner, David Stern. In the 1980s and 1990s, Stern sold the game, its teams, and its stars in the domestic and international markets. He did a very good job.

In addition to promoting the league, the NBA's stars started selling everything else: McDonald's hamburgers, Pepsi, Coke, every sneaker on the planet. Shaquille O'Neal has starred in a movie with Nick Nolte. Dennis Rodman has appeared in news items on *Entertainment Tonight*. Michael Jordan has hosted *Saturday Night Live*. The NBA's stars have blended into the firmament of popular culture.

During the 1998–1999 NBA season, a standoff between management and the players' union halted play for the first three months of the season. When the dispute ended, the NBA immediately sent E-mails and faxes to its twenty-nine team offices about a coordinated marketing strategy to win fans back to the game. In the first month of play, the television ratings for the national games on NBC actually went *up* from the previous year's. The NBA knows how to market.

Secret #23. Know a few star players.

In the NBA, stars rule. Identify two or three. If you know the names of two or three current stars and a few things about them, you will find it much easier to understand the game, learn the names of the teams, and talk about the action.

When you watch a game, quickly determine the star player(s) for each team. (How will you know the stars? Once again, remember those insider tips. **Listen to the announcers and you will be told.**) Then focus your attention on that star. When he has the ball, watch what he does. When he doesn't have the ball, still watch what he does. When the other team has the ball, **still** watch what he does. Very quickly, you will get a feel for the game. (Obviously, you don't have to do this forever or even for an entire game. However, if you watch one player for a few minutes at a time, you can see how he sets up and defends plays.)

> In business, the language of sports is part of being a member of the club. Women need to have this language. They need to know sports. If not, they are on the "sidelines," to use a sports metaphor.
>
> —female management consultant

Even if you don't watch one player (or the game), you still can keep up with the stars. For example, you, the Sports Goddess, live in Seattle. Office talk centers on the SuperSonics. Gary Payton (aka "The Glove") is a star of the Sonics. If you're an energetic Sports Goddess, you can turn to the sports pages and read the first few paragraphs of the game summary. If Payton had a good game, you will be told. If he had a bad game, you will be told. Then, when you're in a meeting and the talk starts on the game, you can say, "I saw that the Glove had a bad game."

Perhaps you don't have the energy, time, or inclination to turn to the sports page. Simply ask, "How did Payton do?"

You'll get a response. You'll participate in the conversation. You'll start connecting with other people on sports.

Start with a few stars. The following list mixes older and younger players. Pick two or three. Follow them in the paper.

Or note their highlights on ESPN or CNN or FOX Sports. Or simply remember the fun fact about each one.

SPORTS GODDESS PROFILE: BASKETBALL STARS

Michael Jordan

His nicknames: "Air Jordan," "MJ."   *SG fun fact:* He was cut from his high school basketball team. When you or a friend or a child suffers a setback, remember this.   *His '98 team:* Chicago Bulls.   *One reason he was a star:* He did just about everything on offense and defense better than anyone else in the history of the game. He won the Most Valuable Player Award five times.   *Watch this move:* He "flew" into the net when making some baskets.   *SG additional note:* Although Jordan has retired, he is arguably still the best player—ever. A Sports Goddess should *still* know about him.

Tim Duncan

SG fun fact: He puts his practice shorts on backward for good luck.   *His '99 team:* San Antonio Spurs.   *One reason he's a star:* He won Rookie of the Year for the '97–'98 season.   *Watch these moves:* Dribbles to the left, then shoots the ball from high over his head. Scores a lot.   *SG additional note:* He's considered one of the more mature younger players. He chose to graduate from Wake Forest instead of "coming out" in the NBA draft after his sophomore year or junior year.

Grant Hill

His nickname: He doesn't have one right now. However, he played on his high school **varsity** team at the age of 13. His teammates nicknamed him "Fetus."   *SG fun facts:* His mother was in Hillary Clinton's class at Wellesley College. His father was a star football player for the Dallas Cowboys.   *His '99 team:* Detroit Pistons.   *One reason he's a star:* In his first NBA season, he received the most votes for the All Star team. (He also shared the Rookie of the Year Award.)   *Watch for these moves:* Like Jordan, he "flies" into the net. Explosive jumper. Very good passer.

Karl Malone

His nickname: "The Mailman" (because he "delivers"). *SG fun facts:* He hunts grizzly bears. He owns a cattle ranch in Arkansas and a fishing lodge in Alaska. *His '99 team:* Utah Jazz. *One reason he's a star:* He is one of only five NBA players in history with more than 25,000 career points and 10,000 rebounds. *Watch this move:* He's known for his baseline "fallaway," a jump shot from the line that separates inbounds from out-of-bounds.

Reggie Miller

SG fun facts: His sister is former USC star, WNBA coach, and television analyst Cheryl Miller. *His '99 team:* Indiana Pacers. *One reason he's a star:* He has scored the most number of three-point shots in the history of the NBA. *Watch these moves:* He has a superb three-point shot. Also, he "trash talks" (intimidates) opponents on the court with his verbal barrage.

Hakeem Olajuwon

His nickname: "The Dream." *SG fun fact:* He played soccer in his native Nigeria. His footwork is considered among the best in the league because of his early soccer career. *His '99 team:* Houston Rockets. *One reason he's a star:* In the 1993–1994 season, he was the first player to win the NBA MVP, the NBA Defensive Player of the Year, and the NBA Finals MVP awards. *Watch these moves:* He's known for his "**dream shake**." When he is close to the basket, he shakes his head and shoulders, spins in the middle of the lane, and (usually) gets off a hook or jump shot. All this moving, shaking, and faking can be tough for opponents to defend.

Shaquille O'Neal

His nickname: "Shaq." *SG fun facts:* His first and middle (Rashaun) names mean "Little Warrior" in Arabic. He has released several rap albums; their titles include *Shaq Diesel.* His father was an army sergeant, and Shaquille spent part of his childhood in Germany. *His '99 team:* Los Angeles Lakers. *One reason he's a star:* He was the youngest player ever in an All-Star game. *Watch these moves:* He slam-dunks with style. It's all part of his "Shaq attack" attitude. He also scores a lot.

Gary Payton

His nickname: "The Glove."   *SG fun fact:* He was voted the NBA's #1 "trash talker" in a *Sports Illustrated* preseason poll. He matured after being named the team captain that season.   *His '99 team:* Seattle Supersonics.   *One reason he's a star:* Payton was named to the NBA's first team (i.e., he was the best at his position) during the 1997–1998 season.   *Watch these moves:* Look at everything he does on defense (e.g., block, rebound).   *SG additional note:* Payton started poorly in the NBA. He didn't play well. He annoyed people with his trash talk. Eventually, he grew into a team leader. His game matured into one of the best overall in the league. NBA insiders point to Payton as a player who developed over the years (in contrast with those who start strong and then fade).

Dennis Rodman

His nickname: "The Worm."   *SG fun facts:* He never played basketball in high school. When he was 20, he was a janitor in the Dallas–Fort Worth Airport. He decided that he would attempt to play basketball on the college level because he had grown eight inches since high school.   *His '99 team:* Los Angeles Lakers.   *One reason he's a star:* Up until the '98 season, he was the league's leading rebounder for **seven** consecutive seasons.   *Watch these moves:* He's known for his rebounds on the court and for his self-promotion off the court.   *SG additional note:* Rodman expresses himself in many colorful ways. He dyes his hair many times in many different shades. He once threatened to sue a company for manufacturing a cross-dressing doll based on his image. He staged his own wedding and was the one wearing the dress! He's interesting, though at times disturbing, to follow.

If you're saying to yourself "What's so great about these guys?", try to do what they do. Go to a basketball court. Hang out with some friends. Fly into the basket like Jordan. Slam the ball through the net like Shaq. Shake, move, and shoot like Olajuwon. You will begin to appreciate the talents of these individuals.

The lazier Sports Goddess who may never get on a court or doesn't want to follow these players, yet wants to be included in the conversation, can simply ask, "What is it about this player that you admire so much?" or "What does he do better in his position than others?" Then listen.

Secret #24.   Understand one basketball rule: *the shot clock.*

You may have heard it in a meeting. "We have 10 seconds left on the shot clock." Or you may have wondered about it watching a game. "1:30 left in the game. 8 seconds left on the shot clock." If you know one rule, and only one, about professional basketball, it should be the shot clock rule.

Here's the rule: **When a team takes possession of the ball, they have 24 seconds to shoot.**

Why is it so important? Picture a basketball game. The team gets the ball. They throw it back and forth. When you, as a Sports Goddess, realize that they have only 24 seconds to shoot, your interest accelerates. The more time they take to set up the shot, the less time they have on the clock. You notice the moves (and the time they take) more.

You will hear about (and see) the game clock. It shows the amount of time left in the quarter. For example, when the clock on the screen shows "3:00," there are three minutes left in the quarter.

Secret #25.   Know the 1, 2, and 3 of scoring in the NBA.

Scoring can be confusing. A player shoots. He scores. The team gets two points. Ten seconds later, another player shoots. He scores. The team gets three. Why?

It depends on where you are on the court when you shoot the basket.

3 points—When a player shoots from **outside** the **three-point arc** (an arc surrounding the basket that in the NBA is 23'9" at its furthest point), his team receives **3** points for the basket. A Sports

Summer Sanders's Bonus Secret—

"Understand the pressure."

Summer Sanders sprinted down swimming, not basketball, lanes during her childhood. She starred in the sport at a young age. She excelled as a swimmer at Stanford and won back-to-back NCAA Swimmer of the Year awards.

Sanders glided through the 1992 Olympics. She won two gold medals—a silver and a bronze—to become the most decorated swimmer of the games. A year and a half later, she retired from the sport. She moved into motivational speaking and talked to high school girls about the benefits of athletic achievement.

She then used her communications major from Stanford to launch her broadcasting career. Today she coanchors the NBA's *Inside Stuff* and is a member of the broadcast staff for WNBA games for Lifetime. She had always admired Michael Jordan and put his poster up in her room. Now, she has reported on him.

Summer brings a unique perspective to comprehending sports as an elite athlete in her own right. She emphasizes that an SGIT should understand the "tremendous pressure" that top athletes face and thrive on. She believes that she relates very well to NBA stars through an understanding of the pressure situations in sports. It's tense. It's an adrenaline rush. It's addictive. Summer says she chose broadcasting as a profession because she felt that the pressure of television came the closest to that of world class athletic competition!

Goddess should refer to this basket as a **"trey"** or a **"three-pointer."**

2 points—When a player shoots from **inside** the three-point arc, his team receives **2** points for the basket.

1 point—When a player shoots from the free throw line, a team receives **1** point for each basket. You always can tell when a player is making a "free throw." Action stops. The player stands on the free throw line (15 feet from the basket) and shoots from a stationary position with no one defending him.

Often an SGIT will hear the term **in the paint** during tense potential scoring situations. If a player is **in the paint**, he or she is in the rectangular area (usually painted) in front of the net.

It would seem more useful to understand the psychology of team sports than to know the players on a team or the daily sports results. I think men expect a team to work a certain way, based on how sports teams operate. When anyone does not observe these rules, male or female, they are thought not to be on the team.

—male executive

Secret #26.   Understand the strategy of shooting.
Intentional fouls.

In the final two or three minutes of a close game, you will become aware of the strategy of scoring.

There will be more fouls. Players commit these fouls **intentionally.** A practical Sports Goddess might wonder why one team provides the other with a scoring opportunity. It's mathematical. The offense has a lower chance of scoring **two** points because they have to shoot two baskets in a foul shot situation (one point for each foul shot) rather than have the opportunity for a two-pointer or a trey. It should be noted that "two baskets" applies only if the foul occurs in the act of shooting or if the team committing the foul is over the limit.

More teams attempt the trey. If a team is behind by two points, they can win with a three-pointer. If a team is down by three points, they can tie with a three-pointer. The fewer seconds left on the game clock, the greater the chance in a close game that a team will go for the trey. (Of course, a team has less of a chance of making this shot because of the greater distance from the three-point arc to the basket.)

Once a Sports Goddess understands these strategic points, the final seconds of the game become more interesting. Fouls take on greater meaning. The need to hit for three is more intense under pressure.

SPORTS GODDESS MOVIE REVIEW

Forget Paris (1995).

Stars: Billy Crystal, Debra Winger.   **SG plot summary:** An NBA referee falls in love with a non–Sports Goddess in Paris. She tries to become a Sports Goddess but finds it hard to be married to a referee.   **SG bonus:** Basketball star Charles Barkley and basketball sportscaster Marv Albert appear in cameos.

Secret #27.   You have to watch only the last five minutes of a basketball game.

You want to say you saw some of a game. But you don't want to watch all of it. In basketball, you don't have to. The final five minutes are enough. It's tougher in other sports. The grand slam home run might occur in the second inning of a baseball game. The seven-in-a-row saves might happen in the first five minutes of the hockey game. However, in many basketball games, a lot of the great action takes place in the final five minutes.

Before you plan to watch for five minutes, you should be aware of something: the last five minutes in an NBA game translate to roughly 20 minutes in real time. So if you want to watch that Lakers-Jazz playoff game and you see that it starts at 2 P.M., tune in at 3:40 P.M. Check the game clock. Most likely, they'll be heading into the final five minutes.

At this point, you will be presented with three possible situations:

a. One team leads by an almost insurmountable number of points (anything over 15). **You can stop now.** Next day, you say, "When I saw that the Jazz were blowing out the Lakers, I turned it off."

Professor David Upton—

"Know what you are saying in business!"

Sports is the No. 1 metaphor in the world of business. Managers read books written by coaches like Pat Riley and Phil Jackson to learn leadership lessons. Companies pay athletes thousands of dollars to inspire the troops at conferences. Meetings of executive "teams" are filled with sports-speak.

The New York Times, 1/18/98

In 1992, David Upton, a gregarious Englishman, began teaching the case method at Harvard Business School. At HBS, 50 percent of a student's grade is based on class participation. When David evaluated many of his students' comments, he noted the reliance on American sports metaphors. Were these phrases precise descriptions of business situations? Meanwhile, his students made him aware of his use of English sports metaphors (e.g., sticky wicket) in his conversation. So he ran an experiment one semester. If his students used an American sports metaphor, they were penalized. If he invoked an English sports metaphor, he was docked. At the end of the semester, he lost. Both sides noted the difficulty of the contest and the domination of sports in the language landscape. Upton said, "I was getting increasingly worried about the fact that sports metaphors tended to exclude the increasing numbers of women and international students in the class. I was also concerned that some of the metaphors sounded good—but were actually fairly banal analogies for the real business situation. So I tried the experiment. Since there were 90 of them and only one of me, I'm sure I let some of theirs slip. Even so, by the end of the semester, I'd apparently used many more 'games of two halves' and 'kicks into touch' than they had 'punted' or 'thrown air balls.' "

b. One team holds a moderate lead (anything between 7 and 15). **Watch it.** Strong teams can score 12 points (six two-point or four three-point baskets) in a short time under pressure.

c. The teams appear close (seven points or fewer is the margin). **Watch it.** Notice the strategic decisions. When do they go for a two-point shot. When do they go for a three-pointer? When do they foul intentionally?

What do you do about overtime? A supreme Sports Goddess always watches. Remember Robin Roberts's insider tip—it's great drama! Overtimes ooze excitement. However, if a busy Sports Goddess doesn't have the time, she will check the final score later. (Think THIN!) Then, the next day, she can say, "I caught the last five minutes of the game but couldn't watch the overtime. I did see the highlight on *SportsCenter*, though."

SPORTS GODDESS BOOK REVIEWS

Once again, I am emphasizing more literary or documentary books. However, business Sports Goddesses should browse basketball shelves for the coaches' books!
The NBA at 50.

Author: David Halberstam.   **SG summary:** This book helps the SGIT make up for lost time! The top 50 players. The top 50 coaches. Lots of pictures. Carefully crafted commentary.

Values of the Game.

Author: Bill Bradley.   **SG summary:** Former NBA star and U.S. senator, Bill Bradley shares the values of the game in ten essays.

Secret #28.   **Pay attention to professional basketball during the playoffs. If you want, skip the regular season.**

The NBA has 29 teams. **Sixteen (55%)** make the playoffs. It's a miniseason. It begins in April and ends in mid-June. The championship team plays four rounds and has as many as 26 games (nearly one third of the regular season). That's a lot of basketball. More than enough for many Sports Gods and Goddesses.

When the regular season ends, a Sports Goddess will hear talk of seeds, first rounds, second rounds, and conference championships. It gets confusing. The best approach is to simplify. **Pick one team. Follow them through the playoffs. If they lose, track the team that beat them. It's the easiest way of learning about the playoff system.** Trust me. It's much simpler than keeping track of 16 teams.

For example, in the spring of 1998, let's say you, the Sports Goddess, picked the Indiana Pacers. Good choice.

First, you knew they were ranked #2 in the Eastern Conference. (In each conference, teams are ranked 1–8, from best to worst. A Sports Goddess's safest bet is to pick a #1, 2, or 3 seed.)

Then you followed them through the **first round, best of five games,** where they faced the #6 Cleveland Cavaliers. They did well. They beat the Cavaliers in the series 3–1.

Then they played the #8 New York Knicks in the **second round, best of seven.** They won the series 4–1. Even a casual Sports Goddess would have heard about the Pacers' Larry Bird's strong coaching skills, Pacer Reggie Miller's trash-talking relationship with filmmaker Spike Lee (a super Knicks fan), Knick Patrick Ewing coming back to play in game 2 after a long layoff due to injury, and Pacer Mark Jackson's **triple double** (he scored in the double figures in the three categories of points, rebounds, and assists).

Then the Pacers faced the Chicago Bulls in the **Conference Championship, a best-of-seven contest.** The series went to **seven** games. The Pacers lost. Then you, as a Sports Goddess, would have followed the Bulls through the **NBA Finals** with the Utah Jazz. You might have rooted for the Bulls because they beat the Pacers, or against them because they beat the Pacers. You would

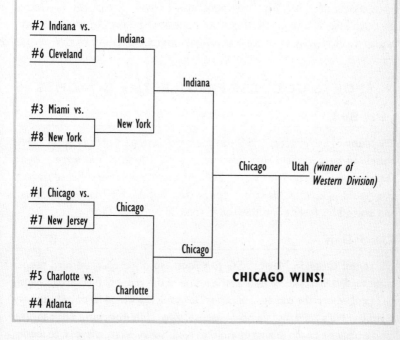

A Sports Goddess's Guide to the 1998 NBA Playoffs—

Pick one team. Follow them until they lose. Then follow the team that beat your original team.

1998 Eastern Conference Playoffs

#2 Indiana vs.
#6 Cleveland
Indiana

#3 Miami vs.
#8 New York
New York

Indiana

#1 Chicago vs.
#7 New Jersey
Chicago

#5 Charlotte vs.
#4 Atlanta
Charlotte

Chicago

Chicago

Chicago   Utah *(winner of Western Division)*

CHICAGO WINS!

have seen or read or heard about Jordan's game- and series-winning shot with just a few seconds left in game 6. Once again, you could have learned this **without ever watching a game.**

Secret #29. Drop the names of a few business gurus who are also known as professional basketball coaches.

While the NBA marketed its star players, and the athletes then hawked everything else, the NBA's coaches started to sell themselves. To corporations as "motivational speakers." To publishing houses as authors of "motivational" books. To other teams as "motivational" (and higher paid) coaches.

Today, Fortune 500 companies call in NBA coaches to inspire their troops. Several NBA coaches have written best-selling **business-oriented** books. Their managerial styles are emulated and discussed by top businessmen. Thus, a Sports Goddess should know a few of the star coaches. However, watch out. Some switch teams more frequently than the players do!

SPORTS GODDESS PROFILE: THE COACHES

Larry Bird

'99 team: Indiana Pacers.   *SG fun fact:* He owns part of the Pacers.   *His coaching personality:* He's low key. A good listener.   *He once played for:* Boston Celtics. Major star.   *SG additional note:* He suffered tragedy at a young age when his father committed suicide. He has written about and shared his feelings on this tough topic in his book *Drive*.

Chuck Daly

'99 team: Orlando Magic.   *SG fun fact:* He once coached high school basketball in Punxsutawney, Pa., the home of the groundhog Punxsutawney Phil (and where the movie *Groundhog Day* took place).   *His coaching personality:* He's fatherly, in a no-nonsense way.   *His coaching philosophy:* He's a player's coach. Manages athletes well. Sells well (to players, to media, to fans). Relies on veteran leadership. Straight and to the point. Doesn't hold many meetings.   *He once played for:* He never played professional basketball.   *He dresses:* meticulously. Favors Hugo Boss.

Phil Jackson

'99 team: He stopped coaching the Chicago Bulls after their sixth championship in 1998.   *SG fun facts:* He practices Buddhism. Meditates. Rides a motorcycle. Who knows when he will ride his motorcycle back into the

game? *His coaching personality:* He's a Zen philosopher, who knew how to yell. *His coaching philosophy:* Jackson attempted to put everything (including losing) into perspective. His teams tended to be graceful and relied on the athletic ability of the players. Of course, his players included such great athletes as Michael Jordan and Scottie Pippen. Incorporated yoga into postpractice ritual. *He once played for:* New York Knicks. Was on championship team. Bench player. *Recent book:* He coauthored *Sacred Hoops* with Hugh Delehanty.

Rick Pitino

'99 team: Boston Celtics. *SG fun fact:* On his wedding night, he left his wife in their room and went down to the hotel lobby to talk about a coaching job. *His coaching personality:* He's hyper. Rarely stands still. *His coaching philosophy:* His teams tend to be aggressive. *Recent book: Success Is a Choice.*

Pat Riley

'99 team: Miami Heat. *SG fun facts:* His father played minor league baseball. His brother spent time in the NFL. Pat opted for an NBA career even though he also was drafted by the Dallas Cowboys. *His coaching personality:* Driven. Obsessed. Motivator. *He once played for:* He won a championship ring with the Lakers in '72. More important, he coached legendary Lakers teams in the 1980s and a very good Knicks team in the early 1990s. *His coaching philosophy:* He's a general. He's a dictator. His teams tend to be very physical, very defense-oriented. *He dresses:* very well. Armani. Appears in *GQ* and on best-dressed lists. *Recent book: The Winner Within.*

Lenny Wilkins

His '99 team: Atlanta Hawks. *SG fun fact:* He's the only individual voted one of the top 10 NBA coaches and top 50 NBA players of all time. *His coaching personality:* He's patient. *He once played for:* St. Louis Hawks and Seattle SuperSonics (best known for those two teams). A big star.

So how does knowing about a few coaches help a Sports Goddess in her everyday life? First, when you watch a game, **look for the coach on the sidelines.** Notice his style. Does he yell? Does he hold back? Second, compare your boss or your professor or a colleague with one of the above-mentioned coaches. This exercise will help you understand why so many corporations hire these coaches as speakers. Is he or she a no-nonsense, fatherly type like Chuck Daly? Or is he or she more contemplative and Zen, like Phil Jackson? Third, consider your own management style. If you don't work, how do you organize your daily life? Do you adhere to a low-key style embodied by Larry Bird? Or are you more driven and obsessed like Pat Riley?

Secret #30.   Know a few basketball dynasties.

History helps an SGIT. While die-hard basketball fans do not mourn the past of basketball in the same way as baseball fans, they do refer to certain teams that won a lot: the Celtics of the 1960s and the 1980s, the Lakers of the 1980s, the Bulls of the 1990s.

Dynasty	Number of Championships	Star	Coach
Boston Celtics	1957–1969: 11 championships including **8 straight**	Bill Russell	Red Auerbach Bill Russell
	1981–1986: 3 championships	Larry Bird	Bill Fitch K. C. Jones
Los Angeles Lakers	1980–1987: 5 championships	Magic Johnson	Paul Westhead Pat Riley
Chicago Bulls	1991–1998: 6 championships	Michael Jordan	Phil Jackson

EXTRA CREDIT   In the 1980s, Larry Bird and Magic Johnson developed a rivalry that spanned the decade. The NBA used their rivalry—and their stardom—to help promote the league.

Fred Hickman's Bonus Secret—

"Listen to the press conferences."

For nearly 20 years, Fred Hickman has carved a distinguished career at CNN and its sister network CNN/Sports Illustrated. With the exception of a three-year hiatus in the mid-1980s, when he worked at a Detroit station, he has been with Ted Turner's network since the very beginning. He approaches sports in a serious, journalistic manner, though he allows himself to have some fun at times. In 1998 and early 1999, when the NBA lockout dragged on for months, he vowed not to shave until it ended. He grew a very long goatee. He has twice won the Cable Ace Award for Best Sportscaster.

Fred's suggestion for SGITs combines his news and his more playful sensibilities: "When you're watching a sports news broadcast, pay attention to the press conferences and the players' interviews. If you start to get bored, look at what the players are wearing. Of course, they may not be wearing anything more than a towel. But if they are, most likely it is on the cutting edge of fashion."

How an SG can use dynastic information: Incorporate these dynasties into your vocabulary.

You've performed eight straight tasks well at work, "just like the Celtics in the '60s."

You've developed a rivalry (professionally or socially!) with someone you consider an equal, "just like Bird and Magic in the '80s."

You've achieved excellence and surpassed everyone else in a certain area, "just like the Bulls of the '90s."

At my former job in management consulting, I was often the one member of the client team that could (and would) discuss sports with clients. Often the other members of my team did not have any knowledge of big-time sports to be able to have discussions about the topic when clients raised it. I found it to be very useful and a good icebreaker with clients, and I think it helped my consulting teammates also. Clients definitely wondered about whether I, as a woman, could really "talk the talk," but after I proved myself, they were very willing to talk sports with me.

—female sports executive

SPORTS GODDESS POWER TALK:

Know your alley-oops from your regular oops. Talk the power talk of basketball.

You want to "talk the talk." You want to know the language so many men and women speak. At home. At business. At parties.

Here are a few of the more popular basketball terms that have crept into business and social vocabulary. An SGIT should pick two or three terms. Learn them. Watch for references to them in the newspaper and on television. Listen for them in sports and in professional and social conversations. Finally, incorporate them into your SG vocabulary.

Defense

Man-to-Man	**Basketball definition:** This is also known as one-on-one. A defensive player is assigned to an offensive player to prevent him from making plays or scoring. **If your boss uses this phrase**—Pick your "man" or "woman." Spend your time with him or her.
Zone Defense	**Basketball definition:** Players defend a zone or an area rather than one designated player. Zone defense is illegal in the NBA. **If your boss uses this phrase**—Determine the location of the zone, as well as your codefenders.

Shots/Plays

Alley-oop	**Basketball definition:** A player throws the ball toward the basket. A teammate jumps up, catches it, and usually dunks it in the basket.

If your boss says, "We're going for the alley-oop here"—Make sure you know whether you are throwing or dunking!

Board

Basketball definition: "Board" equals "rebound." An offensive rebound or board occurs when the player retrieves a shot missed by his own team. Defensive boards or rebounds happen when a player retrieves a shot made by the opposing team.

If your boss says, "You're good on the boards"—When something goes wrong or someone screws up, you catch it.

Free Throw

Basketball definition: A free throw occurs because the opposing team has fouled. The shooter stands at the free throw line, which is 15 feet from the basket. Other players stand on either side of the free throw lane, which runs from either side of the free throw line to the basket. Thus, the shooter has a "free" throw with no one between him and the basket. For every **four** free throws in the NBA, there is **one** miss on average.

If your boss says, "This is a free throw"—You can say, "But even great players **miss** free throws some of the time!"

Full Court Press

Basketball definition: "Press" means pressure. Defense swarms the offense near their (defense's) basket. They are pressing for a "turnover" so they can score a quick basket.

If your boss says, "We're going for a full court press here"—Be prepared to work intensely.

Layup

Basketball definition: A player starts to shoot the ball near the net. A very high-percentage, easy shot.

If your boss says, "This is a layup"—Be sure to perform the job correctly, because he thinks it's an easy assignment.

Slam Dunk   **Basketball definition:** The ball is slammed right through the net. It's a show-off move. But it's very powerful.

If your boss says, "You've made a slam dunk"— You've done something well, in a forceful manner. In addition, everyone knows it.

Bad Shots

Air Ball   **Basketball definition:** An air ball is a ball that doesn't even hit the rim of the basket. A complete miss.

If your boss says, "That was an air ball"—You completely missed the point.

Brick   **Basketball definition:** A brick is a very ugly, very poor shot which "clanks" off the rim or backboard.

If your boss says, "You just threw up a brick"— You should be worried.

SG TIP.   Be aware of the difference between a brick and an air ball. They both are misses, but they're not the same *kind* of miss. A brick is an ugly shot which hits the rim or backboard. An air ball is a complete miss.

SPORTS GODDESS TV GUIDE

NBC rules in pro basketball. Starting in January, it programs NBA games on Sunday afternoons through the rest of the season. It usually runs a pregame and a half-time broadcast that contain interesting features. Hannah Storm, a poised and polished presence, anchors much of their coverage. Check local listings.

The NBA's *Inside Stuff* airs on NBC on Saturdays. It features fun, funky features on the athletes. Check local listings.

TBS and TNT carry a full slate of games during the regular season and early rounds of the playoffs. During the regular season on Mondays, TBS presents a game at 8 P.M., ET. On Tuesdays and Fridays, TNT offers a game at 8 P.M., ET and sometimes a second game on Fridays at 10:30 P.M., ET. Watch for Cheryl Miller, the WNBA coach who analyzes the men's game during her off season.

WOMEN'S PROFESSIONAL BASKETBALL

A Sports Goddess knows:

The league's name—Women's National Basketball Association (WNBA)

The WNBA is divided into—the Eastern Conference (6 teams) and the Western Conference (6 teams)

The regular season runs from—late June to late August

The championship series is called—the WNBA Championship Series

The game is divided into—two 20-minute halves

The shot clock runs—30 seconds (6 seconds more than the NBA)

The 3-point arc is—19 feet, 9 inches, at its highest point (shorter than in the NBA)

The league's slogan is—"We got next."

Women's basketball soared through the 1990s. First, the college game increased in popularity. High-profile TV contracts made news. Top players became stars. Then, the U.S. women's team won a gold medal at the 1996 Olympics in Atlanta. In the year after the Olympics, two women's professional leagues were inaugurated, the **ABL** (American Basketball League) and the **WNBA** (Women's National Basketball Association). Initially, the ABL had more Olympians, higher salaries, and a winter schedule. The WNBA had a few very high-profile players, a strong television consortium (NBC, ESPN, and Lifetime), and a summer schedule with little competition. The WNBA had one other critical advantage. It was backed by the NBA. The ABL filed for

Jackie MacMullan's Bonus Secret—

"Never put down Michael!"

You can read Jackie MacMullan in *Sports Illustrated*. You can watch Jackie MacMullan on CNN/Sports Illustrated. However, whether you read her or watch her, you must listen to her. She packs a tremendous amount of basketball knowledge and insight into each of her columns, articles, and broadcasts.

Jackie starred in basketball in high school and at the University of New Hampshire. She also excelled as a journalist and served as sports editor of the UNH student newspaper. At her graduation, she received the Robert E. Perry Award as the top female student athlete.

Jackie moved swiftly in her chosen profession of print journalism. After graduation, she was hired by the *Boston Globe*, which boasts one of the finest sports departments in the country. Her boss at the time, Vince Doria, recalls her as being "just terrific in every way."

In the late 1980s, Jackie began covering professional basketball. Her factual, tough, and insightful reporting received raves from the journalism community. Soon, she also served as a reporter for ESPN and was a regular on their Sunday morning *Sports Reporters* program.

In 1996, Jackie joined *Sports Illustrated* as a senior writer. She now writes their notes column, "Inside the NBA," as well as lengthier features and profiles. She also contributes reports to and breaks news for the cable network CNN/Sports Illustrated.

Jackie advises SGITs to "Say what you do know. Stick with what you know or believe. Don't try to fake it."

As for basketball, Jackie recommends that you tune in a game during the fourth quarter. She also suggests, "Avoid talking about labor issues like lockouts. It is a waste of time!"

Finally, "Michael Jordan is the standard by which all other players are measured." Think before you criticize!

bankruptcy in December 1998. The WNBA has survived and thrived. In the words of its president, Val Ackerman, the WNBA has become a "league of dreams" for girls and women everywhere.

Secret #31. **Know a few stars of the women's professional game. Talk about their greater accessibility.**

Once again, it's an NBA league. Stars rule. However, Sports Gods and Goddesses like to talk about the greater accessibility of the women stars. Before the game, the players hand out balls to young fans. Sports Gods and Goddesses also like to say that the women have less attitude and more appreciation for the game. They point to the league-holding autograph sessions (for free) with its all-star players. Hopefully, the players won't change with greater exposure!

SPORTS GODDESS PROFILE: STARS OF THE WNBA

Cynthia Cooper

Her nickname: "Coop." **SG fun fact:** She played in Italy for eleven years prior to joining the WNBA. At the same time, she served as a surrogate mother to several of her siblings' children. **'99 team:** Houston Comets. **One reason she's a star:** She was both league and Championship Series MVP in the first two seasons. **Watch these moves:** She's known for crosscourt passes. Good three-point shooter. **SG additional notes:** Cooper dominated the WNBA her first two seasons. Few expected her to excel at this level. She was the star of her team, the league MVP, and the Championship Series MVP. During her first two seasons, her mother battled breast cancer (she died in early 1999). Thus, "Coop" became the #1 player in a professional league, raised many of her nieces and nephews, nursed her mother, and became active in cancer fund-raising at the same time.

Lisa Leslie

'99 team: Los Angeles Sparks. *Her nickname:* "The Flowery Inferno." *SG fun fact:* She started modeling at the age of 10 and is now represented by Wilhelmina, one of the top agencies. *One reason she's a star:* In the Olympics, she led the American team in scoring. *Watch these moves:* She scores with style. She's very graceful.

Rebecca Lobo

'99 team: New York Liberty. *SG fun fact:* In the summer of 1998, she had her hair woven into multiple braids on a segment of the television show *Inside Stuff*. She wore the hairstyle all summer. *One reason she's a star:* She led her University of Connecticut team to the NCAA Championship in 1995. *SG additional note:* Lobo has overcome adversity. After her highly touted college career, she received a tremendous amount of publicity. When the WNBA started, they featured Lobo prominently in their marketing. However, women's basketball insiders said that she was overrated. Lobo had a strong first year and was named to the WNBA second team (i.e., she was second best in the league at her position).

Sheryl Swoopes

'99 team: Houston Comets. *SG fun fact:* She had a baby on June 25, 1997. **Forty-three days later,** she made her WNBA debut. *One reason she's a star:* In college at Texas Tech, Swoopes was the National Player of the Year in 1993. *Watch these moves:* She darts around the court. Goes to the baseline for a layup. Likes to move to the left to make her shot.

Haixia Zheng

'99 team: Los Angeles Sparks. *Her nickname:* "The Female Shaq." *SG fun fact:* Zheng, a major star in her native China, spoke almost no English at the start of her first season. She gradually learned some and has become a fan favorite. *One reason she's a star:* She won the WNBA's first Sportsmanship Award. *Watch this move:* She shoots accurately.

SPORTS GODDESS PROFILE: THE COACH

Cheryl Miller

'99 team: Phoenix Mercury.   **SG fun fact:** Her brother, Reggie, is a star of the NBA Indiana Pacers.   **A few reasons she was a star player:** Many basketball Sports Gods and Goddesses believe she was the best female player ever. She played for the University of Southern California (two national titles) and helped lead the U.S. Olympic team to their first women's basketball gold medal in 1984. She was National Player of the Year three times in a row in college. USC honored her tremendous play by retiring her jersey. The school had never done this for any basketball athlete—male or female—before.   **Her coaching personality:** She's outspoken. Blunt. Brusque.   **SG additional fact:** During the winter you can watch her as an analyst for TNT on NBA games. She was the first woman in such a role.

> **Secret #32.** **Talk about how women emphasize the fundamentals of the game. Know three (just three!) major differences between men's and women's pro basketball. The differences are *more time on the shot clock, zone defense,* and *spirit.***

Men play a power game. They dunk. They drive hard. They jump high. They play **above the rim.** Women emphasize the fundamentals. The longer shot clock allows them more time to pass the ball. They run more plays. Their game relies on skills and strategy. They play **below the rim.** Or so Sports Gods and Goddesses like to think. Of course, some men don't dunk and some women can jump.

However, if you're an SGIT, keep it simple. Think of the men's game as **above the rim** and the women's game as **below the rim.** When you follow or talk about the WNBA, focus on three of its major differences from the NBA.

Shot Clock. Watch (and compare) what the women do with more time on the shot clock. (Once again, you don't have to watch an entire game—just a few minutes of both men's and women's.) Make a note to mention it in conversation: "Yes, the extra six seconds on the shot clock may slow the game down a bit. **But** you have more time to watch the athletes set up plays."

Zone Defense. Women can play one-on-one defense. But in the WNBA, they also can play zone defense. Thus, an SGIT can learn about zone defense from watching the WNBA. Basically, she will see two types of zone defense in the area in front of the basket of the team defending:

2-3   *X=Defense Goddesses*
XXX
XX

1-3-1
X
XXX
X

However, don't worry too much about distinguishing a 2-3 defense from a 1-3-1. Remember those Insider Tips. **Listen to the announcers, and you should be told when a team uses zone defense. And which type. And why they are employing this defense (e.g., to double up on one particularly good shooter).**

EXTRA CREDIT   Zone defense often will force a three-point shot from the outside. (The WNBA's three-point line is 19'9", shorter than the NBA's.) Thus, when you see or hear about zone defense, know that a three-point shot may happen.

Spirit. In the first summers of the WNBA, fans flocked to the games. Arenas rocked. Famous fathers (e.g., Spike Lee) and non-famous parents brought their daughters to watch the women play. Prior to the advent of the WNBA, nearly every celebrated female professional athlete came from an individual sport like tennis or golf. The WNBA's women play a **team sport**, and they receive payment for their labor! Their sense of joy pervades the sport.

Val Ackerman's Bonus Secret—

"Appreciate the achievements of these athletes!"

Val Ackerman has played women's basketball, promoted women's basketball, and now, rules over women's basketball.

A star at the University of Virginia, Val moved to France after her graduation and played for a professional league there. She returned, earned her law degree at UCLA, and began climbing the ladder at a Wall Street law firm. However, she never lost her affiliation with the game. She eventually joined the NBA's legal staff and helped formulate the plan that sent the men's dream team to the 1992 Olympics. She then created a national women's team that toured the United States prior to the 1996 Olympics. In August 1996, she was named President of the WNBA.

Val shares this insight into her league: "Realize how difficult it is to do what they do on the court. The coordination. Speed. Strength. Agility. Stamina. The mental component. So many make it look effortless." In addition, she emphasizes the lessons that can be learned from the WNBA: "It's about empowerment. The league shows what women can accomplish. It's also a unifying aspiration to young girls."

It doesn't take much time to become an SGIT for basketball. If an SGIT chooses to connect to the sport by watching a game, she knows to tune in to the game's last five minutes. If she wants to learn about the personalities of the games, she knows to check out one or two star players *and* one or two star coaches. Finally, if she wants to become a supreme basketball Goddess, she can follow the pros all year: the women play in the summer and the men in the winter!

4

A *SPORTS GODDESS TALKS*
COLLEGE SPORTS

A Sports Goddess knows:

The ruling body for college sports is—the National Collegiate Athletic Association (the NCAA).

The NCAA is divided into—three Divisions: Division I, Division II, and Division III.

In football, Division I is divided into—Division IA and Division IAA.

Each division is divided into—conferences (too many to name here; see below).

BEFORE I OUTLINE each collegiate sport, I must alert you to something crucial, and for many, quite comforting, about college athletics. **A Sports Goddess does not have to talk about all college sports.** Or even most of them. **She only needs to talk about college football and basketball.** Of course, if you played lacrosse or softball or volleyball in college, you most certainly should talk about it. If you want to follow college swimming or tennis or fencing, be my guest. Remember, a true Sports Goddess feels a genuine passion for a sport, any sport, and shares it with others. However, if you simply want to follow, understand, or participate in the college sports culture, you'll be safe if you stick with the big two.

Also, you should be aware that in college sports, **the coach is often the star.** Why? Well, it's college sports. Players graduate. They move on. In most cases, the coach stays. However, it's more than that. The best coaches epitomize the spirit of the college game: sports strategists who shape minds and bodies. Individuals who influence the way these young men and women will conduct their lives. College G & Gs refer to many of these men and women simply as "Coach." It's a term of respect in the college game. An accolade. A position of honor.

Secret #33.   **You have to pay attention only to the top 25 teams in Division I. Even though approximately 600 teams play football.**

At first, college sports seems overwhelming for the SGIT. More than 230 schools play NCAA Division IA and IAA football. Another 360 or so teams play in Division II and Division III. That's approximately 600 teams. And that's just football. How do Sports Gods or Goddesses keep track of all these teams? They don't.

Forget Divisions II and III. (Unless, of course, you or someone you care about goes or went there.) Don't worry much about Division IAA.

In both sports, **the top 25** teams in Division IA rule. Not everyone agrees on the top 25. There are the *AP* (Associated Press) *Top 25*, the *USA Today/ESPN Top 25* the *New York Times Top 25* . . .

Every Monday from September to March, grab *USA Today*'s sports section. During college football season look for two polls: the *USA Today/ESPN Top 25 Poll* (voted on by college coaches) and the *AP Top 25 Poll*. Note the different teams in the top five positions. Talk about them. During the college basketball season, look for the *USA Today/ESPN Top 25 Poll* and the *AP Top 25 Poll*. Note the different teams in the top five positions. Talk about them.

Secret #34.   **Talk about how the college game retains the "purity" and the "essence" of basketball and football. Even though you understand that most top 25 teams play big-time, quasi-professional sports.**

For many, college represents a simpler time with the smell of bonfires, the sounds of a pep rally, and players wearing sweaters with varsity letters. Many fans think that collegiate contests retain the essence of the games.

Many practical Sports Goddesses have difficulty reconciling this talk of "purity" with the reality of Division I football and basketball (men's and women's). After all, the games look just like the pro games. You watch them on the same television networks. You see similar commercials. In many cases, the same announcers call the games. The best players go on to make millions in the professional leagues. So what are the differences besides the fact that unpaid college students play these games?

In college football, the pageantry (college bands playing at halftime; students holding signs painted in team colors; mascots running around the field) contributes to the richness and feel of the game. In college basketball, teams from small schools can often make significant runs throughout the regular season and in the NCAA Tournament of 64. (More on this later.)

Finally, some fans feel "purer" versions of football and basketball are played on the college level. When I try to pin down hard-core Sports Gods and Goddesses on what they mean by this, many hesitate. However, a Football God or Goddess might mention that the college game executes the fundamentals of the sport better. The athletes practice fewer hours than the pros, so they tend to run simpler plays. A Basketball God or Goddess might stress the importance of team play in college ball and the use of the zone defense. The sport places less emphasis on individual statistics than in the pros. In addition, a Basketball God might say that the college women pass more and set up plays better. For all these reasons, college football and basketball are exciting and interesting to watch.

Secret #35.   **Know that the Big Ten conference actually has _eleven_ teams. Know a few things about a few college conferences.**

In college football and basketball, a few conferences distinguish themselves with a number of outstanding football or basketball teams. Learn the names of two or three of these prominent conferences in each sport. For now, skip the rest. Then pick one or two teams in each of your conferences. Remember them and their nicknames. By now you know you shouldn't try to memorize every team at once!

The practical Sports Goddess sometimes does not understand the logic of certain conferences. For example, the **Big Ten** has eleven teams. It was called the Big Ten for so long, they didn't want to tamper with its heritage and history. During the football season, Notre Dame does not play in any conference. During the basketball season, it becomes part of the Big East, a conference of primarily _East Coast_ schools. Notre Dame is in Indiana. (For the geographically impaired, Indiana is not even _close_ to the East Coast.)

Teams join conferences on the basis of school size and geography (though the NCAA's sense of geography and yours might differ!). Thus, in football, the bigger schools tend to form the most prestigious conferences. In basketball, smaller schools can field strong teams due to the requirement of fewer players.

A FEW CONFERENCES FOR THE
SPORTS GODDESS

Big Ten

_____

Characteristics: Big Ten football takes place in the heartland. It is cold during a lot of those games. Big Ten football games exude spirit and pride. Bands blare. Cheerleaders leap. Entire states root for some of these teams. Big Ten basketball provides warmth for a lot of Mid-westerners during chilly winters. In both sports, Big Ten teams play at the highest level in the college game.

Teams and Nicknames: Illinois *Fighting Ilini*, Indiana *Hoosiers*, Iowa *Hawkeyes*, Michigan *Wolverines*, Michigan State *Spartans*, Minnesota *Golden Gophers*, Northwestern *Wildcats*, Ohio State *Buckeyes*, Penn State *Nittany Lions*, Purdue *Boilermakers*, Wisconsin *Badgers*.

Traditionally strong teams: In football—Michigan, Michigan State, Ohio State, Penn State. In basketball—Indiana, Michigan, Michigan State, Ohio State.

SG TIP.   If you want to pick just one conference for both sports, stop here. You can't do much better.

SEC (Southeastern Conference)

Divided into: East and West divisions.

Characteristics: Very big in football. A Sports Goddess will hear some football Gods say, "I'm an SEC football fan," **not** "I'm a college football fan." Football Gods and Goddesses envision warm, sunny fall afternoons when they think of SEC football. They can smell the bar-becue from tailgaters and the gin from their G&Ts. Tennessee won the National Championship in football in the 1998 season. The SEC usually sends several teams to the NCAA basketball tournament. Kentucky won the National Championship in 1996.

Teams and Nicknames: East—Florida *Gators*, Georgia *Bulldogs*, Ken-tucky *Wildcats*, South Carolina *Gamecocks*, Tennessee *Volunteers*, Van-derbilt *Commodores*.

West—Alabama *Crimson Tide*, Arkansas *Razorbacks*, Auburn *Tigers*, LSU (*Louisiana State University*) *Fighting Tigers*, Mississippi *Rebels* or *Ole Miss*, Mississippi State *Bulldogs*.

Traditionally strong teams: In football—Florida, Tennessee. In bas-ketball—Kentucky, Arkansas.

ACC (Atlantic Coast Conference)

Characteristics: Most teams hail from the Southeast. Very, very big in basketball. Some Basketball Gods are "ACC fans." They don't need any other conference.

Teams: Clemson *Tigers*, Duke *Blue Devils*, Florida State *Seminoles*, Georgia Tech *Yellow Jackets*, Maryland *Terrapins*, North Carolina *Tar Heels*, North Carolina State *Wolfpack*, Virginia *Cavaliers*, Wake Forest *Demon Deacons*.

Traditionally strong teams: In football—Florida State. In basketball—Nearly every team has done well at some point. However, North Carolina and Duke have fielded many strong teams over the years. They are major rivals.

PAC (Pacific)-10

Characteristics: Members include some of the larger universities in the West. During PAC-10 televised games, Sports Gods and Goddesses may see shots of the ocean, desert, or woods. These teams play in some beautiful locations.

Teams: Arizona *Wildcats*, Arizona State *Sun Devils*, California-Berkeley *Golden Bears*, Oregon *Ducks*, Oregon State *Beavers*, Stanford *Cardinal* (note—the Stanford Cardinal is **always** referred to in the singular), UCLA *Bruins*, University of Southern California *Trojans*, Washington *Huskies*, Washington State *Cougars*.

Traditionally strong teams: In football—USC, Washington. In basketball—UCLA, Arizona.

Big Twelve

Characteristics: Member schools are all over the place. Texas. Kansas. Colorado. So there's no one dominant identity. However, a Sports Goddess will see a lot of local color. In Colorado, the team's mascot, a buffalo named Ralphie, runs onto the field before football games. Outside an Oklahoma *Sooners* game, a Sports Goddess might see a covered wagon. Most important, both football and basketball are played at the highest level in this conference.

Teams: Baylor *Bears*, Colorado *Buffaloes*, Iowa State *Cyclones*, Kansas *Jayhawks*, Kansas State *Wildcats*, Missouri *Tigers*, Nebraska *Cornhuskers*, Oklahoma *Sooners*, Oklahoma State *Cowboys*, Texas *Longhorns*, Texas A & M *Aggies*, Texas Tech *Red Raiders*.

Traditionally strong teams: In football—Colorado, Nebraska. In basketball—Kansas, Missouri.

Big East

Characteristics: Primarily a conference of East Coast schools. In the 1980s and early 1990s, it was very strong in basketball. Some teams still do well. It never has been a football powerhouse. A Goddess should never say "I'm a Big East **football** fan." Stick with the Big Ten or the SEC in football.

Teams: Boston College *Eagles*, Connecticut *Huskies*, Georgetown *Hoyas*, Miami *Hurricanes*, Notre Dame *Fighting Irish*, Pittsburgh *Panthers*, Providence *Friars*, Rutgers *Scarlet Knights*, Seton Hall *Pirates*, St. John's *Red Storm*, Syracuse *Orangemen*, Temple *Owls*, Virginia Tech *Hokies*, Villanova *Wildcats*, West Virginia *Mountaineers*.

Traditionally strong teams: In football—Boston College. In its pre–Big East days, Miami was very big in football. In basketball—Georgetown, Syracuse, UConn.

Sports Goddess Power Talk: Know a redshirt from a game shirt. Talk the talk of college sports.

Most basketball and football lingo can be applied to college sports. Players shoot bricks. Quarterbacks throw Hail Marys. However, an SGIT will also hear terms that apply only to college sports.

Draft	**Sports definition:** The NFL and the NBA draft the top college players (and sometimes, in the NBA's case, the best high school players) at the end of each season.

The NFL draft takes place in New York City in April, over two days. It's seven rounds and very long. The NBA draft happens in June. It's two rounds and relatively short. **The earlier a player is picked, the more money he makes.**
If your boss says, "You're a first-round pick"— You can say, "Please pay me like one!"

Eligibility

Sports definition: An athlete is allowed to play in college sports for four years.
If your boss says, "You don't have any more time left on your eligibility—worry.

Redshirt

Sports definition: Sometimes an athlete does not play for a year (usually his freshman) in order to retain his eligibility. He or she is "redshirted." The next year, the player hopefully dons a game shirt and joins the team.
If your boss says, "We're redshirting you here"— You're not going to be participating in this project.

Scholarship Athlete

Sports definition: Most top athletes at Division I schools receive athletic scholarships. If they are not eligible to play that sport, they lose the scholarship.

Walk-on

Sports definition: Some athletes do not have scholarships to play their sport and/or have not been recruited. If they make the team, they are referred to as "walk-ons."
If your boss says, "You're a walk-on on this project"—You can say, "Some walk-ons make the pros!"

COLLEGE FOOTBALL

A Sports Goddess knows:

The season runs from—late August to January.

Most games are played—on Saturday.

The championship game—It depends, and the reason why can get confusing. You know all those bowl games you hear about during the holiday season? The Rose Bowl, the Orange Bowl, the Peach Bowl, the Fiesta Bowl, etc. Well, one matters more than the rest. Sort of. More on that later in this chapter.

Secret #36.   **Talk about past coaches in the present tense. Talk about present coaches in the past tense.**

Past and present blur in college football. Today's top coaches are spoken of in hushed, reverential tones. Yesterday's stars are discussed as if they were still coaching (even if they're dead).

SPORTS GODDESS PROFILE: PRESENT LIVING LEGENDS—COACHES

Gary Barnett

Team: Colorado *Buffaloes*.   **SG fun fact:** At the end of the 1995 season when he coached the Northwestern Wildcats, he won **17** Coach of the Year awards.   **One reason he's a legend:** Before 1995, Northwestern had gone **24** years without a winning season, **47** without a bowl appearance, and **59** without a Big Ten title. In 1995, they had a winning season (10–2), they appeared in a major bowl (Rose), and they won the Big Ten. Barnett takes very smart individuals and turns them into even smarter athletes. The next year, they shared the Big Ten title. Eventually, Northwestern started losing with regularity again; however, Barnett's legend appeared unaffected.

Bobby Bowden

Team: Florida State *Seminoles*.   **SG fun fact:** He was featured in a Burger King commercial.   **Coaching style:** He entertains and preaches at the same time.   **One reason he's a legend:** He has coached for more than 30 years, and he won a national championship in 1993.   **SG fun fact:** He has coached for more than thirty years and he won a national championship in 1993.

Joe Paterno

Nickname: "Joe Pa." **Team:** Penn State *Nittany Lions*. **SG fun fact:** He seconded George Bush's nomination for President in 1988. **A few reasons he's a legend:** He's the only coach to have won all four traditional New Year's Day Bowls: Rose, Sugar, Cotton, and Orange. At the end of the 1998 season, he had won more games than any other active coach.

Steve Spurrier

Team: University of Florida *Gators*. **SG fun fact:** He donates money each year to the University of Florida's **women's** athletic program. **Coaching style:** He's verbal. Computerlike mind. Obsessive. Once, at breakfast, he outlined a play with cornflakes. **A few reasons he's a legend:** He won the Heisman as a star quarterback for Florida in 1966. He coached another Heisman trophy winner, Danny Wuerffel, 30 years later. Before Spurrier coached at Florida, the Gators had gone 56 years without an SEC title.

SPORTS GODDESS PROFILE: PAST LIVING LEGENDS—COACHES

Paul "Bear" Bryant

Nickname: "Bear." As a teenager, he reportedly wrestled a bear. Hence, the nickname. **Team:** Alabama *Crimson Tide* (1958–1982). **SG fun fact:** In the movie *Forrest Gump*, Gump plays for Bryant at Alabama. **Coaching style:** He was a disciplinarian. Inspired love. And fear. Teams tended to run more than pass. **Fashion statement:** He was known for his houndstooth hat. **One reason he's a legend:** Bryant won 6 national titles with Alabama and 7 Sugar Bowls. He suffered a heart attack and died 37 days after he retired.

Knute Rockne

Team: Notre Dame *Fighting Irish* (1918–1930). Died in a plane crash in 1931. **Nickname** Knute is his real name! He was born in Norway. **SG fun facts:** He gave motivational talks to car salesmen for additional income. Prior to his death, he had received an offer to play a football coach in a movie musical. **Coaching style:** He was a major motivator. Also a strong

strategist.   ***One reason he's a legend:*** Rockne won 88.1% of all the games
he coached in his career, the highest percentage of any past or present
coach. He led Notre Dame to three national titles. He designed the Notre
Dame football stadium.

In 1940, Hollywood immortalized Knute in *Knute Rockne, All American*,
which starred Ronald Reagan as football star George Gipp, who died at a
young age. In the movie, Rockne's team is behind at halftime. In a speech,
Rockne recounts George Gipp's deathbed request that in a losing situation,
the team should think of Gipp and go out and win. The Notre Dame players
do just that in the movie. They "win one for the Gipper." That's the Hollywood version.

In reality, the Rockne speech apparently happened before the game.
George Gipp may never have asked Rockne to "win one for the Gipper,"
never mind on his deathbed. It really doesn't matter. Know that Rockne
gave the speech. Remember the saying "Win one for the Gipper." You now
have connected to college football.

Secret #37.   Know to talk about "who's #1?" and "who's going to be the national champion?" Know no team is ever really "#1" or the true "national champion."

College football fans debate a lot. They have a lot to talk over.
If a Sport Goddess focuses on two questions—"Who's #1?" and
"Who's going to be #1?"—she can jump right into the discus-
sion.

Every Monday, the question "Who's #1?" is answered. By
about three or four major polls and every football fan with an
opinion. Of course, there often is no agreement. There are too
many teams in Division I to have national standings, as they do
in the pros. Many of the teams with the best records never play
each other. So experts evaluate the teams according to their
won-lost records, the caliber of their opponents, and the strength
of their conferences. Then they rank the top teams. The media
pick the best in the AP poll. The coaches vote in the *USA Today/*
ESPN poll. A computer calculates the *New York Times* poll. In

offices and on college campuses, workers and students debate each other's choices.

Finally, in late October, the Bowl Championship Series (BCS) starts releasing its standings based on calculations of several factors, including polls and strength of schedule. This ranking matters more than others. At the end of the season, #1 and #2 in the BCS poll meet in the National Championship Game. However, it is a ranking based on human evaluation and computer calculation. The top two teams meet in the Championship Game because they were selected by the experts. Not because they beat a series of teams in a playoff system, as in every other major sport. This annoys some people. They would like the top two teams to be decided on the field, not by a computer.

Thus, Goddesses, if you do one thing in the fall, check the AP poll and the *USA Today*/ESPN poll every Monday—you will have more than enough to talk about for a week. Once you note that the AP poll "has Ohio State at #1," you can get into any college football talk with "Do you think they really are #1?"

SPORTS GODDESS MOVIE REVIEWS

Everybody's All American (1988).

Stars: Jessica Lange, Dennis Quaid, John Goodman.   **SG Summary:** Southern college football star and his beauty queen wife navigate through life.   **SG note:** Movie was based on a book by Frank Deford, one of the finest sportswriters of his generation. He has a small cameo.

Knute Rockne, All American (1940).

Stars: Pat O'Brien, Ronald Reagan.   **SG Summary:** It's an idealized version of the life of Knute Rockne, the famous Notre Dame coach.   **SG should watch closely:** the deathbed scene of George Gipp (played by Ronald Reagan). This scene may or may not have happened. However, the line "Win one for the Gipper" has become immortal.

Professor Stephen A. Greyser's Bonus Secret—

"Understand the complexity of the business of sports."

Sports is big business. In 1998, three networks paid $17.6 billion (more than twice the GDP of Luxembourg) for the rights to broadcast NFL games. Corporations own teams, bestow their names on arenas, and purchase title sponsorships to college bowls, golf tournaments, and auto races. The sports world does not escape corporate problems: in the past twenty years, the NBA, NFL, NHL, and MLB all have had work stoppages due to management-labor difficulties.

Professor Stephen A. Greyser at Harvard Business School, a consumer marketing and corporate communications expert, has researched, analyzed, and consulted for a wide range of sports enterprises. He teaches a popular elective course "The Business of Sports." He also was selected to write "And All New England Cheered" an essay commemorating the thirtieth anniversary of the 1967 Red Sox team which won the American League Pennant.

While a recent Georgia Tech study estimated the value of the sports industry at $152 billion, Professor Greyser feels there may be no reliable estimate though, "It's huge and more encompassing than most people would think." He adds, "While the sports industry is often defined as being about teams, leagues, players and their agents, it's also about broadcasting rights, the licensing of merchandise, sports apparel and equipment, product endorsements, and sponsorships of sports teams, and sports-related events."

Rudy (1993).

Stars: Sean Astin.   **SG Summary:** It exalts the Notre Dame mystique. Working-class youth dreams of playing football for Notre Dame despite mediocre athletic and academic ability. Based on a true story.   **SG should look for:** all the Notre Dame exterior shots.

Secret #38.   **Know that one bowl game matters more than the others. Sort of.**

The Peach Bowl. The Cotton Bowl. The Micron PC Bowl. During the holiday season, a Sports Goddess can watch a lot of bowls.

But she doesn't have to. Each year, one bowl matters more than others. Sort of.

It is called "the National Championship Game." A Goddess will know which bowl hosts this game. It is the last game played in the season. It is very well publicized. A rotating series of bowls host it. The Fiesta in Arizona. The Sugar in New Orleans. The Orange in Miami. The Rose in Pasadena. In 1999, the National Championship Game was the Fiesta Bowl on January 4. So a Goddess could have skipped every bowl, including the ones on New Year's Day, watched the Fiesta Bowl, and seen Tennessee win the National Championship.

Why do they play all those games?

Once upon a time, five or six years ago, all those holiday bowl games had very little to do with each other. The bigger bowls got the better teams. At the end of the bowl season, the media voted for their #1 team in the AP poll. The coaches selected their top pick in the *USA Today*/ESPN poll (once known as the UPI poll). If one team was selected the best in both polls, it was named National Champion. If two different teams were picked #1, they split the National Championship. Think about it, Goddesses. Suppose at the end of the baseball season, the media and baseball managers voted for the best team. No play-offs. No World Series. The champion was decided by a vote.

College Football Gods and Goddesses did not like this system. In 1994, the College Bowl Alliance determined that the teams ranked #1 and #2 in the AP poll would play one another in a National Championship Game. The Fiesta, Orange, and Sugar Bowls would host this game in rotation.

Wait, Sports Goddesses. Don't heave a sigh of relief just yet. There was one caveat. After all, this is college football. The Rose

Bowl didn't participate in the rotation. Traditionally, the winners of the Big Ten and the Pac-10 meet in this bowl. A Goddess knows from Secret #35 that these two conferences produce very strong football teams. Even if a Pac-10 or Big Ten team was the best team in the nation (according to the AP poll), it still had to play in the Rose Bowl and not the National Championship Game. So once again, the two top teams (according to the polls) might not play each other. The voters in the polls would determine the National Champion. In January 1998, at the end of the '97 season, Michigan was #1 in the polls. Nebraska was #2. Michigan won the Rose Bowl on January 1. Nebraska triumphed in the Orange Bowl on January 2.

So who was the #1 team in the nation at the end of the season, and the national champion? The AP poll said Michigan. The *USA Today*/ESPN poll named Nebraska.

At that time, Nebraska's coach, Tom Osborne, was retiring. "No fair," Michigan fans said, "he received sympathy votes from other coaches." Nebraska fans retorted, "We played a tougher team." And so on.

So they changed the format once again. The Rose Bowl became part of the Bowl Championship Series. The BCS devised a formula for calculating the top teams in the nation. In late October of 1998, they began to release their standings. Of course, college football fans immediately began debating the merits of the BCS. It was just one more thing to talk about. And at the end of the season, when the BCS's top five differed from the AP's top five, everyone did talk.

On January 4, 1999, the first National Championship Game was played according to the system. #1 Tennessee met #2 Florida State in the Fiesta Bowl. Finally the National Champion was **determined on the field** and not by voters in a poll. Of course, there was one caveat. The AP poll could still vote its own champion. College fans held their breath. However, Tennessee won the game and all the polls. A significant number of College G & Gs even said the system worked. Of course, that was just the first year.

Thus, a Sports Goddess can get out of watching the National

Championship Game by saying, "Until the top two teams are **determined on the field, with a play-off format and not by voters and a computer,** I refuse to watch!"

College Football Gods and Goddesses will understand.

Secret #39. Only three or four games matter each week.

Most weeks, about 20 of the top 25 teams play. Some play each other, some don't. However, **usually**, only four or five games are considered "significant." That's right. Even though somewhere between 200 and 300 NCAA games happen each week, only **three or four really matter.**

A game is significant if it has National Title implications. In Sports Goddess talk, that means if either team is ranked #1 or #2, or might be after the game. The only other reason a game might matter is if it has "bowl" implications. There are plenty of bowls to be filled in college football besides the Big Four (Fiesta, Orange, Sugar, and Rose). For example, there are the Peach, Cotton, and Micron PC Bowls. And the Liberty, Holiday, and Humanitarian, to name a few more.

So how does a Sports Goddess find out which games matter? As always, she can think THIN. She can watch the opening montage of ESPN's *College GameDay* on Saturday at 11 A.M. ET. She can open up *USA Today*'s sports section on Friday. She can surf to *www.cnnsi.com*, and the games will be listed on either the home page or the college football page. She also might find a story or two about college football from *Sports Illustrated* on this site.

During the season, a Sports Goddess will hear of games that involve **traditional rivals**. Sometimes these games matter in the National Title picture. Sometimes they don't. However, they make news because of their rich histories. And College Football Gods and Goddesses love history.

So it behooves the Goddess to know about a few traditional rivals. **Auburn-Alabama**—The state of Alabama splits into two camps during the week before this game. **Notre Dame-USC**—

This game recalls college football's earlier days, when players traveled in style to and from the Pacific Coast by train. They don't anymore. However, the rivalry continues. **Michigan-Michigan St., Michigan-Ohio St., Michigan-Notre Dame**— Sometimes a school has more than one rival. Intrastate. Interstate. Another big football powerhouse. It may seem a bit much for the SGIT. However, even when a team like Michigan is not a contender for the National Title, fans still pay attention to the games against a traditional foe. So more rivals can sustain interest during losing seasons.

SG BOOK REVIEW

A Civil War, Army vs. Navy: A Year Inside College Football's Purest Rivalry.

Author: John Feinstein.   **SG summary:** Gives a Goddess the feeling of the sport in its purest form. Helps her understand the depth of tradition in college football and the significance of rivalries.

Secret #40.   **Even though it is awarded in December, start asking "Who will win the Heisman?" and "Who should win the Heisman?" at the beginning of the season.**

When a Sports Goddess tires of talking about "who is #1" and "who will be #1," she can take a break. Then she can ignite another debate with the questions "Who **will** win the Heisman?" and "Who **should** win the Heisman?"

At the end of the regular season in college football, the Downtown Athletic Club (DAC) in New York City awards the Heisman Trophy to the "best college football player" in the country. The national media and former Heisman winners select the winner.

College football fans love the Heisman. The trophy reeks of the game's history and elite roots. The DAC awarded the first Heisman to Jay Berwanger, of the University of Chicago, in 1935.

That's right. The same university that usually wins Nobel Prizes instead of athletic awards. In 1936 and 1937, the Heisman went to players from Yale. Seven players from Notre Dame have won it. A slew of Army (West Point) and Navy (Annapolis) men have carried the trophy home. The U of Chicago. The Ivies. Army and Navy. The Heisman boasts a rich tradition. But things change. The University of Chicago discontinued big-time football in 1939. An Ivy League player hasn't won since Dick Kazmaier of Princeton in 1951. The last service academy winner was Roger Staubach in 1963.

The practical Sports Goddess would assume that players from such schools, which don't offer football scholarships (with the exception of Notre Dame), wouldn't win any more Heismans. After all, the award goes to "the best college player in the country." The future #1 draft pick. The one who will star in the NFL.

Well, that really doesn't happen. The Heisman is awarded to the player deemed by the voters for various reasons—some very concrete, some very vague—to be the best college football player in the country. But he's usually not the top draft pick. (In fact, 1993 Heisman winner Charlie Ward went on to a professional **basketball** career.) Even if the winner does make it to the NFL, he often does not excel. Of course, exceptions to this rule exist. Former Heisman winners Bo Jackson, Barry Sanders, and O.J. Simpson made it to the NFL—in a big way.

So why do so many College Football Sports Gods and Goddesses obsess about the Heisman? Well, the media make them care. On college football pregame, halftime, and postgame shows, they debate the topic. On most sports pages on Sunday and Monday, a box details the front-runners' performances on Saturday.

A Sports Goddess should know about the Heisman. And the need to talk about it. And that it portends little for the future NFL career of the winner.

As a former national class swimmer in the Ivy League and hailing from Missouri, a Big 8 (now Big 12) hotbed, I thought that I knew everything about college sports before my marriage to a Notre Dame alum. I was wrong. Now, as a member of the Notre Dame family through my marriage, I have a far greater appreciation for the tradition and pageantry of college sports. If you know a little something about Notre Dame, you will be able to understand college sports much better.

—Vicky Gorman Jacoby, banker and
former Ivy League record holder in swimming

Michele Tafoya's Bonus Secret—

"Watch out for 'games of the century!'"

Michele Tafoya has hosted, reported, analyzed, and called play-by-play for college sports for CBS. A California native, she holds a B.A. with honors from UC at Berkeley and an MBA from the University of Southern California.

Michele has proved her versatility throughout her career. She braved and mastered the art of hosting a radio sports talk show in Charlotte, North Carolina; she served as an analyst for men's basketball games for the University of North Carolina-Charlotte's radio broadcasts; and she worked as a sideline reporter on Minnesota Vikings games.

In 1994, she joined CBS Sports. She has covered and reported on NFL games, the NCAA Tournament, men's regular season college basketball and football games, women's regular season college basketball games, and football bowl games. She also does play-by-play for the WNBA. Terry Ewert, CBS's Executive Producer of Sports, says that Michele is "a great journalist. I have never seen anyone who has done more homework!"

To understand college football better, Michele stresses the importance of "reading the polls every Monday morning. Follow the Heisman Trophy each week. Understand that these two college football institutions are the most hotly debated in the sport."

Michele also wants Sports Goddesses to note "that whenever a game is promoted as 'the game of the century,' chances are it's not. Watch it anyway. Most likely it will be 'the game of the year!'"

Secret #41.   Understand the Notre Dame mystique.

Many college football fans revere Notre Dame. Notre Dame is synonymous with Knute Rockne, seven Heisman winners, and tradition-laden games with such rivals as Michigan and USC. To its fans, Notre Dame represents college football. The College Football Hall of Fame is located in South Bend, Indiana.

Many college football fans hate Notre Dame. Notre Dame is synonymous with too much publicity, that overblown "Win one for the Gipper" story, too many undeserved Heismans, and too much media attention in years when the school fields a mediocre team.

A Sports Goddess doesn't have to like or dislike Notre Dame. She just has to understand the aura surrounding the school and its football program. If a Goddess can connect with the Notre Dame mystique, she can relate to the sport of college football.

Turn on the first few minutes of a Notre Dame football game. You'll hear the band. You'll see the famed stadium that Rockne designed. You'll see a shot of "Touchdown Jesus," the mural of Christ on the side of the school's library. Most likely, you will hear a reference to "Win one for the Gipper."

A Sports Goddess should tuck the following ND facts under her wing.

1. **Notre Dame has subway alumni in addition to its regular alumni**. Die-hard Notre Dame fans who didn't go to the school call themselves "subway alumni."

2. **Notre Dame has its own television contract with a network (NBC).** It is the only school in the nation with such a deal. And it hasn't won the National Championship since 1988. (The contract is for its home games.)

3. **The Four Horsemen played for Knute Rockne**. In the Roaring Twenties, the Four Horsemen were part of American popular culture. There was jazz, Babe Ruth, and the Four Horsemen. In 1924, Grantland Rice, a New York

sportswriter, nicknamed the Notre Dame backfield of
Harry Stuhldreher, Jim Crowley, Don Miller, and Elmer
Layden "the **Four Horsemen.**" The name stuck for decades. These four college players have become part of the
lore of the game. They helped Notre Dame to an undefeated season in 1924. Their final victory came in the Rose
Bowl. Don't worry too much about their names. Just know
that the Four Horsemen went to Notre Dame.

Tradition rules at Notre Dame. Change upsets old-timers.
Many Notre Dame G & Gs protested alterations to Rockne's
stadium in the mid-1990s (more than sixty years after its initial
design). However, one man might be amused by the emphasis
on ritual: Coach Rockne. In his day, he was an innovator who
reportedly said, "Tradition is a wonderful thing, but never let
it get in the way of progress."

MEN'S COLLEGE BASKETBALL

A Sports Goddess knows:

The regular season runs from—November to early March.

The week of conference championships is nicknamed—
"Championship Week."

The Division I tournament is nicknamed—"March Madness."
Sixty-four teams compete in a series of playoffs. Most rounds
occur in March.

The final two rounds of the Tournament of 64 are nicknamed—
"The Final Four," for the **four teams** that play in the semifinals
on a Saturday afternoon. The final two teams play the following
Monday night for the championship.

The shot clock is—35 seconds (11 more than the NBA).

*As a man I have been excluded in some cases while women have thrived
because they may know a lot more about college basketball than me.*

—male MBA

Not so long ago, a College Hoops Sports Goddess could root for certain men's basketball players. She could enjoy their development over their four-year college careers. She could cherish their streaks and mourn their slumps. She could reminisce when they graduated. No longer.

The top basketball players (with a few notable exceptions) do not play for very long in college. If they play very well in their first or second year, they "declare early" (basically decide to leave school and resign their scholarship) in the hope of getting drafted by an NBA team. For example, in the 1998 NBA draft, **eight** of the top ten draft picks were underclassmen. Some of the top players do not attend college. They simply go from high school to the draft.

Thus, while a Sports Goddess should pay attention to the high scorer of a college hoops game, she shouldn't become too attached to him. Not until he settles with an NBA team.

Secret #42.   **Just as in college football, follow the true stars of the game: the coaches.**

Watch five minutes of a college basketball game. Most likely, you will see as many shots of and hear as much commentary about the two coaches as about any of the star players. Coaches do a lot on those sidelines. They pace. They yell. They sketch plays. They get into trouble. They're the stars. It usually is their show.

SPORTS GODDESS PROFILE: THE STAR COACHES

Bobby Knight

Nickname: "The General."   *Team:* Indiana *Hoosiers*.   *SG fun fact:* He appeared in the movie *Blue Chips* with Nick Nolte.   *Coaching philosophy:* He's very, very intense. Disciplined. Tactician.   *His teams:* come out playing strong defense. Selfless offense.   *Fashion statement:* He wears a red sweater.   *A few reasons he's a star coach:* He had accumulated 11 Big

Ten championships, 3 NCAA Titles, an NIT championship, gold medals at Olympics and Pan-Am Games through the '99 season. Book written about him, *A Season on the Brink*, became an instant sports classic. **A Sports Goddess also should know:** He coaches in Indiana, a basketball mecca. High school basketball means everything in small and large towns. Thus, he has access to some great local talent. **A Sports Goddess will hear references to:** the chair incident. In 1985, Knight threw a chair across the court during a Purdue game. He nearly hit people in the wheelchair section. He was suspended for one game. He's intense.

Mike Krzyzewski

Nickname: Coach "K." Much easier than pronouncing his last name. It's supposed to be pronounced Roo-shevski. Some say Shoe-shevski. **Team:** Duke *Blue Devils*. **SG fun fact:** He graduated from West Point. It shows. In 1991, after his players had beaten a very good University of Nevada-Las Vegas team, he worried that they would relax too much before the Championship Game. He referred to them as "Fat Cats." He didn't think they were tough enough for the final. He motivated them. They won. **Coaching style:** He's classy. Relies on smart players. Intense. **SG interesting fact:** Due to **stress-related** exhaustion and a back injury, he sat out most of the 1994–1995 season. **One reason he's a star coach:** Duke won back-to-back NCAA Championships in 1991 and 1992.

Roy Williams

Team: Kansas *Jayhawks*. **SG fun fact:** In his early years of coaching, he sold calendars to help make ends meet. One year, he sold **22,000**. He's obsessive. **Coaching philosophy:** He's mature. Practical. Comes across at times as a small town Southern boy (which he was). Always in control. Fanatic organizer. Begins many practices with a thought for the day (e.g., "It's better to chase your dreams than run from your problems.") **His teams:** play all-out defense. Emphasize team play on offense. **One reason he's a star coach:** In his first nine seasons at Kansas, he won more games (247) than any other coach in college basketball history for that length of time.

Secret #43.   Embrace "March Madness."

One month. Maybe a few days on either side of it. That's it. That's all the time a Sports Goddess really has to spend on college basketball.

And Goddesses, it's a great month.

College basketball has a lot of tournaments. Tournaments at the beginning of the season. Holiday tournaments. Tournaments at the end of the season. The ACC Tournament. The Big East Tournament. **However, there is only one NCAA Tournament of 64 in men's basketball.** You don't need to pay attention to any other tournament.

Early in March, a Goddess will hear talk of "Selection Sunday." On this day, the tournament's Selection Committee picks the 64 teams. Many of these teams win their way into the tournament through victories in their conference championships. People argue over the teams selected by the committee. Of course, much debate ensues over teams that didn't make it but should have, and teams that did make it but shouldn't have.

The 64 teams divide into 4 brackets of 16. The committee seeds (i.e., ranks) the teams. The four best teams are seeded #1, one in each bracket. The second best teams are seeded #2. And so on, all the way down to the four worst teams, at #16. The top seed in each region plays the sixteenth seed. The second seed faces the fifteenth seed. Thus, the top seeds have easier matches in the early rounds. Of course, much debate ensues over these seeds. People argue over #2 seeds that should have been #1, and #1 seeds that should have been #2.

The tournament runs over a three-week period. During the first week, eight venues hold the first two rounds. Games go on day and night on CBS TV. Some College Basketball Gods and Goddesses take the Thursday and Friday off (the first two days) to watch these games. They love it. Again and again, an SGIT will hear talk of *the Big Dance*, Sports Goddess slang for the tournament. Sometimes unknown schools will win a round or two. They become known as the *Cinderella teams* of the tournament. Eventually, they lose. College Basketball Gods and Goddesses like to pretend that won't happen during the first week.

Sixteen teams remain after the first two rounds. Sports Gods and Goddesses refer to them as **the Sweet Sixteen**. Some SGITs worry that all this girl talk—Big Dance, Cinderella, Sweet Sixteen—is a ploy to get you into college basketball. It's not. Men use these terms. Honest.

The second week, four different sites host rounds 3 and 4. Sports Gods and Goddesses call these rounds "the Regionals." They are divided into the East, South, Midwest, and West. By the time round 4 arrives on Saturday, only eight teams remain—**the Elite Eight.** They play one more round. Then four teams remain—**the Final Four**.

The next weekend, the four teams, the media, and hundreds of thousands of fans and students arrive at one "neutral" site. The two semifinal games between the four teams take place on Saturday. These games usually offer some great basketball. A Sports Goddess always can catch just the final five minutes of any game. However, she might want to watch a little more of each semifinal. It's only once a year, after all.

The Championship Game is played on Monday night. For many, it seems anticlimactic after the intensity of the tournament!

Round 1	Round 2	Round 3	Round 4	Round 5	Round 6
32 games	16 games	8 games	4 games	2 games	1 game
64 teams	32 teams	16 teams	8 teams	4 teams	2 teams
First Week		*Second Week*		*Third Week*	

SPORTS GODDESS MOVIE REVIEWS

Blue Chips (1994).

Stars: Nick Nolte, Shaquille O'Neal, Anfernee Hardaway, Mary McDonnell. **SG summary:** It portrays corruption in college basketball. Big-time coach looks the other way when boosters (often rich alumni) try to pay stars.   **SG bonus:** It features two NBA stars (O'Neal and Hard-away). College coaches and former champions appear in cameos.

Hoop Dreams (1994).

SG summary: It documents two Chicago inner-city basketball stars who dream of playing college hoops.   **SG note:** Many G & Gs who never pay attention to Hollywood became angered when *Hoop Dreams* was not nom-inated for an Oscar for Best Documentary.

Secret #44.   Know how to fill out a pool sheet.
Intelligently.

In my office, many women participate in football and basketball betting pools for the fun of it, without research or knowledge of the particular sport. Their ratings in the pools are the subject of much discussion.

—female publishing professional

At some point, a Sports Goddess may be handed a pool sheet for the Tournament of 64. Once again, even if you don't want to wager money, fill it out. Throw in your pride. However, look at the following suggestions first!

Keep the *USA Today* special section on the tournament by your side. It comes out the Monday after Selection Sunday. It lists the strengths and weaknesses of all 64 teams. It provides valuable insight for the Sports Goddess.

Start with the easy selections in the first round. #1 always beats #16. #2 almost always wins over #15. #3 almost always claims victory over #14. If #15 upsets #2, most likely it won't be the #15 you picked! Plus, that #15 won't go many more rounds. Everyone thinks that they will. But they never do.

Know that the closer the seeds, the tougher the matchups. And the more likely an upset. #8 vs. #9. #7 vs. #10. #6 vs. #11. Read about each team in *USA Today*. The summary may shed some light on the matchup. For example, if one team has a strong offense and its opponent has a weak defense, think before you select. Even if the team with a weak defense has the more favorable seed, you might want to pick the one with the strong offense.

Almost always, early upset winners lose in the later rounds. So even if you pick a #10 team to win in the first round, it most likely will not make it to the semifinals.

The Final Four Teams usually (though not always) are #1, 2, or 3 seeds.

Finally, start a pool for the women's tournament. You'll double your chances of winning! The same suggestions apply in choosing for the women's tournament as for the men's tournament.

EXTRA CREDIT Championship Week leads up to Selection Sunday. Most conferences hold their tournaments at this time. Tournaments are held by major conferences like the ACC, as well as smaller ones like the MAC (MidAtlantic Conference). A Sports Goddess might surf to one of ESPN's Championship shows at this time. (Remember Chris Fowler, who wrote the Foreword? He hosts most of them. So you'll get information from someone you're familiar with.) You can pick up some tips about how certain teams are playing. Also, you will hear which teams may or may not make it. In college lingo, they *are on the bubble*.

Secret #45.   Know John Wooden. Talk about John Wooden's Pyramid of Success.

One coach stands above all others in the history of college basketball. John Wooden. He coached the UCLA *Bruins* to 10 NCAA Championships. Corporations have made his management principles part of their philosophies. He has inspired legions of men and women coaching at all levels of the game.

A SPORTS GODDESS'S GUIDE
TO THE BRACKETS

#1 _____ vs.

#16 _____   **SG tip.** Stick with #1.

#2 _____ vs.

#15 _____   **SG tip.** Stick with #2

#3 _____ vs.

#14 _____   **SG tip.** You should stick with #3. However, if you
pick #14, make sure you have them lose in one of the
next rounds!

#4 _____ vs.

#13 _____   **SG tip.** You should stick with #4. However, if you
pick #13, make sure you have them lose before the
Elite Eight!

#5 _____ vs.

#12 _____   **SG tip.** Now it starts to get interesting. Pull out *USA
Today*. See how the teams match up. However, re-
member—a #12 team may win the first round but
won't be in the last!

#6 _____ vs.

#11 _____   **SG tip.** Ditto.

#7 _____ vs.

#10 _____   **SG tip.** Here, read very closely. Also, most likely, a
#7 team won't be in the Final Four.

#8 _____ vs.

#9 _____   **SG tip.** Either team could win. However, most likely,
neither one will survive very far!

SPORTS GODDESS PROFILE:
LEGENDARY COACH

John Wooden

His nickname: "Wizard of Westwood." **Team:** UCLA *Bruins* (1948–1975). *He coached such stars as:* Lew Alcindor (who later changed his name to Kareem Abdul-Jabbar) and Bill Walton. *His teams:* emphasized the finesse and beauty of the game. They ran plays. They set up screens. They did not let brute physical strength dominate. *Why he's a legend:* At UCLA, his teams won 10 NCAA titles, including 7 in a row. In addition, he coached 88 straight games *without a loss. His "Pyramid of Success"* is quite popular with business executives and management consultants. During his coaching career, he developed a pyramid of 15 triangles that represented the building blocks of success. He has lectured for such prestigious companies as Arthur Andersen on the philosophy behind the pyramid. He is known for such succinct yet thoughtful phrases as "Discipline yourself, and others won't need to."

SPORTS GODDESS BOOK REVIEW

A Season on the Brink.

Author: John Feinstein. **SG summary:** It chronicles one year in the life of Indiana coach Bobby Knight. An instant classic when it came out in the late 1980s. Acclimates an SG to college basketball.

WOMEN'S COLLEGE BASKETBALL

A Sports Goddess knows:

The regular season runs from—November to March.

The championship tournament is called—the NCAA Tournament of 64.

It operates—just like the men's tournament. You can use terms like *the Big Dance* and *Cinderella teams* for the women. However, the Final Four is held on a Friday and the championship game is held on a Sunday.

Andrea Joyce's Bonus Secret—

"Sports talk makes great gossip!"

If you have watched even a few minutes of the NCAA Tournament on CBS, you may have seen Andrea Joyce. She has hosted the early rounds and served as a reporter in the later ones. Her intelligence, enthusiasm, and knowledge of the sport are her signature.

A Detroit native, Andrea grew up in Big Ten country. After she graduated from the University of Michigan, she began her career in news. However, she quickly moved into sports and worked in such diverse markets as Wichita, Denver, Dallas, and eventually, New York.

In 1989, she joined CBS Sports. For them she covered the Olympics, the NBA, the U.S. Open (tennis), college football, men's and women's college basketball, and the Heisman Trophy show. She has hosted, reported, and analyzed at various times throughout her career.

In addition, Andrea defies the stereotype of the sports-mad husband and the sports-challenged wife. She loves sports. Her husband, the broadcaster Harry Smith, professes indifference. On their first date, he took her to the opera. On their second date, **she** took him to a Tigers game!

Andrea's advice to SGITs is "**If you can gossip well, you can talk about sports!** Sports talk makes the best gossip. Read your local newspapers. You'll find great stuff about your local teams that way. It can make for the best talk around the water cooler. However, **stay honest.** Never try to use lingo you don't understand."

In addition, Andrea suggests that when you follow the NCAA Tournament, try to learn something about the history and the coaches of a few schools. When the star players leave, you'll still have something to talk about the next year.

The shot clock is—30 seconds (5 seconds less than the college men).

Team nicknames start with "Lady"—*Lady Blue Devils, Lady Rebels, Lady Bulldogs.*

College women's basketball shares many similarities with the men's game. Many of the same rules for Sports Goddesses apply. They have the same tournament structure. You can skip the regular season. Coaches rule.

However, a Sports Goddess should appreciate a few things about the women's college game. Many women and men have worked hard to raise the sport's profile during the 1990s. At the beginning of the decade, the women played their semifinal and championship games on back-to-back days so as not to conflict with the televising of the men's games. Now, the women have their own television contract with ESPN for the tournament, and a day off between their semifinal and final games. College Basketball Gods and Goddesses can devote their full attention to the women's matchups. And they do.

Star players stay longer in the women's college game than in the men's. Of course, until the advent of the WNBA, they had no place to play professional basketball in this country. So you can become attached to a dynamic sophomore or freshman player. She probably will be around for two or three more years. The shot clock is five seconds shorter than that in the WNBA and the men's college game. While more men may run faster, in many situations, more women can set up plays and work **as a team** faster.

> ### *Secret* #46. Understand that the *Lady Vols* rule. Know
> ### the star *Lady Vol*: their coach.

Secret #45 told you about John Wooden, the legendary UCLA coach who had seven straight wins in the NCAA Tournament. So what, you think. He last coached more than twenty years ago. I want to see his counterpart now. Well, you can. She's in the women's game, and her name is Pat Summitt.

If you know just one team in the women's game, make it the Tennessee *Lady Volunteers*. Better known as the *Lady Vols*. And if you know one coach, make it Pat Summitt.

The *Lady Vols* have roared through the 1990s. They won three straight NCAA titles (1996–1998). They did not just win the Championship Game in 1998. They set a record for most points in the first half, with 55. They outdraw NBA teams. They are referred to as "America's Team." That's right, just like the Dallas Cowboys. HBO documented them in a special. They have official web sites and marketing rights. They are very, very big.

If Pat Summitt, the coach, has her way, they will dominate the sport for a long time.

SPORTS GODDESS PROFILE: STAR WOMEN'S COACH

Pat Summitt

She has coached Tennessee: since 1974, the year she graduated from the University of Tennessee-Martin.   *SG fun fact:* During her first pregnancy, she began having contractions on a recruiting trip to the home of a prospective player in Pennsylvania. She ended the interview, flew home, and gave birth several hours later. She turned down the pilot's suggestion that they land in Virginia, because she had lost to their team and did not want to give birth in the state.   *Coaching style:* She's an outstanding recruiter. Spots good players early. Tough. Demanding. Pushes players to highest levels of play.   *One reason she's a star coach:* Beyond the three back-to-back NCAA titles in the 1990s, she led the *Lady Vols* to three championships in the late 1980s and early 1990s. She coached the women's Olympic basketball team in 1984, the first to receive a gold medal. She also was a college star and won a silver medal at the 1976 Olympics.   *SG additional fact:* She was the first head coach of a women's team to be featured on the cover of *Sports Illustrated*.   *Recent book: Reach for the Summit* (with Sally Jenkins).

An SGIT can draw a few general conclusions about big-time college football and men's and women's college basketball. She knows to look for the Top 25 teams in each of these sports every Monday in *USA Today*. She's savvy enough to check out, and perhaps pick, a favorite conference or two. Most important, in all these sports, she knows that the true stars are the coaches!

5

A SPORTS GODDESS TALKS
MAJOR LEAGUE BASEBALL

A Sports Goddess knows:

The league's name—Major League Baseball (MLB).

Major League Baseball is divided into—two leagues: the American (14 teams) and the National (16 teams).

The American and National Leagues are each divided into—three divisions: East, Central, and West.

The regular season runs from—April to September.

The number of games in the regular season—162.

The preseason is called—"Spring training" (late February/March).

The championship series is called—the World Series. It's held in October. The American League champion and the National League champion play each other. The World Series champion must win four out of seven games.

Number of players on each team—nine.

The "head coach" is called—the manager.

One nickname for the game—"the National Pastime."

Game summary—Two teams. Nine innings. Each inning is divided into halves. The visiting team bats in the *top* (first) half. The home team bats in the *bottom* half. Each team gets at least three chances *at bat* per inning. When the team at bat makes three *outs* in the inning, the other team comes to bat. If the game is tied at the end of nine innings, the teams play extra innings.

MANY PROMINENT AMERICANS have used baseball as a metaphor for the national identity. Filmmaker Ken Burns (of *Civil War* fame) produced a nine-part series on the game for PBS. Political pundit George Will wrote a book on baseball titled *Men at Work*. The late Bart Giamatti, an Italian scholar and a former president of Yale University, wrote essays on and odes to the game. Prior to his death, this distinguished intellectual was the Commissioner of Major League Baseball.

The practical Sports Goddess often has difficulty with so many intelligent people raising the game to such a high level. After all, baseball players chew tobacco. They spit. They grab—well, you know what they grab. This game tells us who we are as a nation? This game is worthy of honorific odes by Ivy League professors?

Yes and no. Baseball can be a lot of fun. The sport has a rich past and an interesting present. Baseball also can be very boring. Unless a Sports Goddess knows a few secrets for making it more interesting. Then she'll want to play ball.

Secret #47.   Don't talk about baseball, complain about baseball.

The good news for the more cynical Sports Goddesses: sports fans complain about baseball more than any other sport. It is actually okay—in fact, it's appropriate—to moan about the sport. Baseball fans grumble about everything. The designated hitter rule. The new playoff system.

Baseball Gods and Goddesses have a few favorite complaints. An SGIT should learn them and use them.

Complain about the World Series being played at night. Once upon a time, the World Series was played during the day. Schoolchildren could watch it or (even better) listen to it on the radio. They could embrace the sport. Television ruined everything. Now, most games start at 8 P.M. ET or later. This upsets Baseball Gods and Goddesses! Many games last well into the night, past many children's bedtimes.

Of course, Baseball Gods and Goddesses never mention that if children were watching or listening to the games in the better days of the sport, *they were not doing their schoolwork.* Perhaps they were cutting classes. Or the teacher allowed them to listen to the game. Or they weren't watching or listening to the game, but were in class and missing the game, just as they are today.

Complain about how much money players make. Baseball Gods and Goddesses like to think that athletes play for the pure love of the game. It upsets them that so many players make so much money. It really angers them that a player will leave one team for another—for *more money.*

Of course, in the "olden" days, a star player like Babe Ruth made a lot of money. When he was told that he made more than the President of the United States, he said, "I had a better year." He was sold by the Boston Red Sox to the New York Yankees in 1920, a deal that was all about money. However, baseball G & Gs overlook such annoying details and continue to gripe about what they think are inflated salaries.

Complain about the labor strife in baseball. Baseball has had tremendous trouble with the players' union for almost 30 years. Since 1972, play has stopped eight times due to labor issues. In 1994, the World Series was canceled because of a players' strike.

Baseball Gods and Goddesses are rightfully upset about all these troubles. If a corporation had eight work stoppages over a 22-year period, their shareholders would be concerned. However, professional basketball and hockey have also had lockouts in the past few years. Many baseball G & Gs had a very hard time returning to the sport after the 1994–1995 work stoppage. However, most eventually did. They always do.

Complain about how little the players of today care for the game. Baseball Gods and Goddesses worry that the athletes do not respect the game enough and that they do not appreciate the history and tradition of this revered sport. They complain about players treating it *like a job*. Of course, for professional baseball players, it *is* a job.

In 1919, eight White Sox players allegedly conspired with gamblers to throw the World Series. Many would argue that these players did not respect the game. Today, Cal Ripken, Jr., signs autographs for free after games. Mo Vaughn, a star player, wears #42 in honor of Jackie Robinson, the first African-American athlete to play in Major League Baseball in the twentieth century. A practical Sports Goddess would say that these individuals show tremendous respect for the game. However, baseball purists don't get too hung up on details!

Reality intrudes into a baseball purist's world at times. For example, many consider 1998 one of the finest seasons ever. Mark McGwire and Sammy Sosa hit home runs at a record pace. Both beat Roger Maris's record of 61 home runs in 1961. Mark McGwire ended the season with 70 home runs and Sammy Sosa with 66. The New York Yankees won the most games any AL team had ever won and went on to win the World Series. Yankee David Wells pitched a perfect game. Kerry Wood, a rookie pitcher for the Cubs, had a 20 strikeout game, something only one other pitcher had ever accomplished. The Cubs and Giants played an extra game for a playoff spot because they were tied at the end of the regular season. Many Baseball G & Gs paused. They recognized the significance of these achievements. Then some started grumbling again about the troubles of baseball over the winter when star players like Mo Vaughn left his long-time team, the Red Sox, and moved to the Anaheim Angels.

SPORTS GODDESS MOVIE REVIEWS

Angels in the Outfield (1951).

Stars: Paul Douglas, Janet Leigh, Donna Corcoran.   *SG summary:* Angels help a big league baseball manager in a pennant race. Janet Leigh plays an SGIT, a household hints editor-turned-sportswriter. Donna Corcoran portrays a young Sports Goddess, an orphan who prays for her team to win.   *SG bonus:* Baseball legends Ty Cobb and Joe DiMaggio appear in cameos. **SG history lesson:** References run throughout the movie to now defunct franchises (e.g., New York/now San Francisco Giants) and baseball parks (New York's Polo Grounds). **SG fun facts:** Janet Leigh is Jamie Lee Curtis's mother. She also starred in the Hitchcock classic *Psycho*. **Remade**: in 1994 with Danny Glover and Tony Danza. Most sports fans prefer the original.

The Babe (1992).

Stars: John Goodman, Kelly McGillis. **SG summary:** Recounts the life of Babe Ruth (with some embellishing). **SG history lesson:** A Sports Goddess will see Ruth pitch (which he actually did). **SG quote:** When someone tells Ruth he made more than the President of the United States, he responds, "I had a better year." Ruth may or may not have said this. It doesn't really matter. Sports Gods think he did.

The Bingo Long Traveling All-Stars & Motor Kings (1976).

Stars: James Earl Jones, Richard Pryor, Billy Dee Williams. **SG summary:** A team "barnstorms" (stages exhibition matches) during the Negro Leagues era. **SG history lesson:** Serious issues underscore this comedy. Until 1947, African Americans played professional baseball in the Negro Leagues because they were excluded from Major League Baseball. Many wonderful athletes played in these leagues, including pitcher Satchel Paige and catcher Josh Gibson. Billy Dee Williams's character is based on Paige; Jones's character is modeled on Gibson.

Eight Men Out (1988).

Stars: John Cusack, Charlie Sheen. **SG summary:** It depicts the true story of the "Black Sox" scandal. In 1919, members of the Chicago White Sox conspired with gamblers to fix the World Series. **SG should remember the line:** "Say it ain't so, Joe," which baseball fans yell to Shoeless Joe Jackson. Baseball fans love to quote this line.

Field of Dreams (1989).

Stars: Kevin Costner, Amy Madigan. **SG summary:** Iowa man hears a "voice" that inspires him to construct a baseball field on his farm. Father and daughter (a young Sports Goddess) bond over baseball. **SG history lesson:** It recounts the true story surrounding the ban of Shoeless Joe

Jackson from baseball. *SG should remember the line:* "If you build it, he will come."

Major League (1989).

Stars: Tom Berenger, Rene Russo, Charlie Sheen, Wesley Snipes. *SG summary:* A non–Sports Goddess inherits the Cleveland Indians. She tries to ruin the team by hiring the worst players ever. *SG should remember the scene:* where pitcher Sheen walks to the mound to the song "Wild Thing." "Wild Thing" is now an anthem in many baseball parks.

The Natural (1984).

Stars: Robert Redford, Glenn Close, Barbara Hershey. *SG summary:* It portrays the life of a baseball player, "a natural," whose career is cut short by a tragic incident. *An SG will hear the phrase:* "a natural" a lot. It refers to players in all sports who have an abundance of talent. They don't need to learn the game. They're naturals.

> ## Secret #48.   If you show up for work every day in baseball, it's a big deal. Records rule in this sport.

In 1995, the Baltimore Orioles could be seen everywhere. *The Today Show. Nightline. CBS Evening News. People* magazine. The Orioles were not leading their division. They weren't even close. However, one player, Cal Ripken, Jr., was about to break a very important record set by Lou Gehrig in the 1930s. Ripken had not missed a game since May 30, 1982. Not one. On September 6, 1995, Cal Ripken, Jr., played in consecutive game #2,131, one more than Lou Gehrig. According to the baseball rule book, the game and his participation in it became official in the fifth inning. He was given a very long-standing ovation. Networks interrupted prime time programming. The *New York Times* reported it on the front page. It was an historic day.

If you asked Baseball Gods and Goddesses, a few weeks later, *who won the game,* many might have hesitated before answering. (The Orioles did.) It didn't matter. It was the record that mattered.

In 1998, three years later, another major record was about to be broken: *the most home runs in a season*. Roger Maris had set the mark in 1961 with 61 homers, one more than Babe Ruth had slugged in 1927. In 1998, two players, Mark McGwire of the St. Louis Cardinals and Sammy Sosa of the Chicago Cubs, were chasing the record. Mark McGwire's Cardinals were out of contention for postseason play. Sammy Sosa's Cubs were in a tight "wild card" race. However, in both cases, their teams' records were rarely mentioned. ABC News aired a special titled *Chasing History*. Newspaper op-ed pages carried editorials on the meaning of two men going for the record. (In 1961, Maris's teammate Mickey Mantle had a shot at the record throughout the middle part of the season. Many social commentators pontificated on the significance of two men competing against one another and history.) When Mark McGwire tied Babe Ruth's 1927 mark of 60 on a Saturday night, the Sunday morning news and talk shows covered it like a war. Once again, if you asked a Baseball God and Goddess *who won the game*, he or she might have paused. Many of the network newscasts did not get into such minor details. They were too busy showing the footage of the Babe.

Why? Why do so many emphasize individual statistics rather than team victories?

In many ways, baseball is the easiest sport to score. When a runner crosses home plate, his team scores one run. That's it. One run, one point.

Yet, in many other ways, baseball is the toughest sport to score. Because when a runner crosses home plate, numerous other *stats* (i.e., statistics) are being recorded by a true baseball fan. How many runs that player has scored previously. Which player batted him in. Whether the pitcher will be *charged* (i.e., blamed) for the run. And so on. But it doesn't stop there. Baseball fans chart a player's season and career statistics. Then they compare him against other players.

Don't worry, SGITs! You don't have to keep track of the statistics and the records. Trust me. Remember: listen, and you will be told. You just have to understand the significance of statistics in the game. When you know more about them, the game becomes more interesting.

There are a few records that most likely will never be broken. Why? In the earlier days of baseball, most pitchers played the entire game—all nine innings. When they became tired toward the end, they threw weaker balls and batters had a better chance of getting a hit. Today, most pitchers are replaced by specialty pitchers known as *relievers*. They hurl tough pitches. Batters have less chance of getting a hit late in the game than did their counterparts in the early days of baseball.

There are two types of pitchers. A *starting pitcher* begins the game. He usually pitches five or six innings. A *reliever* takes over for the first pitcher. A *middle reliever* starts pitching in the middle of the game. Sometimes a special reliever, known as *a closer*, comes in late in the game, usually when his team is ahead. His job is to *save* the win. If his team is not ahead, then his job is to stop the carnage. *And* if a Sports Goddess hears that a *mop-up reliever* is coming in for her team, she knows that her team is in trouble. Mop-up relievers are there to mop up the damage left by previous pitchers.

Of course, that's the practical explanation. Baseball Gods and Goddesses like to think that the earlier players were just better. Perhaps they were.

A Sports Goddess most likely will never see a network special on these two records being broken.

1. *Joe DiMaggio's 56-game hitting streak*. In 1941, a few months before Pearl Harbor was attacked, Joe DiMaggio hit safely in 56 straight games. Once again, a practical SGIT may shrug her shoulders. "So what!" she thinks. "It doesn't sound like a big deal." It is. First, it recalls baseball's glory days in pre–World War II America. Back then, the best baseball players were not stars. *They were heroes*.

   Second, according to various statisticians, DiMaggio's accomplishment was statistically impossible. No player should have connected with a ball one out of every four or five times in 56 consecutive tries.

Third, it most likely can never happen again. DiMaggio faced tired starting pitchers in later innings. Not hot-shot relievers or closers.

However, many Baseball Gods and Goddesses like to think that DiMaggio would set that record today. Even against those hot-shot relievers.

2. *Rogers Hornsby's .424 batting average (20th century record)*. In 1924, Hornsby hit the ball approximately a little better than 4 times in every 10 tries. A practical SGIT may think, "Four out of 10 doesn't sound too impressive." Actually, it is. Rogers Hornsby set this mark in **1924**. The last time anyone came close to Hornsby was Ted Williams, who hit .406 in 1941.

Once again, with today's top relievers, it is practically statistically impossible to connect with the ball more than 4 out of 10 times throughout the entire season.

If an SGIT starts paying attention to baseball, she might think that Williams holds the record. If a player flirts with .400 during the early part of the season, Baseball Gods and Goddesses talk about him chasing *Ted Williams*, not *Rogers Hornsby*.

In part, Baseball Gods and Goddesses say this because no one will ever come near Hornsby's mark. In part, they say this because they relate to Williams better. He batted .406 in 1941, the same year that DiMaggio hit in 56 straight games. He fought in World War II. He was a hero. So they refer to Williams's record as the modern record. It may not be fair to Hornsby. But, that's baseball. Plus, a true Baseball Goddess knows that Hugh Duffy set the all-time mark of .440 in 1894.

Secret #49. **Think of baseball as a duel between two players: the pitcher and the hitter.**

THE PITCHER

Baseball takes a lot of time. There are a lot of breaks in action. The pitcher throws the ball. The batter swings. *Nothing happens*. The pitcher throws the ball again. The batter doesn't swing. *Still, nothing happens.* By the time something does happen, a Goddess can be gone.

Before you give up—don't. *Think of each pitcher-hitter matchup as a duel.* They psych each other out. One moves ahead, then the other. Eventually one wins, one loses.

A pitcher wants to get the batter out. A batter wants to hit the ball in fair territory and get at least to first base without being thrown out. Each worries about being "inside the lines." A pitcher must throw the ball within the imaginary lines of the **strike zone** (between a player's knees and the letters on his uniform) for it to be considered a strike. A batter must hit the ball within the lines of play for it to be considered a hit. Each player knows his boundaries.

Baseball Gods and Goddesses count the number of strikes and balls. Three strikes, and the batter is out; four balls, and the batter advances to first base. If a pitcher has hurled more strikes than balls, he is *ahead or up in the count.* If the pitcher has thrown more balls than strikes, he is *behind or down in the count.* When the count is "3 balls, 2 strikes," it is a *full count.*

A pitcher will throw a variety of pitches at different speeds. He might throw a *fastball* (which moves quickly), a *slider* (which may veer or *slide* to the side before it reaches the hitter), a *curveball* (which curves as it flies over the plate), or a *knuckleball* (which can swerve over the plate). He may change his speed or his rhythm. At all times, he aims to confuse and frustrate the hitter.

Baseball Gods and Goddesses judge a starting pitcher by three crucial statistics and a closer by a fourth one. An SGIT doesn't have to memorize the stats for each pitcher. Just know which ones matter. If she reads a few paragraphs about the pitcher or watches a few minutes of the game, *she will be told the pitcher's stats.*

1. *Won-Lost Record.* Sometimes an SGIT will see a pitcher's name followed by numbers in parentheses: **Roger Clemens (17–3).** The first number refers to his wins; the second number, to his losses. There's no secret here, Goddesses. If a pitcher has

more wins than losses, then he is having a good season. The wider the margin, the better the season. If a pitcher has more losses than wins, he is having a bad season. The wider the margin, the worse the season.

Most starting pitchers aim to win 20 games each season. Very few, if any, do. Most good starting pitchers win 15 or more.

Two more records that most likely will never be broken:

In 1904, Jack Chesbro won 41 games in one season. Most modern pitchers do not start 40 games each season. The very best pitchers rarely win 41 games in two seasons!

Cy Young won 511 games from 1890 to 1911. He also lost 316 games. Cy Young had several 30+ *winning seasons.* That doesn't happen anymore. He also had several 20+ *losing seasons.* That also doesn't happen anymore.

2. *ERA (Earned Run Average).* Again and again, an SGIT will hear about a pitcher's ERA. For the season. For his career. For one game. ERA sounds confusing. And what's an earned run? What's an unearned run?

An earned run is a run that a pitcher is blamed for.

An unearned run is a run that a player other than the pitcher is blamed for.

ERA is the average number of runs a pitcher is blamed for over nine innngs.

So if an SGIT hears or sees that a pitcher has an ERA of 4.00, she realizes that he gives up an average of four runs every nine innings.

A SPORTS GODDESS'S GUIDE TO ERAs FOR *STARTING* PITCHERS

ERA	A Sports Goddess Should
below 4.00	be very happy
between 4.00 and 4.75	watch
between 4.75 and 6.00	start to worry
higher than 6.00	really worry

Thus, if an SGIT sees that a pitcher for her team has an ERA of 2.80, she should say, "We have a great shot!" If she notes that he has an ERA of 7.00, she should scream, "Get him out of the game!"

3. Strikeouts (also known as K's). Baseball fans love to track the number of strikeouts a pitcher records during each game for the year and over his career. An SGIT can grasp this statistic in the early stages of her training. When she sees 7 under "game strikeouts," she knows the pitcher had 7 strikeouts this game. When she hears that he has 350 strikeouts for his career, she realizes that he has struck out a player on 350 different occasions.

Of course, a pitcher can win a game without throwing a lot of strikeouts. He just looks better when he hurls the K's. Strikeouts indicate power.

A Sports Goddess considers seven or eight strikeouts in a game very good. Twenty is awesome. Roger Clemens, of the New York Yankees, has recorded 20 strikeouts in two different games. Kerry Wood of the Cubs had 20 strikeouts in a game in his first season. They are the only two pitchers to accomplish this feat.

4. Saves or Blown Saves. A Sports Goddess has one more stat that she can use to evaluate a reliever or a closer. Sometimes she will see a minuscule ERA for a closer (e.g., 1.50). She can't compare it with a starting pitcher's because the closer usually throws fewer balls to more tired hitters. Sometimes she will note an enormous ERA for a reliever or closer (e.g., 7.00). It's usually not a good sign. However, once again, it may be higher because he pitched fewer innings. So a Sports Goddess looks for the number of his *saves* or *blown saves*. If a pitcher comes into a game with a lead, and he finishes it without blowing it, he *saves* the game for his team. (That's the easy explanation.) The best closers record between 25 and 45+ saves each season. However, if the pitcher loses the lead, he *blows the save*. The best closers record five or six blown saves a year. The worst closers end up in the minor leagues!

Why Is Baseball on TV?

Some SGITs have difficulty understanding why G and Gs watch baseball on television. At times, nothing happens. The pitcher and hitter just stand there. When something does happen (e.g., a hit), the action is still much slower than football, basketball, or hockey. Once again, a SGIT doesn't have to watch a game. But, if she does, she can concentrate on the duel between the pitcher and hitter. She can ask herself, "Which type of pitch will the pitcher throw next?" She can keep track of the hits, runs, and errors in the game and "score" them in specially designed scorebooks. She can listen to one of today's great baseball announcers (e.g., Bob Costas on NBC, Joe Buck on FOX, Jon Miller on ESPN) and note how he artfully mixes the game's events with a little storytelling, history, and news. Or she can watch a baseball "news" show on her own local TV channel or ESPN's *Baseball Tonight* (M, T, Th, F, Sa 10 P.M., ET; M–Su 12 Midnight; Su 7:20 P.M., ET) which offers scores, news, and baseball gossip. Baseball God and TV producer Jeff Schneider explains why some Goddesses embrace baseball on television: "Baseball is a combination of style, grace, and some pretty cute guys in uniforms. The smell of the grass and the sounds from the stadium make for an emotional bond that permeates through your blood whether male or female from birth. Watching on TV transcends that. It's not the same as being there but it's the next best thing."

THE HITTER

The pitcher works very hard to get the batter out. Meanwhile, the batter tries his best to hit the pitcher's ball out of the playing field for a *home run*. Or at least out into the outfield for a *single, double,* or *triple* (advancing to first, second, or third base).

If she has working knowledge of a few simple hitting statistics, a Sports Goddess's interest in baseball will increase dramatically. Once again, she does not have to memorize the stats for each player! If she reads or watches, she will be told. Each time the hitter comes to the plate, statistics on him flash on the TV screen and on the stadium's scoreboard.

1. BA (Batting Average). This statistic tells a Goddess the average number of times a player hits the ball safely (i.e., he hits it fairly and is not thrown out) for every 1,000 at bats. So if a Sports Goddess sees that a player has a batting average of .300, she knows that he hits the ball approximately 300 times out of every 1,000 at bats. Or 30 times for every 100 at bats. Or 3 for every 10 at bats. A Sports Goddess may think, "Just 3 hits for every 10—so what!"

Actually, .300 is a very good batting average. The best batters usually hit between .325 and .370. Sometimes a little higher. Sometimes a little lower.

Baseball Gods and Goddesses point to the batting average as a metaphor for life. It's one of the game's lessons. Even the best players succeed only 3 out of 10 times.

The next time something doesn't work out, think about batting averages in reverse. The *best* baseball players fail about 7 out of 10 times!

A Sports Goddess's Guide to Batting Averages

Batting Average	A Sports Goddess Should
above .300	be very happy
between .275 and .300	be somewhat happy
between .250 and .275	be cautious
between .200 and .250	worry
below .200	really worry

SG TIP.   The higher the batting average, the better the hitter. The higher the ERA, the worse the pitcher.

If a Goddess has not kept track of a star hitter's season, she can ask a Baseball God, "What's he hitting this season?" or "What is he hitting right now?"

2. RBI's (runs batted in). When the hitter at the plate bats a run in, he receives credit! For example, Wade Boggs of the Tampa Bay Devil Rays comes up to the plate. His teammate is on third base. Boggs hits the ball to the outfield. He gets to first base. The runner comes home and scores. Baseball G & Gs credit Boggs with one RBI. He batted his teammate in.

Sometimes a hitter will drill a fly ball right to an outfielder. It's an easy out. However, if the runner on third base touches the bag after the outfielder catches the ball, he can run home. If he's not thrown out, he scores a run. And even though the hitter is out, he gets credit for an RBI and for a *sacrifice fly*.

The best hitters usually total between 125 and 145 RBIs each season.

3. Home Run Totals. So you've mastered the art of a casual glance at the batting average. You know how to sigh and say, "He flirts with .300 but he never can stay above it for very long." You're tired of checking out RBI counts. So unselfish. So tiresome.

Start looking at home run totals. Home runs represent power. In fact, batters who slug a lot of home runs are known as *power hitters*. Home runs are glamorous. Home runs are very, very easy for the Sports Goddess to keep track of during a game or the season. The statistic that records home runs is known as the **home run total**. If you see a 7 under "HR," it means a batter has hit 7 home runs during the season.

You can compare the hitter with a lot of home runs to the pitcher with a lot of strikeouts. You can get players out and possess a low ERA without striking out a lot of players. You can hit, bat in, and score runs without blasting the ball out of the park. However, high home run and strikeout totals make the hitter and the pitcher seem better. In many cases, they're not. In 1998, Mark McGwire and Sammy Sosa hit the highest and second highest number of home runs **ever** in a season. *Yet neither* *player ranked in the top 10 for batting average in his league.* However, Larry Walker, the National League player with the highest batting average (.363), received very little attention for his accomplishment. Of course, he was not breaking a record. Still, he connected with the ball more times during the season than either McGwire or Sosa!

Hank Aaron hit 755 home runs in his career. For many years, Babe Ruth held this record with 714 career home runs. In 1974, Hank Aaron bested the Babe when he hit home run 715. Aaron finished his career with 755 home runs. To his credit, Aaron continued hitting home runs despite tremendous stress during the final months of his "chase." Sadly, some baseball fans had difficulty with an African American breaking Babe Ruth's home run mark.

More than 25 years later, Aaron's record still stands. However, Ken Griffey, Jr., of the Seattle Mariners was ahead of Aaron's pace at the same stage of his career! If he or anyone ever comes close, don't worry about missing the event. You will be told. By the networks, by newspapers, and by major magazines.

SPORTS GODDESS BOOK REVIEWS

Boys of Summer.

Author: Roger Kahn.   **SG summary:** Kahn chronicles the fabled Brooklyn Dodgers of the early 1950s. Thoughtful. Very literate.   **SG should quote:** the title. A lot. Baseball G & Gs like to think of players as "the boys of summer."

Eight Men Out.

Author: Eliot Asinof.   **SG summary:** Asinof recounts the story of eight Chicago White Sox players who allegedly conspired to fix the 1919 World Series. He renders a sympathetic portrait of the athletes in the days before large salaries.

Men at Work: The Craft of Baseball.

Author: George Will, the political columnist.   **SG summary:** Will examines the different tasks of baseball: hitting, fielding, pitching, and managing. He describes those who excel and those who fail in these functions.

Shoeless Joe.

Author: W. P. Kinsella.   **SG summary:** Iowa farmer hears a voice telling him to build a baseball field in his cornfield. (The movie *Field of Dreams* was based on this book.) Metaphorical. Allegorical. Beautifully written. Appeals to baseball purists.

Secret #50.   Know one baseball rule. *The designated hitter.*

Once, in a lecture, I asked an audience of 50 or so women to raise their hands if they had heard of the designated hitter rule. Nearly every hand went up. Then I asked which baseball league used the rule. Not one person could answer. In the American League, the pitcher does not hit. Instead, a very strong hitter takes his turn at the plate. Most pitchers make it to the major leagues solely on the basis of their pitching abilities. Many do not hit well. Thus, when the pitcher comes up to the plate, he usually strikes out or flies out or is thrown out. The game loses momentum.

The American League instituted this rule to create more excitement. No more "easy" outs. Star sluggers can stay in the game past their prime without having to play defense. Pitchers can rest their arms and their minds while their teams are at bat. So why doesn't the National League use it? Because they choose the more traditional route. Once again, baseball purists obsess about the game's past. Pitchers should hit. Old sluggers should retire. The game should be played as it always has been.

A Sports Goddess should know the designated hitter rule. She also should **take a position on it.** Is she too much of a purist to approve of it? Or does she appreciate the effort to increase the excitement of a game with more chances for hits? Or does she merely ask in a conversation, "What do you think of the designated hitter rule?" No matter which approach she takes, a Sports Goddess will get involved in an interesting baseball discussion.

Secret #51. Know about the "curses" on the Boston Red Sox, Chicago Cubs, Chicago White Sox, and Cleveland Indians.

The baseball season is very long. Too long, for some SGITs. They simply can't follow one team through it. If the prospect of toughing out a long season is daunting, become a fan of the Boston Red Sox, Chicago Cubs, Chicago White Sox, or Cleveland Indians. Why? Because, in the end, **they always lose.** Their fans are convinced that they're cursed. Many use the curse as an excuse not to follow those teams.

The Cubs last won the World Series in 1908. The Boston Red Sox last won in 1918. They defeated the Chicago Cubs. The Cleveland Indians last won in 1948. Thus, if you become a fan of any of these teams, you have an automatic excuse not to follow the season. If they are doing well, you can say, "I can't bear to watch because I know they're only going to break my heart at the end of the season." If they're doing poorly, you can say, "It figures. Forget it."

However, you might want to know why your heart was broken.

Team: Boston Red Sox. *Name of curse:* Curse of the Bambino. *Explanation of curse*: In 1920, the Red Sox management sold star hitter (and pitcher) Babe Ruth to the New York Yankees. Babe Ruth went on to become, well, Babe Ruth. *Evidence of curse:* Since 1920, the Yankees have won 24 World Series titles and 35 pennants. The Red Sox have won no World Series titles and four pennants. More to the point, they have suffered humiliating defeats in each of those World Series (each went to game 7) and in other important games. *1978*. One-game play-off for the Red Sox against the New York Yankees. Winner will play in the postseason. Loser goes on vacation. Bucky Dent, a New

York Yankee, comes to the plate. Dent hit just **4** home runs that season. He proceeds to hit number 5. Red Sox go on vacation. *1986.* Game 6, World Series (versus New York Mets). Red Sox are **one** out away from lifting the curse and winning the World Series. But they don't. After several Mets hits, first baseman Bill Buckner lets a grounder go through his legs and the go-ahead run scores. Needless to say, the Red Sox blow a lead in game 7. They lose the game and the World Series.

Team: Chicago Cubs. *Name of curse:* Billy Goat Curse. *Explanation of curse:* In 1945, William "Billy Goat" Sianis, the owner of the Billy Goat Tavern in Chicago, purchased a ticket for himself and one for his goat, Murphy. The goat was refused admission. In revenge, Billy Goat placed a curse on the Cubs. *Evidence of curse: 1969.* From opening day to September 10, the Cubs are in first place. Unfortunately, the season doesn't end until September 24. The Mets are in first place on that day. New York fans refer to '69 as "the Year of the Miracle Mets." Chicago fans call it the "the Year of the Collapse." *1984.* Game 5, National League Championship Series. A ball goes through Leon Durham's legs, and ends up costing the Cubs the game. The Cubs do not play in the World Series. *1997.* Chicago Cubs lose a record 14 straight games to start the 1997 season. *Attempts to lift curse:* Sam Sianis, the current Billy Goat Tavern owner, has tried to lift the curse. Once, when the Cubs lost 12 straight home games, Sianis walked around the field with a goat.

Team: Chicago White Sox. *Name of curse:* Curse of the Black Sox. *Explanation of curse:* In 1919, the White Sox lost the World Series. In 1921, eight White Sox were banned from baseball for life for conspiring with gamblers to throw the Series. *Evidence of curse. 1920–1998.* White Sox return to the World Series **just once in 78 years (in 1959).**

Team: Cleveland Indians. *Name of curse:* Curse of Rocky Colavito. *Explanation of curse:* In 1960, the Cleveland Indians traded up-and-coming star Rocky Colavito to the Detroit Tigers. The next year, Colavito hit 45 homers and 140 RBI's for the Tigers. *Evidence of curse: 1960–1993.* The Indians never finish higher than third place. And they finish in third place only **once.**

1995. Finally, the Indians make it to the World Series. During the regular season, they bat better than everyone else. In the World Series, they bat poorly. They lose. *1996.* The Indians win the most games (99) during the regular season. They "choke" against the Baltimore Orioles in the divisional play-offs. *1997.* The Indians return to the World Series. They face the Florida Marlins, a team that entered the league in 1993. Cleveland loses. The Marlins become the first expansion team to win a World Series just five years after entering the league.

> **Secret #52.** **Speak in hushed, reverential tones of the Hall of Fame in Cooperstown, New York. Know the names of a few players enshrined there. Know the names of two who are not.**

Cooperstown. The name of the town comes up a lot. When a Baseball God or Goddess refers to the Hall of Fame, he or she needs to say only "Cooperstown" to other G & Gs. They understand immediately.

Most other major sports have a Hall of Fame. They're considered special in each sport. However, the Baseball Hall of Fame operates on another level. It works very hard to preserve the tradition and the spirit of the game in today's world.

SPORTS GODDESS PROFILE: MEMBERS OF BASEBALL'S HALL OF FAME

Tyrus "Ty" Cobb

Nicknames: "Ty," "The Georgia Peach." **Played:** 1906–1928. **Team:** Detroit Tigers (1905–1928). **Position:** Outfield. **SG fun fact:** He invested in the Coca-Cola Company early in the twentieth century. Became very wealthy from this and other shrewd investments. **One reason he was a star:** Cobb still has the all-time highest career batting average, .367. **SG additional fact:** Cobb was one of the most disliked men in sports. A tragedy in his teen years may have played a significant role in his

Bob Costas's Bonus Secret—

"Enjoy baseball today. Beware of the 'field of dreams' poetry about the game."

Bob Costas knows all about baseball curses. He witnessed game 6 of the 1986 World Series between the Boston Red Sox and the New York Mets with the NBC Sports team. In fact, he was in the Red Sox locker room with the trophy, the Commissioner of Baseball (Peter Ueberroth), and the Red Sox owner (Jean Yawkey), because it looked like the Red Sox were going to win the game and the Series. If they had won, it would have been a historic, hallowed moment in baseball history and a powerful presentation and interview. But they didn't.

Fortunately for him and for the American public, Costas survived the wrath of Babe Ruth despite being in the Red Sox locker room on that occasion. For more than a decade, Bob Costas has rightfully shone at the highest point of the firmament of network sports and news. He's anchored Super Bowls, Summer Olympics, and World Series. He's hosted his own late-night interview program, *Later with Bob Costas*; reports regularly for NBC's *Dateline*; and anchors MSNBC's *Internight*. In all his broadcast endeavors, he manages to mix wit with warmth, intelligence with insight, and sincerity with sly, slightly sarcastic twists.

Bob notes, "With the increased coverage of women's sports, not coincidentally, many more female commentators have come onto the scene. No longer are their reports seen as 'the women's point of view,' but instead they are reporting the same news in the same fashion as their male counterparts."

As for baseball, Bob suggests that an SGIT "steer clear of the overemphasis of the 'field of dreams' poetry about the game. That's too soft a view of the sport." Instead, you want to know the real stuff of the game today, like "why the Cardinals' bullpen is so screwed up." Bob continues, "Don't get me wrong—baseball is an interesting game. It has lasted a long time and has a rich history. It has been passed from generation to generation. That gives it a certain romance. That romance is part of the game's appeal but only a part. Too many overblown odes give the game a bad name." The beauty of the game, Bob adds, "is the connection that you feel" today.

later personality. His father suspected his mother of cheating on him. He climbed a ladder to look through her bedroom window. She shot and killed him. She was tried and acquitted of voluntary manslaughter. She claimed that she had mistaken her husband for an intruder. **He was inducted into the Hall of Fame in:** 1936. **He died in:** 1961.

Joe DiMaggio

Nicknames: "The Yankee Clipper," "Joltin' Joe." **Played:** 1936–1942, 1946–1951. Served in World War II from 1942 to 1946. **Team:** New York Yankees. **Position:** Outfielder. **SG fun facts:** Ernest Hemmingway used him metaphorically in his classic *The Old Man and the Sea*. DiMaggio was married to movie legend Marilyn Monroe. Though they were divorced prior to her death, he had roses sent to her grave weekly for many years. **One reason he was a star:** He achieved the statistically impossible by hitting safely in 56 consecutive games. **He was inducted into the Hall of Fame in:** 1955. **He died in:** 1999.

Leroy Robert "Satchel" Paige

Nickname: "Satchel." **Played:** 1926–1953, 1965. **Teams:** Played in the Negro Leagues for most of his career. At the age of 42, he became the oldest rookie in Major League Baseball. He played for the Cleveland Indians (1948–1949) and the St. Louis Browns (1951–1953). In 1965, at the age of 59, made a major league appearance with the Kansas City Athletics. **Position:** Pitcher. **SG fun fact:** Woody Allen and Mia Farrow, in happier times, named their son after him. **One reason he was a star:** At times, he pitched every day in the Negro Leagues because he was so popular. He threw 55 no-hitters during this period. **He was inducted into the Hall of Fame in:** 1971. **He died in:** 1982.

John Roosevelt "Jackie" Robinson

Played: 1947–1956. **Team:** Brooklyn Dodgers. **Positions:** First, second, third baseman. **SG fun fact:** At UCLA, Robinson starred and **lettered in four sports** (baseball, basketball, football, and track). **One reason he was a star:** Robinson truly was a hero. He was the first African-American to play in Major League Baseball in the twentieth century. He made his debut with the Brooklyn Dodgers in 1947. He possessed tremendous strength of character that sustained him during some very difficult times. *His athletic feats:* He was Rookie of the Year in 1947, MVP in 1949, and hit .311 over his 10 seasons. *He was inducted into the Hall of Fame in:* 1962. *He died in:* 1972. He had appeared at the opening game of the World Series several weeks before his death, to celebrate the twenty-fifth anniversary of baseball's integration.

George Herman "Babe" Ruth

Nicknames: "Babe," "Sultan of Swat," "Bambino." *Played:* 1914–1935. *Team best known for:* New York Yankees (1920–1934). *Positions:* Pitcher, outfielder. *SG facts:* Ruth was a major figure in American popular culture during the Roaring Twenties. He womanized, consumed huge quantities of food, and drank way too much. In 1925, he missed a number of games due to an intestinal infection. "Babe's Bellyache" made the front pages of newspapers around the country. At the time, some reporters thought that a sexually transmitted disease might have sidelined him. However, not one word was printed about the suspicion. It was a different time. *A few reasons he was a star:* He began his career as a pitcher. However, he hit so well that his manager switched him to the outfield so he could play in every game. He slugged the ball for many years. He hit more home runs in one season (60) and in his career (714) than anyone else up to that time. He led the league in home runs 12 times in his career. *He was inducted into the Hall of Fame in:* 1936. He was one of the *first five players* to enter the Hall of Fame. *SG additional note:* He adored children. He spent a tremendous amount of time in hospitals and orphanages. *He died in:* 1948, of throat cancer.

Denton "Cy" Young

Nickname: "Cy." Short for Cyclone. *Played:* 1890–1911. *Teams:* Cleveland Spiders (1890–1898), Boston Somersets/Red Sox (1901–1908). *Position:* Pitcher. *SG fun fact:* The Cy Young Award is given to the pitcher considered most valuable in each league. *One reason he was a star:* He is the only pitcher to have won 511 games. Most likely, he will be the only pitcher ever to win 511 games. He also holds the record for most complete games (750). *He was inducted into the Hall of Fame in:* 1937. *He died in:* 1955.

SPORTS GODDESS PROFILE: SHOULD THEY BE IN THE BASEBALL HALL OF FAME?

Finally, an SGIT should know two players who could be in the Hall of Fame. Some Baseball G & Gs would argue that they should be. But they're not. Their exclusion tells the SGIT about the standards of the Hall of Fame and the importance it places on values in the game.

Joseph "Shoeless Joe" Jackson

Nickname: "Shoeless" Joe.   *Played:* 1908–1920.   *Team:* Chicago White Sox.   *Position:* Outfielder.   *One reason he was a star:* He hit the ball very well. He batted over .370 five times. At various times, he led the league in hits, doubles, and triples.   *Why he is not in the Hall of Fame:* He and seven other Chicago White Sox players reportedly conspired with gamblers to fix the 1919 World Series. One year later, he and the other players were indicted by a grand jury; eventually, they were acquitted. However, they all were banned from baseball. Ironically, Shoeless Joe had an outstanding World Series. He played strong defense and hit .375.   *During the trial:* Children reportedly screamed to their hero, "Say it ain't so, Joe."

Pete Rose

Nickname: "Charlie Hustle."   *Played:* 1963–1986.   *Team best known for:* Cincinnati Reds (1963–1968, 1984–1986).   *Positions:* third baseman, outfielder.   *Why he was a star:* He had 4,256 hits in his career. That's more than anyone else, ever.   *Why he is not in the Hall of Fame:* In 1989, Baseball Commissioner Bart Giamatti banned Pete Rose for life from the game of baseball after evidence suggested that Rose may have bet on baseball games. Rose also served time in prison for tax evasion.   *If a Sports Goddess ever wants to ignite a debate among Baseball G & Gs:* She should ask, "Do you think Rose should be in the Hall of Fame?" and follow it up with "Why?" or "Why not?"

> *Secret #53.*   **Mourn the loss of yesterday's stars. However, know a few *future* Hall of Famers. Better known as today's stars.**

Many gifted athletes play baseball in the major leagues today. However, if you listen to Baseball G & Gs, you might not be aware of it. They miss the Babe, Joltin' Joe, Cy Young, and Satchel Paige.

However, an SGIT should know the future Hall of Fame pitchers and hitters. And learn a few things about a few of them.

SPORTS GODDESS PROFILE: POSSIBLE HALL OF FAMERS

THE HERO

Cal Ripken, Jr.

Nickname: "The Iron Man."   *Has played since:* 1981.   *Team:* Baltimore Orioles.   *Position:* Shortstop.   *SG fun fact:* Ripken is very big in Japan! In 1996, he broke the all-time consecutive game record of 2,215, **held by a Japanese player**, Sachui Kinugasa, who set the Japanese mark from 1970 to 1987.   *One reason he is a star:* That record! From May 1982 to September 1998, he played in 2,632 consecutive games. **In addition,** he holds the record for most consecutive errorless games (95) at shortstop.   *SG additional fact:* His father, Cal Ripken, Sr., managed Cal's team, the Baltimore Orioles, in 1987–1988. That's right. His father was his boss. His brother, Billy, played second base next to him from 1987 through 1992.

THE HOME RUN KINGS

Ken Griffey, Jr.

Nickname: "Junior," "Jr."   *Has played since:* 1989.   *Team:* Seattle Mariners.   *Position:* Outfield.   *SG fun fact:* He played on the same team with his father, Ken Griffey, Sr., in 1990. It's the only time that a father and a son started together in the same lineup.   *One reason he is a star:* He hit 13 home runs one April. That's a record for that month.

Mark McGwire

Nickname: "Big Mac."   *Has played since:* 1986.   *Teams:* Oakland Athletics (1986–1997), St. Louis Cardinals (1997–   ).   *Position:* First baseman. *SG fun fact:* McGwire hit 49 home runs during his rookie year, a record. He could have gone for 50 in the last game of the season. Instead, his wife went into labor and he went into the delivery room. *One reason he is a star:* That home run record! In 1998, he hit 70 home runs. He broke Roger Maris's mark of 61 home runs, set in 1961. *SG additional facts:* McGwire spoke in the first public service announcement about the sexual abuse of children. He set up a foundation with $1 million of his own money to fight child abuse.

Sammy Sosa

Has played since: 1989. *Team best known for:* Chicago Cubs (1992–). *Position:* Outfield. *SG fun fact:* He lives in the same apartment building in Chicago as Oprah Winfrey. *One reason he is a star:* In 1998, he hit 66 home runs. He also broke Roger Maris's mark of 61 home runs. However, he doesn't hold the record! Mark McGwire does. Nevertheless, Sosa was the NL MVP for being the most valuable player to his team in the entire league. *A Sports Goddess should know:* Early in his career, he suffered mental lapses. He threw the ball to the wrong base. Or he tossed it to fans in the bleachers, thinking it was the end of the inning. But it wasn't. *SG additional note:* Sosa inspires many because of his tough, poverty-stricken childhood. He grew up in the Dominican Republic and at a young age washed cars on the street for very little money. Today, he gives a tremendous amount of money and time to his native country.

THE HITTERS

Wade Boggs

Has played since: 1982. *Teams:* Boston Red Sox (1982–1992), New York Yankees (1992–1997), Tampa Bay Devil Rays (1998–). *Position:* Third baseman. *SG fun fact:* Boggs is extremely superstitious. For example, he always eats chicken before a game. He never lets anyone else swing his game bat. Once he puts a bat aside, he never uses it again. *Reasons he is a star:* In his first seven seasons, he won five American League batting titles. For seven straight years, he had more than 200 hits. *An SG should look for and talk about:* Boggs's "great eye." He almost never swings at a first pitch, even if it is a strike. Instead, he gets a "feel" for the pitcher. In addition, he rarely goes for a pitch outside the strike zone.

Tony Gwynn

Has played since: 1982   *Team:* San Diego Padres.   *Position:* Outfield.   *SG fun fact:* Sometimes, Gwynn tips the scale. Unkind fans refer to his "Body by Betty Crocker."   *Reasons he is a star:* For several seasons, many Baseball G & Gs thought that Gwynn would end the season with a .400 or better batting average. In 1994, he hit slightly above and slightly below that number all season. Unfortunately, the baseball strike ended the season early. He finished with a .394 average. Through 1998, Gwynn had won eight National League batting titles.   *SG additional note:* A decent, distinguished individual, Gwynn supported the players' strike and never complained publicly about the loss of a potential record.

THE PITCHERS

Roger Clemens

Nickname: "The Rocket."   *Has played since:* 1984.   *Teams:* Boston Red Sox (1984–1996), Toronto Blue Jays (1996–   ). New York Yankees (1999–   ).   *SG fun fact:* A dedicated father, he carries videos of his sons' baseball games with him on the road. He phones home with his critiques. In addition, he lives two miles from former President George Bush in Houston. His home has an indoor tennis court, basketball court, and batting cage. It also has a glass room known as "Rocket's World," which has etchings of famous athletes on the walls.   *Reasons he is a star:* He has recorded 20 strikeouts in one game. Twice. He has won the Cy Young Award (given to the best pitcher in each league) **five** times. For many years, he pitched in Fenway Park, a small ballpark and a hitter's heaven. So his accomplishments are even more impressive.

Greg Maddux

Nickname: "Mad Dog."   *Has played since:* 1986.   *Team best known for:* Atlanta Braves (1993–   ).   *Reasons he is a star:* He has won the Cy Young Award **four** times. He also had an ERA below 2.00 two seasons in a row. No one had accomplished that feat since Walter Johnson in 1919.   *He is known for:* his tremendous control. Hitters contend that

Maddux can pick a spot anywhere in the strike zone and then place the ball there.

Bonnie Bernstein's Bonus Secret—

Know how to say "He hit the ball" like a Goddess!

Bonnie Bernstein can be thought of as the Tiger Woods of sports television. At a very young age, she has rocketed past many veterans on the basis of her talent and intelligence. She presently serves as a reporter and analyst for CBS Sports. In 1998, she was the only woman sitting "in the studio" on an NFL pregame show.

Bonnie speaks sports well. A top gymnast through high school and college, she received the Thomas M. Fields Award for athletic and academic excellence at the University of Maryland. In her short but distinguished career, Bonnie has covered NFL games, the NBA finals, major college football games, and the NCAA men's basketball tournament. She has reported extensively on baseball throughout spring training, the regular season, and the World Series. Her insight and knowledge of the sport brought her early acclaim from insiders in the industry.

Bonnie recommends that a Sports Goddess "learn how to talk the talk" of baseball. For example, she suggests that you become familiar with a few synonyms for "hitting the ball." Don't say "nice hit." Do say *He drilled it* or *He crushed it* or *What a monster shot*! Dropping the proper phrase should make any Sports God look up from the television! As Bonnie says, "It's not who you know—**but how he hit it!**"

Secret #54.   Start paying attention to baseball on Labor Day.

By Labor Day weekend, the haves and the have-nots of the season will have parted ways. Eight teams will make it into the postseason: the six division leaders and two wild cards, one from each league. By thinking THIN, it will be relatively obvious to you which teams will win their division. Which won't. Which races are still being decided. And which teams are competing for the wild card spots.

In addition, a Sports Goddess will be aware of which players may or may not be going for season records. In June, she might hear of a player hitting above .400 or a slugger on pace to hit a certain number of home runs in the season. In September, she will know if that player or any other has a realistic chance.

For example, let's say a Sports Goddess opened the paper on Labor Day, 1998. She would have discovered that Mark Mc-Gwire and Sammy Sosa were chasing Roger Maris's record for most home runs in a season. In fact, she could have turned on the television that day and seen McGwire tie the record against Sosa's team. She would have found out that only one division race remained: Anaheim and Texas in the AL West. She would have noted that Boston led the AL wild card race and Chicago was ahead in the NL wild card race. Both teams were on losing streaks. (Remember the curses on the Red Sox and the Cubs?)

Thus, a Sports Goddess can spend September focusing on the relevant division and wild card races. Once again, she should pick a team and follow it until it clinches its race. Or it falls out of contention. Then she should choose the team that beat her first team.

When the season ends, a Sports Goddess faces three rounds of postseason play. In the first round, in each league, the top four teams with the best and worst records play each other, and the teams with the second and third best records face off. It's a best-of-five series. In the second round, the two teams left in each league battle. This round is known as the League Championship Series (LCS). It is a best-of-seven series. Each LCS champion wins the *pennant* for its league. Then the two *pennant* winners face one another in the World Series, another best-of-seven series.

1998 AMERICAN LEAGUE PLAYOFFS

Round I	ALCS	World Series
	(American League Champion Series)	

NY Yankees vs.

Texas Rangers

       NY Yankees vs.

Boston Red Sox vs.

Cleveland Indians

       Cleveland Indians

                           NY Yankees

Best of Five   *Best of Seven*   *Best of Seven*

SG TIP. If you watch one baseball game each year, make it game 6 of the World Series (if there is one). Game 6 usually turns out to be very competitive. Either one team wins the World Series or the other team stops that team from winning the World Series.

Secret #55.   Know how to read a box score.

Note the language of this secret. I'm *not* saying read a box score every day. (Though a supreme Sports Goddess will want to, by the end of her training!) Simply know *how* to read box scores and line scores. Make this ability part of your arsenal of knowledge. You never know when you can pull it out to impress other Gods or Goddesses.

A box score summarizes how each batter hit during the game, how each pitcher pitched, and how many runs each team scored in each inning. (Remember, baseball fans love statistics.)

Newspapers publish variations on the traditional box score. Most use the following abbreviations. Keep this list handy!

A SPORTS GODDESS'S GUIDE TO BOX SCORE ABBREVIATIONS

Position		Hitting		Pitching	
P	pitcher	**AB**	at bat	**IP**	innings pitched
C	catcher	**R**	runs he scored	**H**	hits he gave up
1B	first base	**H**	hits he made	**ER**	earned runs he gave up
2B	second base	**RBI**	runs he batted in		
3B	third base			**BB**	bases on balls (i.e., walks he gave up)
SS	shortstop	**SO**	strikeouts he made		
LF	left field			**SO**	strikeouts he threw
RF	right field	**Avg.**	his batting average for the season at the end of the game		
CF	center field			**ERA**	his earned run average for the season at the end of the game
DH	designated hitter				
PH/R	pinch hitter/ runner				

Sports Goddess Power Talk:
Know your sluggers from your hitters!

Pitchers/Pitching

Ace   **Baseball definition:** the very best pitcher(s) on the staff
If your boss says, "You're an ace"—You should feel great.

Southpaw   **Baseball definition:** a left-handed pitcher.
If your boss says, "We're looking for a southpaw here"—Volunteer if you're left-handed.

No-hitter   **Baseball definition:** A pitcher gives up no hits in the game.
If your boss says, "I'm looking for a no-hitter here"—Be prepared to excel. Give **nothing** up to your opposition.

Deb Kaufman's Bonus Secret—

"Share the sports pages with your child!"

In February of 1999, I gave a speech based on my research at Wellesley College to the "Mothers of Three Sons" club in Needham, Massachusetts. This organization is comprised of women who have three or more sons and *no* daughters. They have approximately 40 members. In the ensuing discussion, I included several suggestions which grew out of my research and studies. *Don't automatically say "Ask your father" if your child asks you about sports. Use sports to connect with your child and not to disconnect. Don't let football intimidate you.*

The image of a father and a son talking and playing sports has been a popular one in American society. Recently, that image has expanded to include father and daughter (e.g., a father-daughter relationship is at the center of the movie *Field of Dreams*) and even mother and son.

Deb Kaufman presents the image of the future—a mother sharing sports with her daughter. Most mornings, Deb stays at home with her preschool daughter, Madeline, in her Connecticut home. Most afternoons, Deb boards the train for New York City and her job as a reporter and anchor for the Madison Square Garden (MSG) network. She reports on all the professional teams in the number one television market in the country. When Madeline was very young, Deb would hold her while she was reading the baseball box scores and other sports reports in the newspapers. As Deb notes "as babies can only see black and white, she loved the sports pages—and she grabbed and played with paper. It's an easy way to connect your child to sports right away!"

Perfect Game	**Baseball definition:** A pitcher gives up **no hits and no walks, no one on the team makes an error**, and he does not hit the batter with the ball. Very rarely happens.
	If your boss says, "I'm looking for a perfect game"—Be prepared to be better than perfect!

SG TIP.   A perfect game is always a no-hitter. A no-hitter is usually not a perfect game.

Hitting Strategy

Pinch Hitter

Baseball definition: The manager sends in a hitter to substitute for a player at bat. Not a permanent designation like the designated hitter.

Pinch Runner

Baseball definition: The manager sends in a runner as a substitute for someone on base. The runner is usually faster or more likely to steal a base.

If your boss says, "You're the pinch runner here"—Know whom you are replacing. Run faster than him or her.

Sacrifice Fly

Baseball definition: A player hits a ball that is caught in the outfield. The hitter is out. However, if a runner on third tags the base after the ball is caught, and then crosses home plate without being thrown out, the hitter receives credit for a sacrifice fly.

If your boss says, "I want a sacrifice fly from you"—Make sure you know whom you are advancing— and whether he or she is worth it!

Bunt

Baseball definition: A player hits a fair ball a very short distance from the plate. Sports G & Gs will say that a player "lays down a bunt."

If your boss asks you to "lay down a bunt"—Be prepared to make a very small, subtle move—and to move very fast after you accomplish it!

Squeeze

Baseball definition: In a bunt situation, the runner on third must avoid being "squeezed" out by the third base-man and the catcher. When the runner has left third before the hitter has bunted, he faces a *suicide squeeze.* When the runner has not left third before the bunt, he's in a *safety squeeze* situation.

> **If your boss says you will be facing a squeeze situation**—Think before you make your move.

Fielding Plays

Double Play   **Baseball definition:** A double play results in two players being out on the same batted ball.

Triple Play   **Baseball definition:** A triple play results in three players being out on the same batted ball.
If your boss says, "That was a triple play on your part"—You've done something spectacular.
If your boss says, "You hit *into* a triple play"—You've done something very bad.

Fielder's Choice   **Baseball definition:** A fielder "chooses" to throw out a base runner instead of the hitter.

It's very easy to turn the "national pastime" into an "SGIT pastime." An SGIT now knows that statistics (stats) matter in baseball. Most important, she understands that only a few really matter for her viewing or following pleasure: a hitter's batting average (BA) and a pitcher's earned run average (ERA). An SGIT also realizes that many baseball fans feel the game was better in the olden days than in the present, even though some recent seasons have been quite thrilling and among the best ever. Finally, an SGIT recognizes that no matter how great a season the Boston Red Sox, the Chicago Cubs, the Chicago White Sox, and the Cleveland Indians may have, they will inevitably disappoint their fans during either the regular season or the postseason.

6

A SPORTS GODDESS TALKS
HOCKEY

A Sports Goddess knows:

The league's name—National Hockey League (NHL).

The regular season runs from—October to April.

The National Hockey League is divided into—the Eastern (15 teams) and the Western (13 teams) conferences.

The Eastern Conference is divided into—the Atlantic, Northeast, and Southeast divisions.

The Western Conference is divided into—the Central, Northwest, and Pacific divisions.

The number of games in the regular season is—82.

The championship series is called—the Stanley Cup (held in June).

The game is divided into—three periods, each 20 minutes long.

Each team consists of—six players: three offensive players (right wing, center, left wing) and three defensive players (right defenseman, left defenseman, goalie).

The object of the game is—to get the *puck* (small black rubber object that is the equivalent of a ball) into the opponent's net for a *goal*.

Game summary—Two teams play in a rink on an ice surface. The hockey rink is 200 feet long and 85 feet wide. At the end of three periods, the team that has more goals wins the game. During the regular season, if the teams are tied at the end of the third period, they play a five-minute *sudden-death overtime*. The team that scores first during this overtime, wins. If no team scores, then the game ends in a tie. During the play-offs, if the teams are tied at the end of the game, they play *sudden-death overtime* in 20-minute periods, until one team scores and wins. It's called "sudden death" because when one team scores, the other suddenly dies—it loses the game.

One Nickname for the game—"the Coolest Game on Earth."

ONCE, THE NHL played in just six cities (Boston, Chicago, Detroit, Montreal, New York, Toronto) in North America. Six cities with very cold weather. Hockey fans in those cities adored the game, but Sports Gods and Goddesses elsewhere knew little about the sport.

Today, the NHL has expanded to 28 cities (30 in the 2000–2001 season), including such hot climes as Miami and Phoenix. Since the late 1980s, hockey has increased its visibility nationally and updated its image dramatically. Since the fall of the Soviet bloc, many foreign players have joined the NHL and raised the caliber of play. Russians, Swedes, Finns, Czechs, Canadians, and U.S. nationals skate side by side. Former "comrades" flick the puck to freethinking Scandinavians. Many Sports G & Gs now consider hockey cool, hip, and fun.

Why? Well, hockey sells well. Fans in warm weather regions have embraced the game. The NHL now markets itself better. Hockey players skate out onto the ice through the jaws of a shark in San Jose. In addition, in the mid-to-late '90's, FOX-TV broadcast games nationally. This youthful network grabbed viewers' attention through experiments with MTV-like graphics and a glowing blue puck. While FOX no longer televises NHL games (Disney holds exclusive rights), many fans still appreciate its efforts in making the game understandable to a larger population.

You *want* to be a Hockey Goddess. The game is fast. The rules are simple. Most technical terms (e.g., high-sticking, charging) are self-explanatory. Austin Powers, International Man of Mystery (also known as Canada native Mike Myers), adores the game. So should you.

Secret #56.   Know that the Penguins play in the Igloo.

A few hockey arenas have wonderful names or nicknames. The Pittsburgh Penguins play in the Igloo. The Anaheim Mighty Ducks face off on The Pond. The San Jose Sharks skate around in the Shark Tank. The Tampa Bay Lightning streak around the Ice Palace.

Other sports have venues with names that mean a lot to Sports G & Gs. Fenway Park. Lambeau Field. Soldiers Field. Of course, you must know the history of the sport to appreciate the names. Hockey humors its fans and everyone else. These names can be enjoyed by everybody!

The Igloo contains some rich modern hockey memories. While the Mighty Ducks, the Sharks, and the Lightning have yet to make their mark in the play-offs, the Pittsburgh Penguins brought two Stanley Cups home to the Igloo in the 1990s.

In the early 1990s, the Penguins had one of the finest teams in hockey and one of the most admirable players, Mario Lemieux, in any sport. In the late 1980s and 1990s, he won MVP trophies and scoring titles. He led Pittsburgh to back-to-back Stanley Cups in the 1991 and 1992 seasons. In the 1992–1993 season, he was diagnosed with Hodgkin's disease. He took time off for radiation treatments. However, he returned by the end of the season, won the league's scoring title, and helped his team in the play-offs. Over the next few years, he battled a series of injuries. He retired in 1997. For Pittsburgh fans, his talent and his courage are frozen in time in the Igloo.

Secret #57.   Fear the "Grim Reaper" and a few other enforcers.

The Anaheim Mighty Ducks boast about their player Stu Grimson. His name alone chills many Hockey G & Gs. Why? an SGIT may ask. How frightening can a man named Stu, who plays for a team called the Mighty Ducks, be? Very. Grimson serves as an enforcer. A good one. Fans nicknamed him the "Grim Reaper."

Hockey players intimidate each other on the ice. Some extraordinary ones, like Wayne Gretzky, scared off players through their amazing talent. Others *check* (place their body or their stick between their opponent and the puck) very hard. Others battle with their fists. While the NHL has tried to cut down on the number of fights through tougher penalties, they still occur. When there's a brawl on the ice, you'll usually find a team's enforcer.

Most teams have an enforcer. Ideally, he intimidates other players by his size, by his ability to protect his star players, and by his hard checks. Realistically, an enforcer spends a lot of time in the penalty box. His stats differ from other players because he'll have the *most penalty minutes and greatest average number of fights per year.*

In many cases, enforcers live quiet, gentle lives off the ice. Stu Grimson has dedicated his life to Christianity and preaches in his spare time. He has reconciled his religious beliefs with his professional job description. Hockey G & Gs use colorful names when they refer to enforcers. Goons. Bullies. Poor players. The position inspires fear. But not respect.

However, in the 1997 Stanley Cup play-offs, Joey Kocur, a Detroit Red Wing, struck his best blow for enforcers everywhere. Six months before, Kocur had been an out-of-work goon. He played in a beer league in Detroit. Players drank beer before, during, and after the game. In his day, he had been among the best bullies for such teams as the New York Rangers. However, many felt his punching days were over. Still, in midseason, the Detroit Red Wings called him. Thus, he found himself playing in the Stanley Cup finals. In game 1 against the Philadelphia Flyers, Kocur scored the go-ahead goal. This was not supposed to happen. Goons don't get goals. Never mind score big ones in important games. Meanwhile, his fellow bully on Detroit's "Grind Line," Kirk Maltby, also started scoring. Halfway through the series, these two enforcers led the team in points. Maltby made the cover of *Sports Illustrated*. Then other scorers stepped up. They were embarrassed to be outscored by goons! When the Wings won the Stanley Cup, the two bad guys had morphed into good guys to the fans.

Then, the next year, in game 1 of the Stanley Cup Finals, Kocur scored the first goal of the series. Hockey G & Gs were stunned. A Cinderella story in one year is one thing. But two?! The Wings went on to win their second Stanley Cup. Meanwhile, Joey Kocur, the bully from the beer leagues, became a big hero.

SPORTS GODDESS MOVIE REVIEW

The Mighty Ducks (1992).

Stars: Emilio Estevez. **SG summary:** In this Disney movie, a yuppie coaches inner-city kids' hockey team as part of his community service. They do well. **SG additional note:** It's a children's movie. However, Disney's hockey team, also named the Mighty Ducks, debuted soon after the movie. So Hockey G & Gs went out and rented it.

SPORTS GODDESS BOOK REVIEW: GOLDEN OLDIE

The Game.

Author: Ken Dryden, former goalie for the Montreal Canadiens. **SG summary:** Dryden, an Ivy League–educated lawyer, weaves social commentary, sports insight, and political thoughts throughout his book on his years in hockey. **SG additional note:** The book is out of print. Many libraries carry it. Also, certain book web sites take orders for it.

Secret #58.   Glamorize the men behind the fashionable masks—the goalies.

Hockey G & Gs glamorize the goalie in their conversations. They talk about hot goalies and cold goalies and great goalies and gifted goalies. Sometimes, an SGIT doesn't understand. How can a goalie be glamorous? Isn't a goalie the fat kid who can't play any other position?

Not in this sport.

The top scorer can have a bad night and the team can still win. Someone else can accelerate his game and take his place. The best defenseman can have a bad night and the team can escape with a victory. Another defenseman or the goalie can back him up. However, if the goalie lets a few easy shots go by, no one can cover for him. The goals go in. The score goes up. The team loses. The goalie garners praise for a superb performance. He endures scorn for a poor one. An SGIT should always ask, "Who's in net?" or "Who was in net?" when she talks about a hockey game.

Like a pitcher, a goalie has a wins-losses record. Actually, it is a wins-losses-ties record. (Hockey games can end in ties during the regular season; the play-offs are always decided in overtime.) However, a goalie must earn many more wins than a pitcher to be considered great. The best usually win 32 or more games each year.

Hockey G & Gs also look at a goalie's goals-against average (GAA) to evaluate his performance. This statistic tells a Goddess how many goals, on average, he allows in the net each game. For example, if a Goddess sees that a goalie has a GAA of 3.00, she realizes that he gives up an average of three goals each game.

A SPORTS GODDESS'S GUIDE TO GAA

If a Goalie's GAA Is	A Sports Goddess Should
below 2.60	be happy
between 2.60 and 3.25	watch closely
between 3.25 and 3.50	start to worry

| between 3.50 and 4.50 | worry more |
| above 4.50 | panic |

NHL goalies wear face masks that are among the most decorated gear in sports. Some goalies sport masks with symbols (e.g., the St. Louis arch) of their team's city. Others opt for humorous images like Godzilla or a skull. One San Jose goaltender even wanted to have illustrations of computer chips (to represent Silicon Valley) on his mask until he realized they wouldn't be visible to the crowd. So, SGITs, check out those masks.

Of course, it helps to learn the names of a few of the men behind the masks. Hockey G & Gs refer to these gentlemen by several different names besides "the man in the mask." The netminder. The gatekeeper. The hero.

SPORTS GODDESS'S PROFILE: GLAMOROUS GOALIES

Martin Brodeur

Native of: Canada.   *'99 team:* New Jersey Devils.   *SG fun fact:* In 1995, Brodeur blazed through the play-offs. He also became enmeshed in a superstition that was quite time-consuming. When he went to a movie the day or night before a game, the team won. When he didn't, they lost. He tried renting movies. Didn't work. He actually had to be in the movie theater. It may have been a coincidence. However, the Devils did win the Stanley Cup!   *One reason he is a star:* When he wasn't watching movies, he was performing brilliantly for the Devils in the 1995 play-offs.   *Watch for:* his ability to shoot the puck very far down the ice.

Dominik Hasek

Nickname: "The Dominator."   *Native of:* Czech Republic.   *'99 team:* Buffalo Sabres.   *SG fun fact:* He grew up in Communist Czechoslovakia. Came close to staying there and becoming a history teacher.   *A few reasons he is a star:* In 1998, he won the Vezina Trophy (given to the best goalie) and the Hart Trophy (the Most Valuable Player). It was his second year in a row to win the Hart Trophy. Prior to Hasek's back-to-back victories, the last year a goalie won the Hart was 1962. Hasek also helped the Czech Republic win the gold medal in the 1998 Winter Olympics. **SG additional reason he is a star:** One year, no team in the NHL scored more than four goals against him. *And* he let four goals go into the net on just four occasions during the entire season. Some NHL goalies allow five or more goals per game on a regular basis. **SG additional note:** The Dominator can exhibit unusual behavior. During the 1997 play-offs, he grabbed a journalist by the neck, criticized his coach, and missed meetings. Many wondered if he would stay with the Sabres. However, he apologized to the writer, the coach departed, and Hasek's attitude improved. At the end of 1998, he still was considered the best goalie in the game. **Watch for:** his ability to challenge shooters. He stands outside the goal and stares them down.

Patrick Roy

Nickname: "Saint Patrick." **Last name:** is pronounced Roo-ah. **Native of:** Canada. **'99 team:** Colorado Avalanche. **SG fun fact:** He's superstitious. During the 1993 Stanley Cup play-offs, he squeezed a toy elephant before games. **One reason he is a star:** He led the Montreal Canadiens to two Stanley Cup victories. Then he moved to Denver and helped them win the Stanley Cup in 1996. **Watch for:** his "butterfly" style. It's an inverted V formation (i.e., he stands with his arms by his side, not above his head.) He focuses on the bottom of the net, whereas many goalies often deflect pucks with their gloves over their heads.

Secret #59.   Focus on the goalie's nemesis. Seek out the super scorer.

In hockey, one goal equals one game point. Often the game boils down to a showdown between the goalie who can stop that point and the star scorer who can shoot it in. An SGIT should seek out the super scorer on each team. Most likely, he will be a member of an *offensive line* (a right wing, a center, or a left wing). He will not be on the ice all the time. A Sports Goddess should look for his shift (i.e., the period of time he is on the ice with the other two members of his line). She should note her player's moves. When another player has the puck, where is he?

How does he *set up* plays? (Watch him move and pass to other players.) When he has the puck, how does he *handle* it? Does he rush up the ice by himself? Does he pass it? When he goes up against the goalie, how does he fake him?

A star scorer does not always net goals. He also assists his teammates with their goals. The NHL tabulates an individual's scoring points as a combination of goals and assists.

Goals + Assists = Total Individual Points

SPORTS GODDESS PROFILE: SUPER SCORERS

Wayne Gretzky

Nicknames: "The Great One," "Number 99." *Native of:* Canada. *'99 Team:* New York Rangers. *SG fun fact:* He's married to actress Janet Jones. They posed together for the *Sports Illustrated* swimsuit issue. *One reason he is a star:* Many consider him the best player of all time. He scored the most points, goals, and assists *ever* in the NHL. *He retired in:* 1999.

Pavel Bure

Nickname: "The Russian Rocket." *Native of:* Russia. *'99 team:* Florida Panthers. *SG fun fact:* Pavel's father, Vladimir, was a star swimmer for the Soviet Union in the 1968, 1972, and 1976 Summer Olympics. He won a silver and a bronze medal. He competed against famed U.S. swimmer Mark Spitz. *A few reasons he is a star:* He won NHL Rookie of the Year in 1992. In 1998, Pavel ranked #3 on the list of top scorers in the league. *SG should know:* During the 1998–1999 season, he was a holdout (i.e., he did not play) because he wanted to be traded by the Canucks. He spent much of his time in Russia and practiced with the Red Army hockey team.

Peter Forsberg

Native of: Sweden. *'99 team:* Colorado Avalanche. *SG fun fact:* In Sweden, his likeness was put on a stamp. *A few reasons he is a star:* In 1994, he led Sweden to a gold medal in ice hockey in the Winter Olympics.

In 1995, he won the Rookie of the Year Award in the NHL. In 1996, he starred on the Colorado Avalanche team that won the Stanley Cup.

Jaromir Jagr

Native of: Czech Republic.   ***'99 team:*** Pittsburgh Penguins.   ***SG fun fact:*** He has tried to start an all-sports radio station in his native Czechoslovakia.   ***A few reasons he is a star:*** He scored the most points in the 1998 season. Along with Dominik "The Dominator" Hasek, he helped the Czech Republic win the gold medal in ice hockey at the 1998 Olympics.   ***Watch for:*** his aggressive rushes down the ice, his long hair flying from beneath his helmet.

Zigmund Palffy

Nickname: "Ziggy."   ***Native of:*** Slovakia.   ***'99 team:*** New York Islanders.   ***SG fun fact:*** In 1992, he barely spoke English. He learned the language from his teammates and from such American movies as *Cool Runnings*, about the Jamaican bobsled team. Now he listens to Jerky Boys recordings and embraces pop culture.   ***One reason he is a star:*** He ranked fourth on the list of top scorers in 1998.   ***One reason he is not a bigger star:*** He plays for the New York Islanders, who struggled in the late 1990s. Palffy missed the first 32 games of the 1998–1999 season because of bitter contract negotiations with the Islanders. When he returned, he said, "I can't do it all by myself."   ***Watch for:*** his "cannon" shot booming past goalies. His sneaky moves around defensemen to drive into the goal.

Secret #60.   Zone in on one hockey rule. Offside.

The whistle blows a lot in hockey. Every time it does, play stops. It can be confusing for anyone not familiar with the rules. Unless you understand one or two rules of the game, it can be boring. With a few rules under your belt, the excitement increases.

Perhaps the easiest rule to understand in hockey—and the one that makes the game far more interesting to watch—is *offside*. In hockey, five horizontal lines—two in each half and one in the center—partition the playing surface. The *red line* crosses the ice in the center of the playing surface and divides it in half.

At each end, a *goal line* runs across the ice in front of each net. Sixty feet in front of each goal, a *blue line* stretches across the ice. When **an offensive player skates toward the opposing goal, the puck must cross the blue line before his skates do**. When a Sports Goddess watches the player with the puck *rush* (i.e., skate very fast, with the intention to score or set up a shot) into the opponent's zone, she realizes that **he needs to keep the puck just ahead of his skates.** And his teammates need to keep behind the puck as well. If they do not, the whistle blows, play stops, and a face-off (when the puck is dropped between two players from opposing teams) occurs outside the zone. And a great scoring opportunity may have been lost.

Secret #61. Know when to scream "ICE the puck!"

If you watch any hockey game, you will see *icing*. It can be a strategic move. It can be a desperation tactic. When the offense pressures the defense in the end zone, a member of the defending team often *ices* (i.e., shoots) the puck to the other end zone, across the goal line. If the puck goes past the *goal line* and a member of the opposition (except the goalie) touches it with his stick, "icing" is called. Then a face-off is held in the defending team's end zone. A practical SGIT might ask, "Why does a defending player do this if the puck lands back in his own zone?"

He does it so the defense can regroup while the puck sails down the ice.

Therein lies the strategic component of icing. Technically, if a player shoots the puck into the end zone from anywhere behind the red line and it is touched by a member of the opposition, icing will be called. Most often, a Sports Goddess will see icing when a team needs to regroup. When a Sports Goddess watches a game, she knows to scream "Ice the puck" when the going gets tough.

Of course, exceptions exist. **If the defending team is shorthanded due to a penalty (i.e., short a player), then no icing is called.** A Sports Goddess should shout "Get the puck out of the zone" when her team is shorthanded. **If a member of the de-**

fense touches the puck before it crosses the goal line, no icing is called. A Sports Goddess should shout "Skate down there" to her team members after one of them has iced the puck.

> In our industry it's somewhat important to know the basic rules, strategies, and terminologies of the major sports. Salespeople and customers will assume you do, and feel free to use analogies based on these. However, in our industry, professionals have to work a lot of overtime to keep up with their complex, rapidly changing fields—so nobody will assume that a professional is aware of particular sports teams' or stars' performances.
>
> —male manager

Secret #62. On the first day of spring, start thinking hockey. Skip the winter.

Yes, the players skate on a frozen surface. Yes, it's a winter sport. Still, you don't have to pay attention to the sport when it's cold. However, when spring fever sets in, a Goddess's fancy should turn to hockey.

Professional hockey spans all seasons. Training camp commences at the end of the summer. The first two and a half months of the regular season occupy the last two and a half months of the fall. The regular season lasts the entire winter and one or two weeks of the spring. The play-offs run all spring. Then training camp starts about two months later.

On March 20, the first day of spring, begin paying attention to hockey. That way, you'll have a month or so left of the regular season. As in basketball, more than half of all hockey teams make the play-offs. In the final few weeks of the season, an SGIT can follow the last few teams jockeying for the final postseason positions. As in baseball, certain individuals will be going for scoring titles. In the final weeks, an SGIT will be able to focus on the players who have realistic chances for those titles.

With the play-offs, the real season begins. Four rounds comprise postseason play in the NHL. The first round starts in the middle of April, and the last series ends in mid-June. It's two months of hockey, which is more than enough hockey for many Sports G & Gs. The first three rounds are the quarterfinals, semifinals, and finals for the Eastern and Western conferences. Each series is best of seven games. The last round, the Stanley Cup finals, pits the winners of the Eastern and Western conferences against one another.

Just as you would in every sport, pick one team at the beginning of the play-offs. Follow them until they lose. Then track the team that beat them. Until they lose. And so on.

Hockey play-offs contain several sportsmanlike traditions. At the end of every play-off series, the players of both teams stand in a line and shake each other's hands. Of course, some bandaged fingers and fists touch the hands that hurt them during the series. At the end of the final game, the winning team skates the Stanley Cup around the ice. Later, players and lucky fans sip champagne from the cup. Some years, victorious players display the cup in their backyards during summer barbecues.

Secret #63. Revere the legend and lore of *les Canadiens*. Also known as the Montreal Canadiens.

In the NHL, *les Canadiens* rule. They're classy. They're rich in tradition. Many fans speak French. The Canadiens encapsulate hockey history. If an SGIT knows a few things about the "Habs," she will understand the sport a little better.

Since the NHL was founded in 1918, the Montreal Canadiens have won the Stanley Cup 23 times. That's a winning percentage of 25 percent! In addition, since the 1920s, the Canadiens have won the cup at least once in each decade.

The Canadiens used to play at the Montreal Forum. The Forum contained cherished memories. Banners. Team uniforms. The ghosts of great players from the past. Now the Canadiens skate around the Molson Centre. It's a high-tech arena built with luxury boxes, and it has a corporate sponsor. Fans have embraced the new arena if not the recent rough seasons of the

Canadiens. Perhaps because they moved all the nostalgia into
their new home. Or it could be because the seats are much more
comfortable. Or because the building is named after a beer company. Canadien fans may be classy, but they're still sports fans.

**The Canadiens' uniform has an H on it surrounded by a big
C.** The C stands for Canadiens. The H is for hockey. Many
Hockey G & Gs will tell the SGIT that the H represents "Habs"
or "Habitants," two nicknames for the Canadiens. (A habitant
is a French-Canadian farmer.) Don't be fooled.

**An Ivy League–educated lawyer guarded the net for the
Canadiens in the 1970s. He did very well.** Ken Dryden was one
of the best goalies ever in the game. He also was one of the
smartest athletes to play professional sports. He skated through
Cornell University academically and athletically. He captured
the Rookie of the Year Award in 1972. He won the Vezina Trophy five times. In the middle of his career, he took a year off to
clerk in a Toronto law firm. He returned to hockey. He starred
some more. Then he quit the sport at the age of 31. Like Jim
Brown in the NFL, he left near his peak. He moved to Cam-
bridge, England, for a while and wrote an intelligent, insightful
book on hockey.

**A player named "The Flower" scorched the NHL in the
1970s and early 1980s.** Guy LaFleur (his last name means "the
flower" in French) won scoring titles. He bagged MVP trophies.
He helped the Habs to several Stanley Cups. Off the ice, "The
Flower" partied very hard and drove cars very fast. His professional and personal reputations made up for an easy-to-pick-on
name by macho sports fans. In 1988, after he had been elected
to the Hall of Fame, he came out of retirement, played for the
New York Rangers and Quebec Nordiques, and scored more
goals. His final goal, number 560, came against the Canadiens
in 1991.

**Maurice "Rocket" Richard helped the Canadiens roar
through the 1940s and 1950s.** Even today, an SGIT will hear
certain players compared with Rocket Richard. In many ways,
he was the definitive Canadien. In *The Hockey Sweater*, by Roch
Carrier, all the children in a French-speaking town idolize

Rocket. They wear sweaters with a number 9, just like his. They tape their hockey sticks just the way he does. They put grease in their hair, just as he does.

Richard was the first player to score 50 goals in a season. Only very good players reach that total today. However, they play an 82-game season; Richard accomplished this feat in a 50-game season. That's an average of one goal per game. Only Wayne Gretzky has achieved a higher average.

A popular player, the Rocket possessed a fiery temper. In 1955, he hit an official during a game. The president of the NHL, Clarence Campbell, suspended him for the rest of the season and the play-offs. When Campbell showed up at a game in Montreal on St. Patrick's Day of that year, a riot took place in the Montreal Forum and continued all night on the streets of the city.

Montreal loves its Canadiens.

Secret #64. Exclaim, "Do you believe in miracles?!"

Now and then, an SGIT will hear the phrase "Do you believe in miracles?" from Hockey G & Gs. It will be shouted. It will be exclaimed. Al Michaels, the ABC Sports Announcer, contributed this phrase to sports lore. The year was 1980. The venue was the Lake Placid Winter Olympics. At that time, Russia (the Soviet Union) was considered the enemy. Prior to the Olympics, it had invaded Afghanistan. Hostilities percolated beneath the icy surface of the Olympic rink.

In previous Olympics, the Soviet Union had won the gold medal four straight times. In 1980, they were expected to collect their fifth. The best hockey players in the USSR played on the USSR Olympic team. The best hockey players in the United States worked on NHL teams. They were not in Lake Placid. The players on the U.S. team were all nonprofessionals.

The United States and USSR faced off in the semifinal. The game was tied with only ten minutes left. Then, Mike Eruzione, a U.S. player, scored the go-ahead goal. Nine minutes left. Eight minutes left. Seven. Still, no Russian goal. With only a few seconds remaining, when it became obvious that the United States would win, ABC's Al Michaels exclaimed, "Do you believe in miracles?!"

Two miracles occurred. The United States beat the USSR. Then they went on to capture the gold medal.

At the time, the victory symbolized much to Sports G & Gs everywhere. The United States vs. the USSR. Capitalism vs. communism. Good vs. Evil. Al Michaels's phrase served as shorthand for this event. The game became known as "the Miracle on Ice."

Linda Cohn's Bonus Secret—

"Size doesn't matter"

Linda Cohn has pioneered new ground for women in sports as a player and as a reporter. In grammar school, she followed the New York Rangers and Giants. In high school, she played on the **boys'** ice hockey team. In her mid-twenties, she became the first full-time female sports anchor for the ABC radio network. Soon after, she landed at ESPN. She now anchors *SportsCenter* and LPGA golf events. Linda packs her intelligence, insight, and genuine enthusiasm for sports into all of her highlights and events. In 1998, the *St. Petersburg Times* named her one of the 10 best *SportsCenter* anchors ever.

Linda still loves hockey. When the New York Rangers won the Stanley Cup in 1994, she attended game 7. That night, after the victory, she sipped from the Stanley Cup. She ranks the win as one of the top three events of her life (alongside her marriage and the births of her children).

Linda offers this "secret" to understanding hockey better: **"Size doesn't matter!** The little guy in the corner can be as effective as the big player in front of the net. Watch how a smaller player digs the puck out of tough situations. Note how he sets up shots from the outside. In hockey, the little guy can be the king!"

Sports Goddess Power Talk:
Know your Lady Byngs from your Lord Stanleys. Talk the talk of hockey.

The beauty of the language of hockey lies in its clarity. Nearly every phrase (e.g., power play, hooking) evokes an image. Most images reflect the sports meaning of the term.

Perhaps the Canadian heritage of the game is best captured by the Stanley Cup and the Lady Byng Trophy. In 1892, Lord Stanley, Canada's governor-general, donated the cup named for him. He wanted it to be awarded to the "leading hockey club" in Canada. Ironically, Lord Stanley never saw a Stanley Cup game because he returned to England before it was awarded for the first time in 1893. In 1925, Lady Byng, the wife of the governor-general of Canada, started presenting a trophy, named after her, to the hockey player who combined sportsmanship with a high standard of playing. Her cup, awarded each year, adds a classy, gentlemanly air to an often brutal and combative game.

Penalties	(**SG Note**: Hockey does not have fouls. It has penalties.)
Power Play	**Hockey definition**: When a player receives a penalty, his team plays *shorthanded*. His opponent's team is on a *power play*. **Power Talk:** Perhaps hockey's greatest gift to professional jargon! **If your boss says, "We're in a power play situation here"**—You should find out how many more players you have on your side than the opposition has.
Penalty Box	**Hockey definition**: It's where a player sits during his penalty. If he receives a **minor penalty,** he resides in the penalty box for two minutes. If he earns a **major penalty,** he spends five minutes in the box.

Howie Schwab, a sports executive, always vowed that his future bride would take a sports test prior to their marriage. In the movie *Diner*, the fiancée of one of the lead characters must take a football test prior to her marriage. Sports G & Gs quote the scene where she nervously answers the questions. In 1990, a real-life *Diner* quiz scene occurred in a conference room in Connecticut. Sure enough, after Howie became engaged, he informed Jodi, his betrothed, of her destiny. To her tremendous credit, she showed up on the appointed day and faced a room of *sports journalists*. She not only had to answer football questions, she had to respond to queries about a multitude of sports. She survived. In fact, she thrived. She performed better than the poor fiancée in *Diner*. At one point, she was asked by a prominent sportscaster which league awarded the *Lady Byng Trophy*. She laughed. She hesitated. However, she gave the correct response. She talked the talk. Howie then walked the walk down the aisle.

If your boss says, "You're in the penalty box"— Ask whether you have committed a major or a minor penalty!

General Hockey Talk

Boards   **Hockey definition**: The boards are the wall around the hockey rink. Hockey players enjoy slamming each other against the boards.
If your boss tells you that you're "against the boards"—Ask him if you have room to dig yourself out. Of course, you always can start a fight!

Breakaway   **Hockey definition**: The player with the puck "breaks away" from the other players and no one stands between him and the goalie.
If your boss tells you that "you're on a breakaway"—You may be expected to score!

Face-off   **Hockey definition**: The official drops the puck between two opposing players.
              If your boss says you will be "facing-off" against an opponent—Make sure you know who is dropping the puck and whom you are facing off against.

Hat trick   **Hockey definition**: A player scores three goals in one game.
              If your boss tells you that you have "scored a hat trick"—You have done three things in a row well!

Penalty   **Hockey definition**: If a serious infraction has been
Shot   committed against a player—usually when he has been illegally checked on a breakaway—he receives a penalty shot. He starts at center ice and then goes one-on-one with the goalie.
              If your boss says, "I'm giving you a penalty shot here"—Make sure you know whom you are going up against one-on-one!

Pipes   **Hockey definition**: Pipes are the goal posts.
              If your boss tells you, "You hit the pipe"—You came close to scoring but missed.
              If your boss says, "You hit *between* the pipes"—You scored!

Shutout   **Hockey definition**: When one team does not score any goals, the other team **shut them out.** The goalie receives credit for a *shutout.*
              If your boss tells you, "Shut them out"—You can't let anything go by.

These days, even if an SGIT lives in the middle of a desert, she can still follow hockey with the proliferation of teams across the country. She realizes that the "coolest" player on the team may be the goalie, with his specially designed mask, and the "baddest" player on the team is always the enforcer. She understands that "les Canadiens" refers to the most pedigreed team in hockey and not to the nationality of many of the players. Finally, she knows that she really doesn't have to start following this winter sport until the play-offs begin in the spring!

7

A SPORTS GODDESS TALKS
GOLF

A Sports Goddess knows:

Professional male golfers play on—the Professional Golf Association (PGA) tour.

Professional female golfers play on—the Ladies' Professional Golf Association (LPGA) tour.

Professional Senior golfers play on—the Senior Professional Golf Association (SrPGA) tour.

The PGA tours—have golf tournaments most weeks from January to November.

Game summary—Most rounds of golf on the professional tours consist of 18 holes. The object of the game is for each golfer to get the ball, through a series of strokes, from the *tee* (i.e., the starting point) of each hole into an actual hole that is marked by a flag. Most tournaments have a series of 18-hole rounds. The golfer with the lowest score at the end of the series wins the tournament.

I wish I played golf. That is the conversation in the CEO/boardroom that you must participate in.

—female executive search professional

IN MY SURVEYS, I kept hearing about the importance of golf: professionally, socially, and culturally.

Golf can be considered a journey. One player and one ball (maybe three or four) travel together around an 18-hole course. Some Golf Gods and Goddesses consider it a Zen experience because of the woods, grass, and nature. Other G & Gs approach it with more angst than a high-powered board meeting.

You need to know how to talk about golf. Know how golf is played. Know how to watch a few minutes of golf. Find one or two interesting things about the game. Latch onto them. It can be Tiger Woods mania. It can be comparing different swings. It can be the accomplishments of female golfers. Once again, golf knowledge can give an edge to a Goddess in her personal and professional arenas.

Secret #65.   Understand why Golf Gods and Goddesses watch the game on television.

I'm not saying that *you* have to watch it on television. However, many SGITs simply do not understand why networks televise golf. They can understand the broadcasts of football or basketball, even if they don't watch them. They can appreciate the shared sense of community with baseball. However, they simply can't comprehend why anyone would spend hours looking at a golf course when they could be on one.

By watching televised games, Golf G & Gs can study the moves of the great players. "Fine," an SGIT thinks, "but what do they watch for?" A Golf God or Goddess focuses on the *swings* of the players, the *golf clubs they choose in different situations,* and *how they maintain composure* during tense moments. Thus, an SGIT should note these factors during a broadcast. Compare the swings of two different players. Check which club (e.g., a 7 iron or a 9 iron) different players use in the same situations. You'll know what clubs they select because the announcers will tell you. See some golfers sweat. Watch others remain calm. Note one or two details. Then comment on them.

Most golf courses have lots of grass, some sand traps, and some water hazards. Are all golf courses alike? No. The great ones differ in design and style. Some courses boast fast *greens* (the area around the hole with manicured grass) that play tricks with the ball. Some contain narrow *fairways* (the long stretch of rougher grass leading up to the hole), which means the player must work harder to keep the ball from the woods. Some place *water hazards* near the hole. Some are packed with *sand traps*. Sand traps are also known as *bunkers*. Classic *links-style* courses incorporate weather elements in their design. These courses tend to have very few or no trees. Many architects situate them near the ocean. This style of course originated in Great Britain.

Golf Gods and Goddesses fawn over favored and famed courses. In Monterey, CA, *Pebble Beach* and *Cypress Point*, two revered golfing sites, are situated by the ocean. *St. Andrews* in Scotland hangs over the sea. Golf G & Gs may never play these legendary courses, but they can stroke through them vicariously via television.

Secret #66. **Know your birdies from your eagles! Understand scoring and handicapping in golf.**

A SPORTS GODDESS'S GUIDE TO SCORING GOLF

Par—Recommended score on a hole

Birdie—A Golf Goddess shoots 1 *under* par

Eagle—A Golf Goddess shoots 2 *under* par

Bogey—A Golf Goddess shoots 1 *over* par

Double bogey—A Golf Goddess shoots 2 *over* par

Triple bogey—A Golf Goddess shoots 3 *over* par

Snowman—A Golf Goddess shoots 8 (a snowman) on a hole. A Golf Goddess's nightmare.

Each hole in golf has a recommended score (the number of times you hit the ball from the tee to the hole). It is called *par*.

Jim Nantz's Bonus Secret—

"Golf espouses the lessons of life."

If an SGIT tries just a few suggestions in this book, she will undoubtedly cross paths with Jim Nantz, the distinguished CBS Sports broadcaster. He has been, and continues to be, at all the major venues in sports. Jim has hosted and reported from the Winter Olympics, the Final Four, CBS's *NFL Today* show, the U.S. Open (tennis), and the Masters golf tournament. In addition, he had a very prominent and visible role in the golf movie *Tin Cup*.

Jim notes that golf "is a sport that espouses the lessons of life: patience, discipline, humility, and integrity."

Also, in order to understand the protocol of a television golf broadcast, Jim says, "Know why we [i.e., the announcers] whisper during the broadcast." It's a frequently asked question. After all, football, basketball, baseball, and hockey broadcasters do not lower their voices during the telecast. Jim adds "The hushed tones are not a result of a false sense of drama. It is out of total respect for the players. The sport demands tremendous concentration. Players are taught to play in silence. We sit right above them. And our voices, unless we whisper, can disturb their play.

For example, if a Golf Goddess plays a hole with a par of 5: she *pars* the hole with a score of 5; she *birdies* the hole with a score of 4; and she *bogeys* the hole with a score of 6.

However, golf equalizes the score of players with differing abilities through the *handicap system*. Excellent golfers and top amateurs are known as *scratch* golfers. Golf G & Gs expect them to par each hole based on their ability. Professional golfers are better than scratch.

Most golfers possess *handicaps*. "Handicap" may not be the most politically correct word these days, but golf uses it. A handicap allows a Golf Goddess to deduct a certain number of strokes at the end of her round. For example, if a Golf Goddess shoots an 86 on an 18-hole round and her handicap is 10, she deducts 10 strokes from her score to arrive at a *net* score of 76. If the course has a par of 72 for 18 holes, she would have shot 4 over par according to the handicap system. An SGIT can also think about the handicap system in another way. If your handicap is 5, and the par for the course is 72, then you are expected to shoot a 77 on the course.

Bottom Line—**The higher the handicap, the worse the golfer.**

Secret #67.   Read and talk about the leader board.

Of course, a Sports Goddess does not have to watch a golf tournament to follow golf. She can turn on the tournament in the last five minutes (this is in real time) of a broadcast to find out the day's summary and the *leader board*.

A leader board tells Golf Gods and Goddesses which players lead a tournament. In a newspaper, most look like this:

Par 72 6,842 Yard (36–36) Million Air Country Club Course

Tiger Woods 70–70—140−4

Justin Leonard 72–72—144 E

Mark O'Meara 73–72—145 +1

An SGIT knows from the information provided in the sports section that a Golf God should shoot a 72 on this course. That's par. Tiger Woods, in his first two rounds, made 4 *under par*. Justin Leonard, in his first two rounds, shot *par* and is *even*. Mark O'Meara has gone 1 *over par*. In addition, an SGIT should use the proper phrasing to talk about the Golf Gods on top of the leader board. Tiger Woods leads the pack by four *strokes*. O'Meara is *five strokes behind the leader*, Tiger Woods.

On television, in the middle of a round, an SGIT might see a leader board that looks like this:

Tiger Woods −4 16th

Justin Leonard E F

Mark O'Meara +1 17th

The number on the left usually refers to the golfer's score for the entire tournament up to the last hole played. The number on the right refers to the hole the golfer is on at that moment. Here Woods is 4 under for the tournament and on the 16th hole. Leonard has finished at even par. O'Meara is on the 17th hole, 1 over par. You should listen for a minute or two to hear what the announcers have to say about the score. If, by any chance, the score is for just that round, *you will be told* by phrases like "O'Meara is shooting one over par *today*."

Secret #68.   Know your woods from your irons.

Golfers select different clubs depending on their position on each hole. When they tee off, most (though not all) use *woods*. These clubs drive the ball far. When Golf G & Gs find themselves on the fairway, most choose *irons*. These clubs lift the ball higher and send it a shorter distance than woods. When Golf G & Gs sink the ball in a sand trap, they usually grab a *wedge*. These clubs dig the ball out of a tough situation. When a Golf Goddess plays on a green (the area surrounding the hole), she picks a *putter*.

When a Golf Goddess chooses a wood or an iron, she has several options. She can select a 1, 2, or 3 wood on a 3, 4, 5, 6, 7, 8, or 9 iron.

The lower the number of the club, the farther the ball will go. The higher the number, the higher in the air the ball will go.

When a Golf Goddess watches the game on television, she will hear numerous debates about which club the golfer should use in each situation. She will see the golfer consult with his or her *caddy* (the person carrying the golfer's clubs) about the selection of a club. She should remember the club used on one or two crucial shots. Then she can note it in conversation. "I saw that Tiger pulled a 3 wood" or "Justin grabbed a 7 iron."

Secret #69. Distinguish a long game from a short game.

Again and again, an SGIT will hear references to a Golf God "who has a great *short game*" or a Goddess "who plays a terrific *long game* but loses it on the short game."

Two types of games push the ball into the hole. The *long game* involves driving the ball from the tee or way back on the fairway. The *short game* gets the ball onto the green from a short distance or *putts* it into a hole. The long game depends on power. The short game relies on accuracy and concentration.

Some players achieve renown for their powerful long game. They crack the ball far. However, their strength does not serve them well when they near the hole. Others putt with precision. However, their technical accuracy does not help when they have to drive the ball. Long games require the use of woods or irons with low numbers. Short games use irons with higher numbers or the putter.

Sports Goddess Power Talk: Know the difference between the eighteenth and nineteenth holes!

Front Nine   **Golf definition:** the first 9 holes of an 18-hole golf course. Often used in metaphors for life—"You're on the front nine."

Back nine   **Golf definition:** the last 9 holes of an 18-hole golf course. Also used as a metaphor for life—"You're on the back nine."

Nineteenth Hole   **Golf definition:** There is no 19th hole on an 18-hole golf course. The term refers to the clubhouse bar. When "the nineteenth hole" is used as a metaphor for life, it usually means you've gone to the clubhouse bar in the sky.

Duffer   **Golf definition:** A duffer is a bad player.
If your boss says, "You're a duffer"—Worry!

Divot   **Golf definition:** the ground a Golf Goddess digs up during her shot.
If your boss says, "Clean up the divot you left from that project"—You did not do something neatly.

Gallery   **Golf definition:** The gallery consists of fans who stand on the side of a golf course and watch the golfers.
If your boss says, "I'll need a gallery here"—He may be looking for supporters, not a place to put up paintings!

Mulligan   **Golf definition:** A Golf Goddess attempts a shot again. Mulligans usually occur on the first tee.
If your boss says, "Take a mulligan"—Make sure you're not being penalized.

Shank   **Golf definition:** Technically, a shank occurs when the hosel of the club (where the club head meets the stick) hits the ball and it flies 90 degrees to the right of the target. However, *shanking* is more than a series of shanks. It is a *state of mind*. It is a disease. Some golfers, even the very best professionals, go through *shanking* phases. No matter what they do, they seem to shank every few shots.
If your boss says, "You shanked that"—You did not hit your target. Just hope that it was a one-shot shank.

Yips **Golf definition:** A Golf Goddess misses an easy putt due to jerky, nervous movements.
If your boss says, "You have a case of the yips"—Your nerves are getting the better of you.

MEN'S GOLF

A Sports Goddess knows:

The four major tournaments are

The Masters—played at the Augusta National Golf Club in Augusta, GA, in April.

The US Open—played at a different course each year in June.

The British Open—played at a different course in Great Britain each year in July.

The PGA Championship—played in the United States each year in August.

Secret #70. Master the Masters.

Each April, the Masters Tournament is played on the same course in Augusta, Georgia. Tradition seeps through the television coverage. Magnolias frame the leader board on television. Spring scenes segue into the coverage of most holes. Semiserious music plays on the way into and out of commercial breaks.

The Masters reflects both the positive and the negative history of golf. The course radiates beauty. Superb players have stroked their way to victory on it. In 1997, Tiger Woods emerged as a global Golf God when he won the tournament at the age of 21. Forty percent of all TV sets in the United States were tuned in to his final round. However, Woods was not only the youngest winner of the tournament; he was the first victor of African-American heritage. (His ancestry is African American, Thai, Chinese, Caucasian, and American Indian.) In fact, he was only the fourth competitor of African-American heritage ever in the tournament. Augusta National, the host club, did not accept black members until 1991.

Bobby Jones, the top U.S. golfer in the 1920s, founded the tournament. Jones epitomized the gentleman golfer. He graduated from Georgia Tech at 18, earned another degree from Harvard at 21, and passed the bar exam after three semesters at Emory Law School. However, Jones's golf career outshone his academic one. He won the British Open three times and the U.S. Open four times. He built Augusta National after he retired in 1930. Soon after, he started inviting a few friends—a few masters—for a tournament. By the mid-1930s, the tournament had achieved prominence.

Golf Gods and Goddesses praise the course's design. The 11th, 12th, and 13th holes challenge golfers each year. Golf G & Gs refer to these three holes as *Amen Corner*. Players say "Amen" when they complete the trio.

For many years, the Masters had been considered the toughest ticket to get in sports because most Masters "badges" are held by Augusta families. These badges have been left in wills and divided up in divorce settlements. Scalpers reportedly have received as much as $10,000 for one. An Augusta travel director committed suicide in April 1997, when he couldn't deliver the correct number of tickets to his clients.

When a Goddess talks of the Masters, she also should refer to it as *Augusta* or *Augusta National*. She should ask throughout the week, "Who will wear the green jacket?" The winner always dons one after his victory. She should speak of the tournament's heritage and history. She also should be aware of it.

Secret #71.   Understand "Tiger Mania."

In 1997, Tiger Woods strode through the golf season. He smiled from the covers of magazines. He spoke on numerous newscasts. A famous sportswriter penned a book on him. Tiger was 21.

Why all the attention? Well, he's very young. He's handsome. He's talented. However, he's more than a photogenic athlete who won a few tournaments. He's a genuine prodigy, as gifted as a child at golf as Mozart was at music. His presence changes the sport more each year.

SPORTS GODDESS GOLF PHENOM

Tiger Woods

Nickname: None! When Woods turned 21, he legally changed his name to Tiger (his given name was Eldrick).   *SG fun fact:* At the age of **three,** he appeared on TV on the *Mike Douglas Show* and putted with Bob Hope.

   His golf game: relies on his awesome talent. He plays very aggressively and takes risks with his shots.   *One reason he's a star:* He doesn't just win. He wins big. When he won the Masters, he set a tournament record with an 18 under par 270. His margin of victory—13 strokes—was the widest in modern golf history.   *His impact on the sport:* has been huge. His youth lures young fans. His ethnic background (African-American father, Thai/Chinese mother) diversifies a white sport and attracts an eclectic crowd in his galleries. Finally, he has enriched golf. Literally. Television ratings increased more than 50% for the final rounds of the four majors in 1997. That year, the Associated Press estimated his economic impact on the game at **$653.5 million.** While he had a quieter 1998, with no wins in any major, he was just 22 years old. Golf G & Gs look to him as the future of the sport.

SPORTS GODDESS MOVIE REVIEW

Caddyshack (1980).

Stars: Chevy Chase, Rodney Dangerfield, Bill Murray.   *SG Summary:* Golfers act up on a country club course. Many Golf G & Gs enjoy this movie.   *An SG will not learn about:* professional golf. However, she can pick up some golf talk and have a laugh at the same time.

Inga Hammond's Bonus Secret—

"Watch. Go to a tournament. Play!"

Inga Hammond grew up watching golf, baseball, football, and basketball. A true Sports Goddess, she was the only woman in her sorority at Indiana University who had a subscription to *Sports Illustrated*. After her graduation from IU, she gravitated toward news. She quickly became a top news anchor and reporter in such major markets as Seattle and Minneapolis. She received awards and accolades for her journalistic skills.

In 1995, Inga made a very gutsy decision. She still loved sports. So she moved from a major news anchor position in Seattle to a weekend sports job in Phoenix. She took a 65% pay cut. Her risk reaped many rewards. Within six months, she became the station's sports director and #1 anchor. Within one year, she was hired by CNN/Sports Illustrated as one of the top anchors for the network. Jim Walton, the president of CNN/SI, saw her as "the next star." In her broadcasts, Inga integrates her strong news background with her passion for sports.

Inga has reported from baseball spring training, NCAA regionals, the World Series, and the Masters. She views the Masters as "a religious experience" because of its emphasis on ritual and tradition. (She's the daughter of a Presbyterian minister, so this statement carries credibility.)

Inga emphasizes that to understand golf, an SGIT should realize "it's not just a game, it's a Zenlike experience." In addition, she suggests that to learn the names of golfers, you should watch the first round of a major championship (the Masters, U.S. Open, British Open, or PGA Championship). You usually will see a major player or two struggle and an unknown player having a great day. Also, if "you have the opportunity to go to a professional tournament, don't follow Tiger Woods or Greg Norman—you'll only see the heads of other spectators." Instead, Inga recommends that you "find someone you've never heard of and follow them . . . you'll get an up-close look at the strategy of the game and a greater understanding of its difficulty."

Finally, for you business Goddesses out there, *learn to play the game*. Inga says, "The 'old boys' club makes many a business deal on the golf course—make sure you're there with the movers, shakers, and duffers!"

WOMEN'S GOLF

A Sports Goddess knows:

The four major tournaments are

The Dinah Shore Classic—held in Palm Springs, CA, in March.

The LPGA Championship—held in the United States each year during late spring.

The U.S. Women's Open—held at a different course each year during the summer.

The du Maurier Classic—held at a different course in Canada each year during August.

Secret #72.   Revere *current* female players in the Hall of Fame.

In baseball, basketball, and football, a player must be retired for five years before he can be elected to the Hall of Fame. In hockey, he has to have been away from the game for three years. Almost always, a Goddess will never see a Hall of Famer play after he's been named to the Hall of Fame in those sports. (Guy LaFleur of hockey was a notable exception.) But she can in women's golf. Present golfers can play their way in to the Hall of Fame during their active years. It's not easy. The LPGA has set up a points system for its Hall of Fame. A player is awarded 2 points for a major championship victory, 1 point for a regular tour victory, 1 point for a Vare Trophy (low stroke average), and 1 point for a player-of-the-year award. If they have played for at least 10 years, won at least 1 major title, Vare Trophy or player-of-the-year, and earned 27 "points," they make it into the Hall of Fame. Some very good players can go for years without a victory. (They continue to be considered a top player because they "finish" in the top 2 or 3 or 10.) In men's golf, an active player can also make the Hall of Fame but he must be at least 40 years old. He also needs fewer victories—10 victories in regular tournaments or 2 majors. Ladies' golf doesn't have the age requirement. However, the LPGA Hall of Fame is considered one of the toughest halls to make it into because they require so many victories. (And they recently relaxed the rules.) Only a few active stars make it to the Hall of Fame. And the media make a big deal of these lady Hall of Famers, more so than in men's golf. A Goddess should know one or two of their names and watch for them.

SPORTS GODDESS HALL OF FAME PROFILES

Betsy King

Entered Hall of Fame: in 1995. *SG fun fact:* She has received a humanitarian award for her work with Romanian orphans. *Why she's in the Hall of Fame:* Betsy King joined the tour in 1977. However, she didn't win a tournament for seven years. Once she started, she never stopped. She won two more tournaments that year. By 1995, she had racked up 30 wins in 11 years, including 5 majors.

Nancy Lopez

Entered Hall of Fame: in 1987, at the age of 30. *SG fun fact:* Lopez is married to Ray Knight, a sports broadcaster and a former major league baseball player and manager. At one point, he caddied for her! *Why she's in the Hall of Fame:* She was a child prodigy at golf. She won the New Mexico Women's Amateur Championship at the age of 12. In 1978, her rookie year, she captured nine events, five in a row.

Patty Sheehan

Entered Hall of Fame: in 1993. *SG fun fact:* She's the daughter of the 1956 U.S. Olympic ski coach. She excelled in skiing at a young age but switched to golf when the family moved to Nevada. *One reason she's a Hall of Famer:* She reached the $1 million mark in earnings faster than any other woman at the time. *SG additional fact:* She founded a home for troubled teenage girls in northern California.

Secret #73.   **Praise the Pak woman.**

In 1997, 21-year-old Tiger Woods roared through men's golf with his record-breaking performance at the Masters. In 1998, 20-year-old Se Ri Pak stroked through ladies' golf with back-to-back wins in two majors.

Golf Gods and Goddesses had prepared themselves for Woods. After all, he made the cover of *Golf Digest* at the age of 5. Se Ri Pak surprised Golf G & Gs. She did not start playing golf seriously until the age of 14 in her native South Korea. Only six years later, Pak's golf game grabbed global attention.

SPORTS GODDESS FEMALE PHENOM PROFILE

Se Ri Pak

SG fun facts: Se Ri starred in track-and-field events at a young age. Her father made her run through a local cemetery even at *night* to help her control her emotions. At the end of 1998, she was named the **top female athlete of the year** by the Associated Press over such popular sports stars as figure skater Tara Lipinski and sprinter Marion Jones. **A few reasons she's a star:** In 1998, she won four tournaments, including the LPGA and the U.S. Women's Open. During her victory at the Jamie Farr classic, she shot a 61 on the second round. It was the lowest score for 18 holes in LPGA history! **An SG should look at:** Pak's powerful swing. She drives the ball far. In the early stages of her career, her short game lacked precision. However, her athleticism and stoicism carried her through to victory.

SPORTS GODDESS BOOK REVIEWS

Fore! The Best of Wodehouse on Golf.

Author: P. G. Wodehouse. **SG summary:** series of short stories written by a master of British humor.

Murder on the Links.

Author: John Logue. **SG summary:** murder at the Masters. **SG bonus:** It may not be the best murder mystery ever written. However, an SGIT will learn about the Masters.

The Soul of Golf.

Author: William Hallberg.   *SG summary:* A writer travels around the country and attempts to find the soul within golf and himself.

SENIORS' GOLF

A Sports Goddess knows:

The four major tournaments are

The Tradition—played at the Golf Club at Desert Mountain in Scottsdale, AZ, in the spring.

The PGA Seniors' Championship—played at a different site each year in the spring.

The U.S. Senior Open—played at a different site each year in the summer.

The PGA Sr. Players Championship—played at a different site each year in the summer.

A professional becomes eligible for the senior tour—on his 50th birthday.

A few years ago, many Golf Gods and Goddesses preferred to follow the Senior tour. The players packed more personality into the game. In addition, Golf G & Gs couldn't let go of certain players. Today, fewer Golf G & Gs disparage the regular tour with the emergence of superstars like Tiger Woods. Still, the Senior tour offers two great reasons to know something about it.

Secret #74.   Revere two golden oldies from seniors' golf.

Arnold Palmer. Jack Nicklaus. For many G & Gs, these men defined the game of golf at different times in the 1960s, 1970s, and 1980s. They breathed life into the staidness of the sport with their powerful presence and graceful games.

SPORTS GODDESS GOLDEN OLDIE PROFILES

Jack Nicklaus

Nickname: "Golden Bear."   *SG fun facts:* Nicklaus is a renowned golf course   *designer.*   *Why he was a star:* Many Golf G & Gs consider Nicklaus the best golfer ever. Tiger Woods still has years to match Nicklaus's feats. Nicklaus netted 18 major championships and became an ardent student of the game. In 1986, he captured the Masters at the age of 46, a tournament he first won at 23.   *His playing style:* Nicklaus played a calculating game. He measured risk against opportunity. Sometimes he didn't go for the most aggressive shot and just played it safe.

Arnold Palmer

Nickname: Arnie. His fans in the gallery were known as "Arnie's Army."   *SG fun facts:* Palmer last won a major tournament on the regular tour in 1964. Two decades later, he was still one of the highest-paid athletes because of his endorsements.   *One reason he was a star:* Palmer looked like an athlete. In the 1960s, many golfers did not! He exuded charisma and charm. He also won seven major championships.   *His playing style:* Palmer charged. He played very aggressively, usually going for the tough shot even if it cost him. He specialized in the come-from-behind win.   *What he did for sports:* Palmer teamed with marketing guru Mark McCormack early in his career. The two helped create modern sports marketing through the clever use of endorsements, launching product lines, and broadcasting tournaments. McCormack's firm IMG (International Management Group) became synonymous with sports marketing. McCormack wrote a book—*What They Don't Teach at Harvard Business School*—that businessmen love to quote.

In today's business world, knowing a little bit about golf can go a long way. An SGIT can connect to golf in many different ways. She can watch seasoned Senior golfers like Palmer and Nicklaus or hotshot phenoms like Tiger Woods and Se Ri Pak.

She can learn about the game on television and never pick up a golf club. Or she can play the game and never watch it on television. She can respect tradition and revere *the Masters*. Or she can embrace LPGA events. Young or old. Male or female. Traditional or modern. Golf offers the SGIT a lot of options to follow the game. All she has to do is pick one.

8

A *SPORTS GODDESS TALKS*
EXTREME SPORTS

A Sports Goddess knows:

Major championships include—ESPN's Summer X Games and Winter X Games; NBC's Gravity Games.

The Summer X Games are held in—late June/early July.

The Winter X Games are held in—late January.

The Gravity Games are held in—July.

I'm in children's book publishing, so we sell books to boys and girls, and so it behooves us to know what sports KIDS think about and what they are interested in buying.... Sports knowledge—like all popular culture knowledge—is VERY important.

—female publishing executive

EXTREME SPORTS EMPHASIZE energy and edge. Competitions contain chilling challenges. Individuality inspires many athletic performances.

In the 1990s, extreme athletes have altered urban landscapes and rural areas. Skateboarders screech around venues ranging from New York City's Union Square to skateboarding parks in Huntington Beach, CA. Mountain bikers bomb past hikers on remote trails. These athletes achieve athletic excellence by re-defining and reinterpreting more traditional sports.

Kristina, a Wellesley student in one of my research groups, embraced Extreme sports. "You can get in on the ground floor," she explained. "No one else knows that much about them either!" You may decide that's the best approach for you, too.

Secret #75. Know the difference between "vert" and "street."

If an SGIT spends even a few minutes on Extreme sports, she will hear two terms. Again and again. *Vert* and *street*. *Street* and *vert*. What do they mean? *Vert* is short for "vertical." Vert competitions take place on a *half-pipe*. This metallic structure resembles half of a very big, curved pipe.

Skateboarders, mountain bikers, and in-line skaters perform routines on these half-pipes. In early Extreme sports history, circa 1970, California skateboarders whizzed around empty swimming pools. Or so Extreme legend tells us today. These half-pipes incorporate the feel of those pools. They serve as a surface for the Extreme athlete to demonstrate his or her stuff.

Street refers to a street or a road. You have seen skateboarders and in-line skaters weave by you (and perhaps annoy you) during a drive. Or they have roared past you during a walk.

Of course, in many competitions, a *street* does not resemble a regular road. It has twists and turns and ramps and ruts. However, its origins lie in the city streets where the first feats of these Extreme athletes were performed.

Secret #76. Stun your soulmate, roommate, and workmates. Summarize summer Extreme sports for them.

Don't try to learn all the Extreme sports of both seasons at once; choose one or two. Start with the Summer X Games. In the short history of X sports, they have a little more tradition than the Winter X Games.

Serena Altschul's Bonus Secret—

"Sports participation is an integral part of your ongoing education."

Serena Altschul, a news anchor for MTV, exudes energy and health. A passionate sportswoman, she enjoys participating in a wide range of athletic endeavors. She golfs, sails, plays tennis, hikes, enjoys yoga, practices the Pilates method of exercise, and even bowls. She has tried such Extreme sports as snowboarding and catamaran sailing. She has been photographed on a Hobie Cat sailboat for the cover of Condé Nast's *Women's Sports & Fitness for Women*. She believes that "Sports enable women to function more clearly" and notes that both the "mental and physical pieces" make you feel better all day long. In addition, she finds that participation in a diverse group of sports enables her to provoke interesting conversations.

Serena attended an all-girls high school in New York City. Despite the urban location, she managed to be a jock. She played lacrosse and competitive soccer. She recalls the challenge of learning squash. "I came in not knowing anything about the sport, and through it sharpened my abilities to concentrate and focus." She considers sports then and now as "an integral part of an ongoing education," and equates the outcome of learning about a sport with the "rewards of a good grade. When you're finished, you have made something that you're proud of."

SPORTS GODDESS EXTREME SUMMER SPORTS PROFILES

In-line Skating

Reason for name: the skates that the athletes wear. They have wheels or rollers **in a line.** Do not refer to the skates as Rollerblades. Do not call the competitions "Rollerblade races." An Extreme Goddess always says *in-line skates* and *in-line competitions*!

Competitors: compete on vert and street courses. In-line skaters perform routines on the half-pipe and the street courses. Think figure skating. (Though the athletes probably don't!)

Judges: evaluate these athletes on style, spins, and the difficulty of their **tricks.** Also on how much of the pipe or the course they cover in their performance. As in figure skating, judging can upset both competitors and fans.

One in-line skating trick to watch for: Miller flip. The skater flips backward and spins 360 degrees at roughly the same time.

In competitions: In-line vert and street skating also are referred to as *aggressive in-line.* It sounds more extreme.

Skateboarding

Reason for name: the skateboards that athletes perform on. The skateboard is a valuable piece of athletic equipment. Manufacturing details, board dimensions, and materials matter. Street boards differ from vert boards.

Competitors: compete on vert and street courses. Skateboarders also perform routines on the half-pipe and the street courses. Some competitions have "doubles," which feature skaters flipping and showing off tricks in pairs.

Judges: evaluate the athletes on style, spins, and the difficulty of their tricks. In addition, they rate doubles on how well they complement and contrast with one another.

One skateboarding trick to watch for: goofy. When a skateboarder rides with his right foot forward on the board. When he rides with his left foot forward, he is riding *regular.*

Sky Surfing

Reason for name: One athlete surfs in the sky while his teammate films him with a video camera. Prior to the surfing and shooting, the team has jumped out of a plane. *The surfer* performs a series of flips and tricks.

Judges: rank the teams on difficulty and presentation. (Once again, if you know figure skating, think about it here.) In the X Games, the first set of marks rates the surfer's technical achievements. The second set evaluates the surfer's artistic merits and the cameraman's work.

One sky surfing trick to watch for: layout. When a surfer flips from a vertical to a horizontal body position.

One interesting footnote to the sport: In the 1995 X Games, surfer

Rob Harris and cameraman Joe Jennings won the gold medal. Harris died during the shooting of a commercial several months later. One year later, Jennings competed with a new partner and scattered Harris's ashes during a jump.

Street Luge

Reason for name: It resembles the sport of luging in the Winter Olympics. But in street luge, athletes lie on their backs on a specially designed skateboard and shoot down a street course at speeds of around 100 mph.

   Competitors: are called *pilots*. At first, the casual Goddess may not understand how the athlete pilots the board. However, if he sits up slightly, drags his feet, or moves his hands, he increases resistance. A Goddess will hear a lot of talk of *aerodynamics* and *physics. A Goddess should watch:* whether a pilot moves out at the start of the race or hangs back. Sometimes, if he stays back, he may pick up speed from the *draft* of the competitors ahead.

   A Goddess also should watch for: one pilot passing another on the course. It can get dicey.

Sportclimbing

Reason for name: It would be called rock climbing, except that nature didn't place sheets of rock in the middle of the X Games and fancy gyms in New York and Los Angeles.

   Competitors: are called *sportclimbers* or *climbers. The two major competitions:* are in difficulty and speed. In *difficulty*, climbers race up a face with a series of holds (indents they should touch). They rack up points through a combination of speed, control, number of holds they hit, and if they clip into a *carabiner* (an aluminum ring with snaps) at the highest hold. In *speed*, two competitors race against the clock (not each other) up a wall. Basically, after a qualifying round, the fastest time wins. *A Goddess doesn't want to see this move:* screamer. Sportclimbing technical term for a very bad fall.

Wakeboarding

Reason for name: the specially designed board (basically a snowboard with fins at both ends) that athletes use in competition. They ride in the wakes of powerboats.

Wakeboarders: spin, twist, and fly around during their routines. At the X Games, they submit a list of tricks and must perform them in order. They set the speed of the boat, usually between 18 and 22 mph.

Judges: ride in the boat in front of them.

A Goddess should watch for: surface 360. Boarder stays on the water while turning 360 degrees.

Wakeboarding has one of the better chances: of any summer Extreme sport to become an Olympic sport. Some G & Gs think it resembles snowboarding, already a Winter Olympic medal sport.

Secret #77.   Let winter Extreme Sports chill you.

Competitors shoot down icy mountains on bikes. They surf off ramps, spin around, and settle down in the snow. They speed snowmobiles over icy circuits. Summer Extreme sports seem scary. Winter Extreme sports chill fans.

SPORTS GODDESS EXTREME WINTER SPORTS PROFILE

Snow Mountain Biking

Reason for name: Athletes ride mountain bikes with spiked or thick, knobby tires straight down a course in the snow and ice.

Competitors: compete in **dual downhill** and **dual speed**. A dual downhill course resembles a slalom with bikers weaving in and out of gates and around obstacles. Dual speed involves bikers going down a steep incline (e.g., 45 degrees) side by side at speeds that can reach 90 mph. They compete against each other and the clock.

Watch for: more braking in dual downhill as bikers navigate the course. More braking leads to more crashing.

Skiboarding

Name refers to: two short skis that athletes use in competition. Skis are a combination of traditional skis and snowboards. They have tips on either end, which allows for forward and backward jumping.

Competitors: perform a series of tricks and spins.

A Skiboarding Goddess should watch for: the **yoda**! A yoda occurs when a skiboarder goes to a cross-legged position in the air.

Snowboarding

Reason for name: the specially designed board with built-in bindings that the athlete performs on.

Competitors: compete in **half-pipe (vert), slopestyle, big air,** and **boardercross** (known as Boarder X in the X Games). In **half-pipe**, competitors perform tricks and spins during a planned program. **Slopestyle** appeals to the laid-back snowboarder. The athlete negotiates an obstacle course and shows his stuff during his run. There are usually no compulsory tricks or jumps. Judges evaluate the athlete on tactical abilities. In **big air**, competitors shoot down a long ramp, jump approximately 30 feet in the "big air," then twist, turn, spin, and land. Booming music rocks the athlete and the program. He or she is judged on difficulty, execution, and jumping technique. In **boardercross**, several snowboarders at a time negotiate a snowy obstacle course.

A Goddess should watch for: big air snowboarding competitions at Summer X Games on man-made snow.

Ice Climbing

Name refers to: high (e.g., 60 feet) walls of man-made ice that the athletes scale during competition.

Competitors: compete in **difficulty** and **speed**. Resembles sportclimbing events. Athletes use **ice axes** to help them during their runs.

Secret #78.   Hail the Hawk and a few other Extremists.

Extreme athletes tackle tough terrain. They challenge themselves and others through their physical feats. While their sports and styles seem unorthodox at first glance, a Goddess soon realizes their greatest similarity to other world-class athletes. Extremists seek excellence in every performance.

SPORTS GODDESS EXTREME ATHLETES PROFILE

Katie Brown

Extreme sport: sportclimbing.   *SG fun fact:* A devout Christian, she carries a Bible with her on the sportclimbing circuit.   *One reason she's a star:* In 1996, at the age of 15, she won the gold medal for difficulty in sportclimbing at the Summer X Games.   *Her demeanor:* is very low key. That's unusual for an Extremist.

Tony Hawk

Nicknames: "The Hawk," "MJ" (because he is the Michael Jordan of Extreme sports).   *His sport:* vert and street skateboarding.   *A Goddess should know:* The Hawk is the Man of Extreme sports. In the early years (the 1980s), he etched skateboarding on the sports landscape. *Thrasher* magazine, a bible for Extreme fans, named Hawk the skater of the decade. Today, fans mob him. Media outlets monopolize him. Extreme endorsers seek him out.   *One reason he is a star:* He's won golds in vert solo and doubles at the X Games.   *SG additional note:* He's not a typical Extreme athlete. He's old (past his 30th birthday!). He's married. He's a businessman. He has some mainstream tendencies. However, if you know one Extremer, make it the Hawk.

Shaun Palmer

Extreme sports: He was a world champion snowboarder. Now excels in mountain biking.   *SG fun fact:* Tattoos cover his body. Many depict Cadillacs, his favorite car.   *Why he is a star:* He won snowboarding World Championship four times. Then captured mountain biking slalom World Championship.   *SG additional fact:* Palmer possesses tremendous athletic ability. Extreme G & Gs point to him as an athlete who can be compared with more mainstream stars like Michael Jordan and Troy Aikman.

Michael "Biker" Sherlock

Nickname: Even though his nickname is "Biker," he is best known for street luging.   *Extreme sport:* street luge.   *One reason he is a star:* He has won luging golds in the X Games.   *Watch for:* his blistering passes.

Rat Sult

Nickname and only name known by: Rat.   *Extreme sports:* street luge. Winter mountain bike.   *SG fun fact:* When he was a child, he ran his "big wheel" up on ramps.   *One reason he's a star:* He's a dual Extreme athlete. Has won gold and bronze medals in street luge.   *SG additional fact:* He suffers for his sports. He has dislocated his shoulder 12 times and broken his foot, leg, and wrist.

SPORTS GODDESS POWER TALK:
KNOW YOUR BACON FROM YOUR CHEESE GRATER.

Here's your big chance, SGITs. You not only can become fluent in X sport talk very quickly, **you also may be the first among your friends and colleagues to talk Extreme in your office or on your campus.** You can set the standard!

Bacon	**Extreme definition:** from *street luge.* Refers to a very rough road surface with hazards. A slightly less rough road surface is known as *scrambled eggs.* **If a Sports Goddess says to her boss, "We're facing the bacon here"**—He or she should expect tough times.
Brainless	**Extreme definition:** from *in-line skating.* When the skater flips backward while turning 540 degrees. **If a Sports Goddess says to her boss, "That was brainless"**—She actually is complimenting him or her. But she better let her boss know it!
Cheese grater	**Extreme definition:** from *sportclimbing.* An Extreme athlete falls and then scrapes down the surface. **If a Sports Goddess says to her boss, "I'm pulling a cheese grater"**—She is in trouble and she is hurting.

Suzy Kolber's Bonus Secret—

"Feel a genuine passion for the athletes!"

Suzy Kolber has covered many sports—including pro football, college football, major league baseball, and pro hockey—for ESPN and FOX. She approaches each assignment with insight, intelligence, and her trademark enthusiasm. Yet she becomes most animated and passionate when she reports on her beloved X sports.

Suzy grew up in Pennsylvania. At the age of 10, she was on the front page of her local paper in Philadelphia when she became the first girl in the United States to join an organized football team. She attended the University of Miami, a major sports power. At Miami, she was a bat girl for the baseball team! For several years, she worked behind the scenes in television as a sports producer in Miami. Next she moved to Dallas and hosted a weekly show on the Cowboys. Soon she was tapped to host ESPN2's flagship newscast during the network's start-up phase. Two years later, she was coanchoring the X Games on ESPN. In all of her journalistic endeavors, Suzy conveys the humanity of the athletes in addition to reporting the results of competition.

Suzy's secret for following and understanding Extreme sports is to have a "genuine passion" for the athletes. **Understand and respect their athleticism, drive, and dignity.** She certainly possesses tremendous feeling for the achievements of these men and women. When she reports on Extreme sports, she provides viewers with small, telling details that distinguish the performances. In sport-climbing, she notes the use of every muscle and every joint (even the fingernails) in a run. In in-line skating, she points out the athleticism and acrobatic achievements involved in spins and tricks. She knows and empathizes with these individuals because she participates in such Extreme sports as mountain biking. Her reportorial work in this field has brought her and the sports tremendous respect.

Fakie   **Extreme definition:** from many sports. An Ex-
                     tremist moves backward while maintaining the same
                     stance.
                     **If a Sports Goddess notes that a client is pull-
                     ing a "fakie"**—He or she is retreating.

Wad   **Extreme definition:** from *street luge*. A pilot
                     crashes into a large group of spectators.
                     **If a Sports Goddess says to her boss, "We're
                     looking at a wad"**—She's preparing him or her
                     for a disaster.

An SGIT does not have to be a member of Generation X to
enjoy Extreme sports. She can be in her teens, she can be in her
seventies, or she can be anywhere in between. The energy, excitement, and enthusiasm generated by these sports transcend
generations. An SGIT can select a "mainstream" Extreme sport
to follow, like snowboarding, or a more "extreme" Extreme one,
like sky surfing. And once she picks an "extreme" sport or two,
she will connect not only to cutting-edge athletic competition
but also to contemporary music, fashion, and popular culture.

9

A SPORTS GODDESS TALKS
TENNIS

A Sports Goddess knows:

The best male professionals play on—the Association of Tennis Professionals (ATP) tour.

The best female professionals play on—the Women's Tennis Association (WTA) tour.

The four major tournaments are

Australian. Played at Flinders Park in Melbourne during late January.

French. Played at Roland Garros Stadium in Paris. Starts in late May.

Wimbledon. Played at the All-England Club in Wimbledon. Starts in late June.

U.S. Open. Played at the U.S. National Tennis Center in Flushing Meadow, New York. Starts in late August.

The four majors are—coed! Both men and women play in their draws at the same time.

Each major tournament is played over—a two-week period.

ONCE, SPORTS G & Gs talked of tennis whites, tea services, and manicured courts when they discussed the game. Today, tennis tackles tradition. Monica Seles wore a sheer black tennis dress at the 1998 U.S. Open. Andre Agassi has sported long hair some years and almost no hair in other years. While you can still find a cup of tea at Wimbledon, you also can buy Thai food.

Tennis cycles in popularity in the United States. In the late 1970s and 1980s, U.S. players like Chris Evert and John McEnroe ignited its popularity. Then the game receded a bit from the public consciousness. Today, Pete Sampras, Lindsay Davenport, and upcoming stars Venus and Serena Williams vie for America's attention with athletes from other sports. Each aims to be the best in the game.

Secret #79.   Watch the singles. Skip doubles.

When you follow professional tennis, focus your attention on the singles matches in the tournaments. Skip the doubles and the mixed doubles. No one talks about them. No one really cares about them. In certain major tournaments, you might be shown a few minutes of a doubles match—if a singles match has been rained out.

If *you* play tennis, you may double up with a partner. You can meet more people and build more sports relationships through doubles. You can learn more about teamwork and strategy through doubles. If you attend a professional tournament, you might want to watch a doubles match for tips. However, when you follow tennis in the newspaper or on television, zoom in on the singles.

Jana Novotna epitomizes the sorry status of superb doubles players. For years, she excelled in doubles. With various partners, she won the doubles championships at several majors. She also won a silver medal in doubles and a bronze in singles at the 1996 Olympics. Yet Tennis G & Gs referred to her as a "choker." She couldn't win a "big one," a singles championship at one of the four major tournaments. Nothing else really matters.

In 1993, Novotna came close at Wimbledon. However, she blew a third-set lead to Steffi Graf. During the awards presentation, she sobbed on the shoulder of the Duchess of Kent. For years, everyone recalled her tears. However, in 1998, she re-deemed herself. She finally triumphed on her third time in the finals at Wimbledon. She laughed. The Duchess of Kent smiled. Tennis G & Gs proclaimed her a winner.

Secret #80. **Distinguish your deuces from your tiebreakers. Know how to score tennis.**

Tennis names some points: Love. Deuce. Tennis numbers others: 15. 30. It's quite simple. If you understand the system.

A SPORTS GODDESS SCORES TENNIS

Points
_____

Love.   Zero. The start of a game.

5 or 15.   The first point won by a player.

30.   The second point won by a player.

40.   The third point won by a player.

Deuce.   The players are tied at 40. A player must win **two** points more than her opponent to win a game.

Advantage.   The point after a deuce. If the server wins the point, it's *advantage in*. If her opponent wins the point, it's *advantage out*. At a tournament, it will be announced as the advantage of the player who won the point. For example, a Goddess will hear "advantage Hingis" or "advantage Sampras."

Win.   If the individual with the advantage wins the next point, she wins the game. If the other player captures the point, the game returns to deuce. A player must win a game by two points.

SG TIP.   Sometimes, a Goddess will hear a statement like "Hingis won the game at love." This means her opponent did not score any points during the game.

Games/Matches

Set.   Whoever wins **six games first,** wins the set. Of course, there are exceptions. If the score in games is 5–5, then the winner must win **two games more** than her opponent. (Thus, she needs to win 7–5 or 8–6 or 9–7 . . .) In professional tennis, when the score reaches 6–6, a tiebreaker ensues. The first player to reach **seven points** wins the tiebreaker and the set. If the points are tied at 6–6, then a player must win by two points (e.g., 8–6 . . .)

Match.   In professional tennis, a player must claim two out of three sets to win the match. In the four major tournaments, the men (and only the men) must win three out of five.

SG TIP.   When a tennis Goddess wins a match, the announcer says, "Game, set, match" and the name of the player. (For example, "game, set, match, Ms. Hingis.")

Secret #81.   Know the different playing surfaces of the four majors.

Tennis Gods and Goddesses elaborate on the different playing surfaces of the majors. An SGIT will hear about the hot red clay of Roland Garros (French Open) or the burned-out grass of Wimbledon.

Balls react differently on each surface. Athletes must move differently on each surface. Certain athletes play beautifully on clay but stumble on grass. Others slam around hard courts with ease but are stymied on clay. If a Sports Goddess familiarizes herself with the surfaces of the four majors, she will understand the sport of tennis better.

Tournament	Court Surface	What It Means
Australian	Hard court. Rebound Ace. (Has rubber in it.)	Medium-fast surface. Ball bounces evenly. On hot days, rubber can stick to players' shoes.
French	Clay (it's very red!)	Ball moves slower. Points go on much longer. Players need to "slide" on the clay.
Wimbledon	Grass	Very fast. Ball bounces erratically.
U.S. Open	Hard court. Deco Turf (acrylic cement).	Fast surface. Ball bounces evenly. In New York, players complain about noise and crowds.

SG EXTRA CREDIT   Sometimes an SGIT will hear about synthetic surfaces or "carpets." These can be found in indoor facilities and are rolled out like carpets. The WTA Championship at New York City in November is played on the carpet at Madison Square Garden.

Secret #82. **Know which stars shine on the different surfaces.**

Grass court Gods. Clay court specialists. All-around players. A Tennis Goddess uses these terms to describe the stars of the tennis circuits. An SGIT should learn the names of a few tennis stars, their surface specialties, and one or two other facts.

Sally Jenkins's Bonus Secret—

"Tennis is played in a square. It's about geometry."

If any woman ever writes the great American sports novel, it may well be Sally Jenkins. The daughter of former *Sports Illustrated* writer Dan Jenkins, Sally graduated from Stanford University with a degree in English. After graduation, she migrated to the *Washington Post* and then to *Sports Illustrated* as a senior writer. She covered such sports as college football, golf, and, most notably, tennis. However, her reportorial work in tennis mined stories far deeper than the world of teenagers in whites winning weekly tournaments. In one acclaimed cover story, she revealed Mary Pierce's history of emotional abuse by her father.

She now surveys the world of sports for Condé Nast *Women's Sports & Fitness.* Her articles range from a series of succinct, substantial summaries of the top female athletes of the year to probing profiles of such popular tennis stars as Martina Hingis and Venus Williams. She has written several highly acclaimed sports books, including one on football and women and two with Tennessee women's basketball coach Pat Summitt.

Sally says, "As with any sport, women have been reared with the notion that they don't understand tennis as well as men. They should realize, 'I'm perfectly capable of understanding this. It's not genetic.' "

She offers this insight into the sport: "The game is played in a square. It's about geometry. It's about hitting the ball where the opponent isn't. There are four or five basic strokes. There are four corners to the court. It's about the application of math." As for the women's game, "You can't tell a champion by her body. Lindsay Davenport, the 1998 U.S. Open Champion, was always treated as the Big Girl. She's 6 feet, 3 inches tall and 175 pounds. Aranxta Sanchez Vicario, who wrenched the #1 ranking from Steffi Graf, is short and squat."

Finally, Sally notes that tennis has earned the reputation of being "complicated, elite, and hard," and it has never truly gone public. Yet it can be played on an inner-city court with no equipment other than the racket and balls.

SPORTS GODDESS TENNIS GODDESSES PROFILE

Lindsay Davenport

Surface specialty: hard courts.   *Native of:* United States.   *SG fun fact:* Her father was on the U.S. Olympic volleyball team.   *One reason she is a star:* She won the Olympic gold medal in 1996 and the U.S. Open in 1998.

Steffi Graf

Nickname: "Fraulein Forehand."   *Surface specialty:* Graf is known as an all-around player. She has won all four Grand Slam tournaments several times. In fact, in 1988, she won a Grand Slam by winning all four majors in one year.   *Native of:* Germany.   *SG fun fact:* She has modeled for *Vogue* and for the swimsuit issue of *Sports Illustrated*.   *A few reasons Graf is a star:* Through 1998, Steffi Graf had won 21 majors. At one point, she spent 186 consecutive weeks in the #1 ranking.   *A Tennis Goddess should look at:* her forehand.   *SG additional note:* Graf has played through tremendous adversity. She has suffered a series of injuries. Her father served time in prison for income tax evasion. She has battled back from everything.

Martina Hingis

Nickname: "Swiss Miss."   *Surface specialty:* Through 1998, Hingis had mastered everything but clay.   *Native of:* Czech Republic. Moved to Switzerland as a child.   *SG fun fact:* Hingis's mother, a tennis fan, named her daughter after fellow countrywoman Martina Navratilova.   *One reason she's a star:* At the age of 16, she was the youngest player to win three Grand Slams in one year.   *A Tennis Goddess should know:* Hingis possesses power! She serves, she returns, and she hits powerfully from both sides.

Jana Novotna

Surface Specialty: grass! Jana plays a serve-and-volley game well suited to the Wimbledon courts.   *Native of:* Czech Republic.   *SG fun fact:* After she won Wimbledon in 1998, she had tea with the president of the Czech Republic in his castle.   *One reason she's a star:* She won Wimbledon on her third visit to the finals.   *A Tennis Goddess should note:* Jana serves and usually runs up to the net to put away her opponent's shots. She stands out among the women for this style of play.

Aranxta Sanchez Vicario

Surface Specialty: Sanchez Vicario is renowned for her clay court capabilities. At the age of 17, she beat Steffi Graf in her prime to win the French Open. She knows how to slide on the clay and when to return the ball with style.   *Native of:* Spain.   *SG fun fact:* Aranxta comes from a tennis dynasty. Her brothers Javier and Emilio have played on the men's tour.   *One reason she's a star:* Through 1998, she has won the French Open three times and the U.S. Open once.

Monica Seles

Surface specialty: Seles wins on everything except grass!   *Native of:* Yugoslavia. She's now a naturalized U.S. citizen.   *SG fun fact:* In her early playing years, Seles changed her hair color many times. She began life as a brunette, switched in her early career to blond, changed to black, then moved on to brown.   *One reason Seles is a star:* In 1993, at the age of 19, she had already won 8 majors. She was stabbed in the back by a crazed Steffi Graf fan. She took time off from tennis after the incident. Though she won the Australian Open in 1996, she still struggles to regain her form.   *A Tennis Goddess should watch:* Seles hitting the ball very, very hard. She also is known for her grunts, which at times distract her opponents.

SPORTS GODDESS TENNIS GODS PROFILE

Andre Agassi

Surface Specialty: grass and hard courts.   *Native of:* United States.   *SG fun facts:* His father boxed for Iran in the 1948 and 1952 Olympics. When Agassi won a gold medal in singles at the 1996 Olympics, he embraced his father immediately after the victory. He was married to Brooke Shields.   *One reason he's a star:* He's won the Australian Open, Wimbledon, and the U.S. Open.   *A Tennis Goddess should note:* Agassi returns his opponent's serves very well.

Yevgeny Kafelnikov

Surface specialty: clay.   *Native of:* Russia.   *SG fun fact:* After he won the French Open, he quickly returned to Russia for a meal cooked by his mother, Valentina, a former top-ranked junior player.   *One reason he's a star:* He won the French Open in 1996 and the Australian Open in 1999.   *SG additional note:* He plays a lot of singles and doubles. Could achieve more slams on all surfaces in the future.

Richard Krajicek

Surface specialty: grass.   *Native of:* Netherlands. Of Czech descent.   *SG fun fact:* Daphne Deckers, the mother of his child, is a Dutch model and actress. She appeared in the James Bond film *Tomorrow Never Dies*. At the 1996 Wimbledon, the British tabloid press focused on her many facial contortions during his matches.   *One reason he's a star:* He won Wimbledon in 1996.   *A Tennis Goddess should look at:* Krajicek's height (6'5") because it gives him an edge when serving.

Patrick Rafter

Nickname: Chick Magnet (named by fellow tennis players).   *Surface specialty:* hard courts.   *Native of:* Australia. Now lives in Bermuda.   *SG fun facts: People* magazine named him one of the ten sexiest men in sports. Once, at the Australian Open, several young women held up a banner that said "Rafter is sex!"   *One reason he's a star:* He won back-to-back U.S. Opens.   *A Tennis Goddess should look at:* his serves. He can place his first serve anywhere. Tennis Gods consider his second serve one of the best in the game.

Pete Sampras

Surface Specialty: grass and hard courts. Through 1998, Pete had not yet mastered clay and never had been victorious at the French Open.   *Native of:* United States.   *SG fun fact:* He has dated actress Kimberly Williams, the star of *Father of the Bride*. One year at Wimbledon, he blew kisses in her direction and patted his heart.   *One reason he's a star:* Through 1998, he had won 11 majors.   *A Tennis Goddess should note:* Sampras serves superbly. When he is "on," his serve can be impossible to return.

Secret #83.   Understand the seeding system. Know about "wild cards."

Tournament officials assign *seeds* or rankings to the top 16 players. The best player is seeded #1. The second best player is seeded #2. And so on.

The seeds serve several purposes. They alert the Sports Goddess to the best players. If a player is seeded #4, the Sports Goddess knows that he or she is considered the fourth most likely player to win the tournament. In addition, seeds structure the draw of players. Seeds do not play other seeds in the first round of major tournaments. Thus, the top players will have easier matches at the beginning. Tournament officials don't want their stars to face each other or to lose in the early rounds!

Now and then, an SGIT will hear about a **wild card** player. Wild card players tend to be stars from a few years ago. They may have taken time off, been injured, retired, or haven't been doing too well. Tournament officials admit them to draw crowds.

Secret #84.   Know that many men's points end very quickly. Know that many women's points go on a very long time.

In men's professional tennis, most players *serve and volley*. This means that when one player serves, he immediately runs up to the net and *volleys* the remaining points. Today, some of the top men's best serves have been clocked faster than **130 mph.** Often, opponents can't hit them back. If they do, the server usually can win the point **at net** with a strong volley. Thus, most men's points consist of a serve, a return, and a volley. That's it. It's powerful. But not very interesting.

Most women play tennis differently. The strongest professional players rarely serve above 100 mph. (Though Tennis Goddess Venus Williams has hit several faster than 120 mph.) While these serves challenge the receiver, most can be returned. In addition, most women do not come up to the net to **volley** and end the point faster. Instead, they stay at the baseline and hit from there. Thus, many women's points can go on for several minutes as they **rally** back and forth. It can be more interesting than men's tennis. It can also become monotonous.

Sports Goddess Power Talk

Ace	**Tennis definition:** A Sports Goddess serves the ball within the boundaries and her opponent can't even touch it with her racket.
Bagel	**Tennis definition:** When a Sports Goddess loses a set 6–0, she has been *bageled*. (A bagel looks like a zero.) **If your boss says, "You were bageled"**—You lost. Badly.
Break or Broken	**Tennis definition:** Players alternate serving the ball into the opponent's side of the court. One player serves one game, the other player serves the next. Good players are expected to win on their serve. If their opponent wins, then the opponent has **broken** their serve and is **up a break**.
Default	**Tennis definition:** A player withdraws from a match either before or during it.
Let	**Tennis definition:** When a player's serve hits the net and then goes into the service court within the boundaries, she takes a **let** or a free serve. **If your boss says, "That's a let"**—Try again.

Lucky Loser   **Tennis definition:** A player loses in the qual-
                         ifying rounds of a tournament but gains admit-
                         tance because of the withdrawal of another
                         player.
                         If your boss says, "You're a lucky loser"—
                         You're going to be playing even though you re-
                         ally shouldn't be!

Tennis has often been portrayed—sometimes fairly, sometimes unfairly—as an elite sport. However, it is a sport that any
SGIT can follow and most can play. There are many public
courts all over the United States. If an SGIT chooses to become
a Tennis Goddess, she has several options. She can pick one
major (e.g., Wimbledon) and track the results through the fort-
night of play. She can watch or know about the final matches
of all four majors. She can keep up with the women's game or
with the men's game or both. Or she can learn more about the
sport's beautiful people like Patrick Rafter or up-and-coming
female star Anna Kournikova!

10

A SPORTS GODDESS TALKS
BOXING

A Sports Goddess knows:

Boxer fight in—weight divisions.

Each weight division—has a champion. Also referred to as the "champ."

Each fight with a champion is called—the *championship* fight or the *title* fight.

The champion's major opponent is known as—the *contender*.

The champion receives—a "title belt." It's really a belt. A big one.

Most sanctioned bouts last—12 rounds for men; 10 for women. If a boxer is knocked down and can't get up, the fight ends. The boxer has either been *knocked out* (*KO'd*) (if he is knocked down and "out") or *technically knocked out* (*TKO'd*) (if the fighter is conscious but can't get up or can't properly defend himself).

Sport summary—Two competitors wearing boxing gloves face off in a square area bounded by ropes, known as a *ring*. Each professional round lasts three minutes for men and two minutes for women. A bell starts and ends each round. During the round, each competitor attempts to land a series of punches above his opponent's waist. A boxer will try to KO or TKO his opponent to end the fight. If he doesn't, at the end of the fight, a group of judges will add up their points for each boxer by round and declare a winner, or a draw (a tie).

A BOXING MATCH consists of two men or, nowadays, two women. They fight with their fists, their feet, their minds, and nothing else. A boxer has no teammates. No equipment besides his gloves. Not much of a uniform. All he or she has is sheer brawn and quick thinking.

Some Sports G & Gs rave about boxing. The sport symbolizes power, beauty, and pure athleticism. Others disdain it. They consider it brutal. Ugly. Violent.

Boxing fascinates many Americans. Some classic movies (e.g., *The Champ, Raging Bull*) have captured the soul of the sport. Some legendary authors (e.g., Ernest Hemingway, Norman Mailer, Joyce Carol Oates) have portrayed its grit and guts. One boxer, Muhammad Ali, has claimed to be the most recognized person on the planet!

Secret #85.   Weigh the different divisions. Then focus on the heavyweights!

Boxers fight boxers their own size. They have no choice. The sport is divided into weight classes. Fighters fight within those divisions. An SGIT will hear of a great middleweight or a superb bantamweight. If she wants, she can follow fighters in each division. But that's only if she's very motivated.

Start watching boxing with the heavyweights. In fact, at first, focus on the Heavyweight Championship fights. They occur a few times each year. They receive tremendous publicity weeks in advance in the sports pages, on sports web sites, and on sports telecasts.

Most of the great, memorable fighters in boxing history—Joe Louis, Muhammad Ali, George Foreman, Mike Tyson—were heavyweights. Heavyweights not only are physically bigger than other boxers, but their fights, their spirits, their stories also seem larger than life.

Today, most heavyweight fighters weigh in between 200 and 250 pounds.

SG EXTRA CREDIT There are three major sanctioning bodies in boxing: the World Boxing Association (WBA), the World Boxing Council (WBC), and the International Boxing Federation (IBF). Sometimes a boxer is champion of all three sanctioning bodies in his weight class. Then he is known as the *undisputed champion* of his weight class.

In boxing, many tough and tragic tales unfold outside the ring. Many boxers escape physically from rough, impoverished backgrounds. Some can't shed the wounds of their early years. Some successful boxers can fight their opponents in the ring but not the demons within themselves. A Boxing Goddess should know two of today's heavyweights.

SPORTS GODDESS BOXING PROFILE

Evander Holyfield

Nickname: "The Real Deal."   *SG fact:* Holyfield preaches Christianity. He has sported biblical sayings on his boxing robe.   *SG additional fact:* Holyfield does not always practice what he preaches. In 1998, he admitted to fathering three children with three different women (including his wife) during the previous year. Holyfield's father abandoned him at a very young age, and he has worked in programs with fatherless children.   *Why he is a star:* He has won heavyweight titles on several different occasions.   *He began his career:* in the cruiserweight class, one rung below the heavyweight division. Boxing G & Gs often debate whether he's a "real" heavyweight.

Mike Tyson

Nickname: "Iron Mike."   *SG history:* Tyson had a tough childhood in the Brownsville section of Brooklyn. He was mugging people by the age of 13. He ended up in a reformatory. A top boxing trainer, Cus d'Amato, saw his boxing potential. He moved Tyson to his home in the Catskills and began training him. D'Amato died in 1985. The next year, Tyson won the WBC heavyweight title. Some boxing experts predicted that he would hold the title for years. However, Tyson couldn't fight his way out of numerous personal problems. He married and divorced the actress Robin Givens, who told Barbara Walters that he was "scary." In 1990, he lost his title when he was knocked out by a pudgy James "Buster" Douglas. In 1992, he was tried, convicted, and sentenced to jail for raping a beauty pageant contestant.

After he finished serving his sentence, he returned to boxing and eventually won the WBC and WBA heavyweight belts. In 1996, he lost the WBA belt to Evander Holyfield, and he had to relinquish the WBC belt for not fighting the major challenger, Lennox Lewis. In 1997, during a rematch with Holyfield, Tyson bit Holyfield on the ear and spit the flesh out on the mat. He was disqualified. The Nevada State Athletic Commission revoked his license to fight. A little over a year later, his license was restored and he was allowed to return to the ring.

In January of 1999, he won his first fight after being relicensed against Francis Botha. One month later, he was back in jail. This time, he was sentenced to prison on two counts of a misdemeanor assault resulting from an altercation with two motorists over a minor car accident.

SPORTS GODDESS MOVIE REVIEWS

The sport of boxing stirs the souls of many filmmakers and writers. The ring abounds in rough, rich stories. Many translate well onto the big screen.

The Champ (1931).

Stars: Wallace Beery, Jackie Cooper. Beery won an Academy Award. *SG summary:* A down-and-out boxer builds relationship with his son. A Sports Goddess will cry. *Remade:* in 1979 with Jon Voight, Ricky Schroder, Faye Dunaway.

Raging Bull (1980).

Stars: Robert De Niro, Cathy Moriarty, Joe Pesci. *SG summary:* It depicts the tough, brutal life of boxer Jake La Motta. De Niro won an Academy Award.

Somebody Up There Likes Me (1956).

Stars: Paul Newman, Pier Angeli.   **SG summary:** It's the true story of Rocky Graziano's rise from New York City streets to prizefighting success.

When We Were Kings (1996).

SG summary: documentary on 1974 championship fight between George Foreman and Muhammad Ali in Zaire (aka "The Rumble in the Jungle"). It won the Academy Award for Best Documentary.   **An SG should note:** social commentaries from George Plimpton, Spike Lee, and Norman Mailer.

Secret #86.   Understand the Ali mystique

A Sports Goddess will hear the phrase "transcended the sport" about certain athletes: Jackie Robinson. Michael Jordan. Muhammad Ali.

Ali's accomplishments and adventures outside boxing often brought him as much fame and notoriety as his feats within the ring. His career coincided with the civil unrest and turbulence of the 1960s and 1970s. At various times, his life collided with his era.

Muhammad Ali, known then as Cassius Clay, first came to athletic prominence when he won a gold medal at the Rome Olympics in 1960. In 1964, he claimed the heavyweight title for the first time after he beat the reigning champion, Sonny Liston. He won the heavyweight World Championship on three separate occasions. He fought Joe Frazier in the early 1970s in three memorable bouts including the legendary "Thrilla in Manila." He won the championship for a third and final time in 1978, defeating Leon Spinks. He retired in 1979. However, he came out to fight the new champion, Larry Holmes, in 1980, and lost to him. In 1981, after one more loss to Trevor Berbick, he left boxing permanently.

Ali impacted America in ways beyond his athletic feats. In 1942, he was born Cassius Clay, the son of a sign painter, in Louisville, Kentucky. In 1964, he converted to the Muslim faith and changed his name to Muhammad Ali. He still hands out pamphlets with Islamic prayers on them. In the 1960s and 1970s, he often spoke in rhyme. The Oxford poet's society invited him to speak. In 1967, because of his religion, he was a conscientious objector to the war in Vietnam and refused to report to his draft board. He was stripped of his title and sentenced to prison for draft evasion. The Supreme Court eventually overturned the sentence. In the 1980s, his speech slurred and his waltz slowed. Illnesses shut down certain abilities. However, his mind remains sharp. When he lit the Olympic torch in Atlanta, he moved the world without words.

SPORTS GODDESS BOOK REVIEWS

The Fight.

Author: Norman Mailer.   **SG summary:** It documents events leading up to the 1974 championship fight between Muhammad Ali and George Foreman in Zaire. Contains plenty of social commentary.

Muhammad Ali & Company.

Author: Tom Hauser.   **SG summary:** Hauser has written many books on and with Ali. He's obsessed. This volume contains a selection of his writings. It helps the SGIT connect with the Ali mystique.

Shadow Box.

Author: George Plimpton.   **SG summary:** During the 1960s and 1970s, Plimpton, a former *Sports Illustrated* writer and social commentator, attempted to play different sports and then wrote about his experiences.

Sparring with Hemingway.

Author: Budd Schulberg.   **SG summary:** Schulberg edited and wrote on boxing for many years. He really did spar with Hemingway! This collection of essays examines boxing from a social perspective.

Secret #87.   Know two women boxers!

First, boxing appeared in benign forms in health clubs. Kick boxing. Aero boxing. Women pounded punching bags. Then a female match showed up on a boxing undercard. (An undercard is the series of fights prior to the "main event" of the evening.) Now women hold their own title matches. They box for their own belts. March with their own entourages. And face the same health issues as their male counterparts.

SPORTS GODDESS PROFILES: FEMALE BOXERS

Jane Couch

Nickname: "The Fleetwood Assassin."   *Native of:* United Kingdom. *Former profession:* factory worker.   *SG fun fact:* She beat a London policewoman in her pro debut. "It was brilliant to flatten one and get paid for it," she told the media.   *Enjoys boxing because:* it took her away from drink and drugs. "I was a slob living off beer, fish and chips, and rock," she told an English newspaper.   *Why she's a star:* She was the first female fighter to receive a boxing license in the United Kingdom.

Christy Martin

Nickname: "The Coal Miner's Daughter."   *Former profession:* schoolteacher.   *SG fun fact:* She became a boxer in the late 1980s when friends dared her to enter a "tough woman" contest. She won.   *Reportedly earned in 1998:* More than $100,000 per fight.   *Why she's a star:* she was undefeated in the 1990s until December 1998, when she lost to an unknown, Sumya Anani.

Secret #88.   Talk "the tale of the tape."

The "tale of the tape" evaluates the two boxers according to measurements. Boxing G & Gs look at it ahead of time to assess the two boxers. Pound for pound. Inch for inch.

Mary Ann Grabavoy's Bonus Street—

"It's a matter of degrees."

In 1992, media outlets everywhere covered Mike Tyson's rape trial. Mary Ann Grabavoy Heaven stood in the center of the coverage. A lawyer, she integrated her legal, sports, and journalistic training in her reports for ABC Sports.

Mary Ann excelled as a gymnast and a student during her youth. She graduated from Notre Dame magna cum laude and from Notre Dame Law School as a White Scholar in law, government, and human rights. She has spent her career as an on-air reporter and a behind-the-scenes producer for NBC Sports, ABC Sports, ABC News, and ESPN.

While Mary Ann has covered every major team sport and many Olympic sports, she has always gravitated toward boxing. In 1993, she broke the story of AIDS in boxing. In an Emmy Award–winning report, she interviewed Ruben Palacio, an HIV-infected fighter, in the slums of Medellin, Colombia. Palacio, a former world champion, was forced to relinquish his crown after he tested positive for HIV.

Mary Ann's secret to understand boxing better: "It's simply a matter of 'degrees'—a law degree, a psychiatry degree, a medical degree, and a divinity degree."

She notes that reporters rarely spend much time on what goes on **inside the ring** because of all the drama on the outside!

When an SGIT reads the tale of the tape, she should focus on two or three stats. Who has more knockouts? Who's heavier? Who's bigger across the chest? A Sports Goddess can get some great information with the tape!

A SPORTS GODDESS'S MODIFIED VERSION OF A TALE OF THE TAPE: 1997 EVANDER HOLYFIELD–MICHAEL MOORER FIGHT

Holyfield		Moorer
33–3	Record	39–1
24	Knockouts	31
34	Age	29
214	Weight	223
6' 2½"	Height	6'2"
77½"	Reach	78"
43"	Chest (normal)	42½"
45"	Chest (expanded)	44"

If a Sports Goddess compared Holyfield and Moorer according to the tale of the tape before this fight, she might have given the edge to Moorer. He was younger, heavier, and had more knockouts and fewer losses. Or she might have favored Holyfield's larger chest and greater height. Holyfield won this fight with a TKO in the eighth round.

SPORTS GODDESS POWER TALK

Decision	**Boxing definition:** When a boxing match lasts 12 rounds without a knockout or a technical knockout, the judges decide the winner.
	If your boss says, "You won by decision"—You didn't knock your opponent out but you escaped with victory.

Below the Belt **Boxing definition:** A punch below the waist is illegal!

If your boss says, "That was below the belt"—You can respond, "I thought it was legal."

Rope-a-dope **Boxing definition:** Ali devised this boxing strategy near the end of his career. A boxer stands against the ropes, covers his face with his hands, and lets his opponent punch away. Ideally, the opponent grows tired and the boxer on the ropes knocks him down. He may look like a dope against the ropes, but in many cases, he wins.

If your boss says, "Use the rope-a-dope"—You're going to look cowardly for a while. However, you may win in the end.

Sweet Science **Boxing definition:** A popular nickname for the sport.

If your boss says, "We're talking the sweet science here"—Be prepared to box.

The sport of boxing evokes powerful feelings in many people. Some worship the sport and see a raw, primal beauty in it. Others disdain it and feel it should be banned. As a Sports Goddess, you can learn about the sport without ever watching a bout. You can rent some of the superb movies with boxing themes or you can read some of the outstanding books or commentaries on the sport. You may end up being fascinated by the sport or repulsed by it. Most likely, you will not feel indifferent about it.

11

A SPORTS GODDESS TALKS
HORSE RACING

I think my most interesting experience was at a work breakfast where I sat at a table of about six men and one woman. The conversation was about some horse race that had happened over the weekend and the men were embarrassed (and said so) that this was all they could talk about, and the women were uncomfortable because they hadn't a clue about what was being discussed. Awkward for everybody!

—female media executive

A Sports Goddess knows:

That there are three very big horse races each year.

The Kentucky Derby. Held on a Saturday in early May at Churchill Downs in Louisville, KY. The track is 1¼ miles long.

The Preakness Stakes. Held on a Saturday in the middle of May at Pimlico in Baltimore, MD. The track is 1³⁄₁₆ miles long.

The Belmont Stakes. Held on a Saturday in June at Belmont Park in Elmont, NY. The track is 1½ miles long.

If a horse wins all three races—he wins *the Triple Crown*.

All the horses in the Triple Crown races are—three years old.

Mint juleps. Big, beautiful hats. Catered parties on manicured lawns. When many Sports Goddesses envision a horse race, they conjure up such scenes. Of course, some more cynical SGs may let their minds wander to other images. Deadbeat dads gambling their wages at the track. Dirty stands. Lots of peanuts.

The neophyte Goddess should stick to the three big horse races each year. You will see every Sports Goddess fantasy: models, actors of the moment, great clothes. And some fine horse racing.

Secret #89. **Drop the name of one of the greatest athletes of the century. *Secretariat*.**

In racing, the horse is the athlete. A jockey may push and prod the horse. A trainer may work him out. However, the horse runs the race.

When *Sports Illustrated* cited its 40 greatest contributors to sports in 1994, they included Secretariat: a horse. But a great one. And a phenomenal athlete. Other horses won more races and earned more money. But no other animal, and few human athletes, sported Secretariat's style.

SPORTS GODDESS PROFILE: HORSE RACING'S SUPERSTAR OF THE PAST

Secretariat

Born: in Virginia, in 1970. *SG fun fact:* When he died in 1989, he received a front-page obituary in the *New York Times*. *SG amazing fact:* His autopsy showed that his heart was more than twice the size of a normal horse's heart. *Why he was a star:* He won the Triple Crown in 1973. Set a track record at the Kentucky Derby. Won by an amazing 31 lengths at the Belmont. *Sired:* more than 300 offspring.

Charlsie Cantey's Bonus Secret—

"The horse is the star—in every way."

Charlsie Cantey cuts a credible figure in the male-dominated world of horse racing. For nearly 20 years, she has served as a sideline reporter on Triple Crown races, first for CBS Sports and now for ABC Sports and ESPN. She asks probing questions, analyzes, and even attempts to pick the winner!

Charlsie's horse sense comes from her extensive experience with the equine world. A native North Carolinian, she showed horses competitively during her youth. After her graduation from George Washington University, she worked for a prominent race horse trainer in New York. She eventually moved into television commentary. In addition, she recently set up her own training stable at the Laurel Park track. Through the 1998 season, she had three dozen winners in three years, including three stakes winners.

Charlsie shares this secret to understanding the world of horse racing better: "The horses are the stars. They are athletes. They share all the similarities with human athletes except for scratching and spitting. They exhibit starlike behavior. They are prone to aches and pains and off days. The trick for the Sports Goddess is to determine the horse's condition on the day of the race. How does he look in the paddock? How does he perform during the warm-up? Is he on his best game today?"

Secret #90.   **Look for the morning line or a handicapper's picks on the Internet or in the newspaper. Know how to pick which horses will win, place, and show.**

A track's handicapper predicts in the **morning line** what odds the betting public will give a horse. The top horses usually receive the best odds.

For the three Triple Crown races, you can see if the morning line is posted on the respective web sites of the tracks: Kentucky Derby (*www.churchilldowns.com*), Preakness Stakes (*www.pimlico.com*), and the Belmont Stakes (*www.nyracing.com*). Or you can surf to the Daily Racing Form (*www.drf.com*) or a sports site (*www.espn.com*), which should list the odds for the race.

A SPORTS GODDESS'S GUIDE TO MORNING LINES AND/OR HANDICAPPER'S PICKS:
1998 Preakness

Post	Horse	Trainer	Jockey	Odds
1	Spartan Cat	R. Dutrow	R. Wilson	30–1
2	Black Cash	P. Byrne	S. Sellers	20–1
•				
•				
•				
11	Real Quiet	B. Baffert	K. Desormeaux	5–2

A Sports Goddess should know that horses do not come in first, second, or third. They *win* (first), they *place* (second), and they *show* (third). When a Goddess makes her selections, she always should pick win, place, and show. So how does a Sports Goddess use a morning line to pick who will win, place, or show?

First, she looks at the odds. For example, she sees odds of 20–1. A Sports Goddess can interpret those odds to mean that for every 20 times the horse runs that race with that field on that day, he will win once. If a Goddess puts down $1 on the winning horse, she will be paid $20.

The lower the odds, the better the horse. The higher the odds, the more money a Sports Goddess makes if the horse wins.

Second, a Sports Goddess should evaluate the **post** position. If a horse races in one of the lower inside posts (i.e., 3, 4, 5, or 6), he is considered to have a very good chance. If he races from one of the high outside posts (i.e., 10 or 11), he has a poorer shot. He actually has to race a few more furlongs. However, in this race, post position didn't matter. Real Quiet (#11) won.

Third, if a Sports Goddess has the opportunity, she should look at the horse before the race. (Remember Charlsie Cantey's Bonus Secret: **The horse is the athlete!**) Does he look in shape? Does he prance proudly into the gate? Or is he expending unnecessary energy by foaming at the mouth or giving his trainers a tough time?

Fourth, a Sports Goddess should know that the morning line may change in the days leading up to the race. In this Preakness Race, the favorite, Coronado's Quest, withdrew (was **scratched**) the day before the race. The odds for some of the horses, such as Real Quiet, changed for the better.

Fifth, many Sports Gods and Goddesses pick a horse by its name. I can't recommend this method on mathematical grounds. Those oddsmakers know a lot. However, as long as a Sports Goddess knows she should look at the horse, his odds, and his post position, she can justify her pick of any horse. ("Well, I like the name Classic Cat, and he's racing from the third post.")

Finally, very savvy Horse Racing Goddesses will drop the name of certain *jockeys* (the individual who rides the horse in the race) and *trainers* (the individual who supervises the horse's racing career). Once again, if an SGIT reads a few paragraphs on an upcoming race or listens to a report or two, she will be told of the association of an outstanding jockey or trainer with a particular horse.

SPORTS GODDESS PROFILE: FEMALE JOCKEY

Julie Krone

SG fun fact: On her wedding day, she rode in six races before the evening ceremony.   *One reason she's a star:* She became the only female jockey to win a Triple Crown race when she rode the longshot Colonial Affair to victory in the 1993 Belmont Stakes.   *SG additional fact:* Julie Krone was considered the top female jockey for many years. However, at the peak of her career, she suffered several falls that left her with 3 plates and 21 screws in her body. **She retired in:** 1999 as the winningest female jockey in racing history.

SPORTS GODDESS BOOK REVIEW

Come to Grief and other Dick Francis Mysteries.

Author: Dick Francis.   **A few more titles:** 10 Lb. Penalty, Flying Finish, Comeback.

Secretariat (The Making of a Champion).

Author: William Nack   **An SG will read about:** the greatest horse of all time.

SPORTS GODDESS POWER TALK: KNOW YOUR STUDS FROM YOUR GELDINGS.

Handily	**Horse Racing Definition:** Racing handily means racing without using a whip. **If your boss says, "You're dealing with that situation handily"**—he or she may mean that you're not beating up your employees.
Handle	**Horse Racing Definition:** The handle is the amount of money bet on a race or a daily card (all the races that day) or in the year. **If your boss says, "That's our handle"**—That's the entire amount you are wagering.
Racing Silks	**Horse Racing Definition:** The silks are the jacket and cap worn by a jockey. **If your boss says, "Nice racing silks"**—You're dressed to compete.

Horse Terms

Gelding	**Horse Racing Definition:** A gelding is a castrated male horse.

Stud   **Horse Racing Definition:** A stud is a male horse used for breeding. The best can sire several hundred foals.

SG TIP. In social and professional situations, never say "gelding" when you mean "stud," and vice versa.

If a Sports Goddess devotes six and a half minutes to horse racing each year, she could watch all three of the Triple Crown races. That's right: all three races for three-year-olds total approximately six and a half minutes of viewing time. It's the shortest live event (with the exception of certain races in track and field) out there. Of course, an SGIT may not want to watch horse racing; she may opt to talk about it instead. She can think THIN and learn the favorite horse in the upcoming race. She can check out the morning line or a handicapper's picks and place her bet in an office pool or party hat. Or she can tune in to the prerace shows, where she will see the beautiful people of the moment, and relate to the sport in this way.

Finally, if a Sports Goddess wants a little more horse racing throughout the year, she should pay attention to the Breeders' Cup in the fall. Since 1984, the Breeders' Cup has been held in November at a different track each year to determine the sport's "major champions." Seven races are held that day in different classes. If a Sports Goddess chooses to watch or read about the Breeders' Cup, she will see how the winners of that year's Triple Crown races perform (if they are entered), and she can learn about the top two-year-olds who will be racing in the Triple Crown races the next year. She also will hear a lot about "the Horse of the Year," a race as hotly contested and debated as the Heisman Trophy in college football. So, Horse Racing Goddesses, think about paying attention to this colorful, competitive autumn event.

12

A SPORTS GODDESS TALKS
AUTO RACING

A Sports Goddess knows:

The two major types of auto racing in the United States are— stock car and Indy car.

The major stock car circuit in the United States is—National Association of Stock Car Auto Racing (NASCAR).

The major Indy car circuit in the United States is—Championship Auto Racing Teams (CART).

Another Indy car circuit is—Indy Racing League (IRL).

Most NASCAR races are held on—oval tracks (drivers make left turns on these tracks).

CART races are held on—a mixture of oval tracks and twisty road courses (drivers usually make right turns on these courses).

IRL races are held on—oval tracks.

The "crown jewel" on the NASCAR circuit is—the Daytona 500 (500 miles). Held at the Daytona International Speedway in Daytona, FL, in February.

The NASCAR season runs from—February to November.

The "crown jewel" on the Indy car circuit was—the Indy 500. It's held on Memorial Day weekend in Indianapolis each year. In 1996, the track's owner, Tony George, set up a rival league, the IRL (Indy Racing League), and used the Indy 500 for this new league. CART set up a rival "crown jewel" race, the U.S. 500, in Brooklyn, MI.

The CART season runs from—March to October.

The IRL season runs from—January to October.

I KNOW MANY Supreme Sports Goddesses who initially have difficulty with auto racing. It seems dirty. Environmentally questionable. Unfathomable.

Then they visit a racetrack. The cars blur by. The engines roar. The gasoline burns. Adrenaline surges. Though it sounds unhealthy, it can be quite appealing. The Daytona Speedway holds 150,000 fans. More than 350,000 Auto Racing Gods and Goddesses flock to the Indy 500. The sport entertains many.

It's very easy to be an Auto Racing SGIT. In February, find out who won the Daytona 500 and by how much. In May, determine the victor of the Indianapolis 500 and by what margin. If the IRL and CART still hold separate championships, determine the winner of the U.S. 500 in July. You're done!

Secret #91. Know the difference between a stock (NASCAR) car and an Indy (CART) car! Know one driver of each type of car.

The NASCAR circuit has Southern roots. The CART circuit has Midwestern roots. NASCAR drivers race for the Winston Cup (the trophy awarded to the driver with the most points at the end of the season). CART drivers compete for the PPG Cup. While these facts differentiate the two circuits, the primary difference is the type of car raced on each circuit.

NASCAR drivers operate stock cars. The wheel structure looks similar to the one on your car. In fact, stock cars resemble sports cars. They're just slimmer, sleeker, speedier, and more souped-up.

In the early days of NASCAR, the drivers drove their cars

to the track. Today, they drive specially designed automobiles at speeds in excess of 200 mph.

CART and IRL drivers race with Indy cars. The wheels are on the outside of the car and they have no fenders. They do not look like your car or any other automobile on a regular road on this planet.

SPORTS GODDESS BOOK REVIEW

Wide Open: Days and Nights on the NASCAR Tour.

Author: Shaun Assael. **SG summary:** Documents one year in the life of three NASCAR drivers. Captures thrills, dangers, and competitive spirit of the sport. Also digs into the personal lives of those in the sport.

SPORTS GODDESS PROFILE: NASCAR DRIVER

Dale Earnhardt

Nickname: "The Intimidator." **SG fun fact:** Many consider him the finest NASCAR driver ever. Yet he never won the Daytona 500 until 1998. The day before the race, he visited with children from the Make-a-Wish Foundation. A little girl in a wheelchair gave him a lucky penny. He taped it to his windshield and won for the first time in 20 tries! **One reason he's a star:** He has won the Winston Cup seven times. In 1997, a panel of 28 NASCAR experts voted Earnhardt the greatest driver of all time. **Earnhardt excels:** in the business arena. In 1994, he assumed ownership of his marketing rights by purchasing Sports Image, Inc. Several years later, he sold Sports Image for $30 million.

SPORTS GODDESS PROFILE: CART DRIVER

Jimmy Vasser

SG fun facts: He collects antique luggage. Has flown with the Navy's Blue Angels. **Also follows:** the NASCAR circuit. **Started racing at:** the age of six in quarter midget cars. **A few reasons he's a star:** He won the

PPG Cup in 1996. Also triumphed in U.S. 500 the same year.   *In his personal life, he drives:* a '57 Thunderbird.

SPORTS GODDESS POWER TALK: KNOW YOUR BLACK FLAG FROM YOUR CHECKERED FLAG.

Pit
Auto racing definition: The pit is where a crew works on a car during a race.
If your boss says, "We're making a pit stop"— You're still in the race. You're expected to emerge from the pit stop in better condition.

Black Flag
Auto Racing Definition: Track officials disqualify you. You must leave the area immediately.
If your boss says, "You have been black-flagged"—View this very negatively. Leave quickly.

Checkered Flag
Auto Racing Definition: When the winner crosses the line, the checkered flag drops.
If your boss says, "You took the checkered flag"—You won.

Red Flag
Auto Racing Definition: A red flag is displayed when a crash or other accident has occurred. Cars must return to their pits.
If your boss says, "The red flag has dropped"— A disaster has happened.

Yellow Flag
Auto racing definition: When poor track conditions prohibit cars from driving at their fastest speeds, a yellow flag is displayed,
If your boss says, "I've dropped the yellow flag"—Hold back.

Lyn St. James's Bonus Secret—

"Auto racing demands 100% from the driver!"

When Lyn Carusso went into business with her husband, she wanted a different name from his for professional reasons. So she changed her name to Lyn St. James because she thought so highly of the actress Susan Saint James. She carried this name with her into another profession, auto racing.

While other high school girls in Ohio cheered the men on in football, Lyn drag-raced against the guys. After graduation, she began racing with a souped-up Pinto. In 1992, she qualified for the Indy 500, the most prestigious race for Indy car drivers. She was only the second female driver in the history of the event. She finished 11th and was named Indy Rookie of the Year. She is a past president of the Women's Sports Foundation and has started her own foundation for young racers, especially women.

Lyn stresses the importance of the Indy 500 in the world of auto racing: "It's our Olympics, our Super Bowl." It is "hallowed territory." She characterizes auto racing as a sport that uses "100% of the driver's capacity in all areas." Mental. Physical. Emotional. In addition, it demands "100% of our mechanical capabilities." It's very technical, yet requires "feeling the car. The driver becomes one with the car. The vehicle is an extension of us." Together, the two form the athlete.

Pole Position

Auto racing definition: The pole is the first, and usually considered the best, position to start the race. Whoever wins the qualifying heats sits in the pole position.

If your boss says, "You're sitting in the pole position"—You're in a better position than your colleagues and competitors at the start of the race.

Auto racing has a loyal and passionate following. As an SGIT, you can dabble in the sport or you can embrace it. You can choose between stock and Indy car racing. Or you can follow both. If you want to, you can even learn about *Formula 1*, the international open-wheel circuit, which holds races around the world. Whether you are enthralled by the speed of the cars, intrigued by the strategy of driving, or simply interested in checking out the point standings of the drivers on their respective tours every few weeks, you will be relating to one of the most popular spectator sports in the country.

13

A *SPORTS GODDESS TALKS*
SOCCER

A Sports Goddess knows:

The World Championship is called—the World Cup. It's held every four years. The United States hosted the women's World Cup in the summer of 1999; the next women's World Cup will be held in 2003. Japan and South Korea will cohost the next men's World Cup in 2002.

The sport is called—football in most countries.

The international ruling body is—Fédération Internationale de Football Association (FIFA).

The international game is divided into—45-minute halves.

The league's name in the United States is—Major League Soccer (MLS).

Major League Soccer is divided into—the Eastern Conference (six teams) and the Western Conference (six teams).

The regular season runs from—March to October.

The championship trophy is called—the MLS Cup.

The number of players on each side—11.

The object of the game is—to get the ball into the opponent's goal.

Game summary—The game is played on a large *field* or *pitch*. The team with more goals at the end of the game wins. In regular international games, if the game is tied at the conclusion of the second half, the game ends in a *draw*. However, if a winner must be determined, then two 15-minute periods of sudden death *overtime* are played. If the game is still tied, then a *tiebreaker* is played. Each team has five penalty kicks (a player goes one-on-one with the goal keeper). At the end of the round of five kicks, the team with more goals wins the game. Or the shootout continues until one team finally scores.

> I worked in an international trade finance group where the sport that was most discussed was soccer/football/World Cup. In these conversations, Americans of both genders were at a big disadvantage.
>
> —female banker

SOCCER BOASTS THE largest number of fans on this planet. Approximately 1.7 billion people watched the 1998 World Cup final. The United Nations has 185 member countries; FIFA, soccer's international ruling body, claims 203 member nations. Most important, more than 200 million men and women are registered to compete in the game throughout the world. Hundreds of thousands more play casually.

An SGIT may choose World Cup soccer as her favorite sport. She can point to the tournament's pageantry, political intrigues, and worldwide popularity as reasons. She can state that U.S. professional sports just can't compare. It makes her sound classy. Smart. Politically savvy. She doesn't have to mention that she also embraces the sport because the World Cup (for both sexes) is awarded only **once** every four years.

Secret #92.   Seek out the striker. Learn how to say "goooooal" when he or she scores!

During the World Cup, U.S. television stations often run a highlight clip featuring Andres Cantor, a Latin American sports announcer. When a player scores, Cantor screams, "Gooooooal," "Gooooooal," "Gooooooal!" He's been on David Letterman. He's published a book in English. He's a soccer icon.

In soccer, the striker often scores the most "gooooals." He or she usually plays in the middle of the field and in front of the goal. The best defensive player on the other team usually *marks* or defends him or her. View the striker as the high scorer in basketball and hockey.

There are several ways to score in international championship competition. A player can kick the ball into the goal during the game and the overtime. Usually that's when Andres screams "gooooal." In addition, if one team commits a serious foul, the other team may be allowed a *free kick* or *penalty kick*. No one stands between the kicker and the keeper. Finally, if the game is tied after the overtime, each team alternates taking penalty kicks. After the five kicks for each team, the team with more goals wins. Or they keep going until one team scores. *Some Sports G & Gs consider soccer's penalty kicks after an overtime among the most tense and thrilling moments in all athletic competitions.*

Secret #93.   Praise Pelé.

Edson Arantes do Nascimento may not be the easiest name to remember in casual conversation. However, **Pelé** is. In the 1950s, 1960s, and 1970s, this Brazilian superstar stormed through the sport. He helped popularize soccer in the United States. He starred in the North American Soccer League (NASL). Pelé is considered by most soccer aficionados to be the finest player ever. He defines the sport for them.

SPORTS GODDESS PROFILE:
SOCCER LEGEND

Pelé

Nickname: Pelé believes it came from his childhood soccer pals. But he doesn't really remember!   *SG fun fact:* His father named him Edson after Thomas Edison.   *SG amazing fact:* The war in Biafra was halted for three days when Pelé played there.   *SG political fact:* From 1994 to 1998, Pelé served as Minister of Sport in Brazil.   *A few reasons he was a star:*

He played on three victorious World Cup teams. No other soccer player has accomplished this feat. He scored 1,281 goals in 1,365 professional appearances.

SPORTS GODDESS POWER TALK: KNOW YOUR RED CARDS FROM YOUR YELLOW CARDS.

Penalties

Yellow Card

Soccer definition: A ref holds up a yellow card to warn a player for unsportsmanlike or dangerous behavior.
If your boss says, "I'm giving you a yellow card"—You are being warned.

Red Card

Soccer definition: A ref holds up a red card to indicate that a player is being thrown out of the game.
If your boss says, "I'm giving you a red card"—You are being fired.

Plays

Banana Kick

Soccer definition: a kick that has a curve trajectory. Usually used to get the ball over or around the defender or goal-keeper.
If your boss says, "That was a banana kick"—You can ask if you scored the goal!

Bicycle Kick

Soccer definition: A player kicks the ball backward and over his own head. Requires a certain amount of acrobatic skill.
If your boss says, "That was a beautiful bicycle kick"—You can say, "I'm trying to show off!"

Diving Header

Soccer definition: A player dives for the ball and it bounces off his head near ground level.
If your boss says, "That was a diving header"—You made a valiant effort to get the job done.

Emilie Deutsch's Bonus Secret—

"Choose your style in soccer: Latin or European!"

During the 1996 presidential campaign, the phrase "soccer mom" represented a special interest group. The Sunday morning TV shows debated the emergence of the "soccer mom" as a voting bloc; op-ed pages pontificated on its meaning. In 1998, Emilie Deutsch, an ABC Sports executive, offered her own wry twist on the term "soccer mom." As the birth of her third child neared, she was deeply involved in the production of soccer's World Cup.

Emilie can understand the political implications and nuances of the World Cup matchups. She graduated from Stanford University with a degree in international relations, after having served as sports editor of the *Stanford Daily*. She briefly worked as an on-air sports anchor in California. However, Emilie gave up on-air glamour for the off-air prestige of working for ABC's Olympic units and, later, for *Wide World of Sports*. During her career at *Wide World of Sports*, she has spanned the globe on numerous productions. Emilie has received six Emmy Awards, including one for a special on athletes and addiction, and another for a four-part series on the first "unsupported" (without supplies being airlifted in) sled-dog expedition across Antarctica.

From 1994 to 1997, Emilie made a significant contribution to women and sports journalism. She developed, produced, and supervised *A Passion to Play*, a landmark series of specials on female athletes, and the first show on network TV devoted to women's sports issues in 20 years. *A Passion to Play* tackled such tough, topical issues as the injuries to female boxers, celebrated the achievements of African-American sports heroines, and explored the world of female athletes in such "adventure" sports as ice climbing and kayaking.

Emilie draws on her experience in the international arena in her suggestions for understanding World Cup soccer better. First, "The language of international soccer is a dialect unto itself. The person in the net trying to keep the opposing team from scoring is never called the goalie, but rather *the goalkeeper* or *keeper* for short. Football isn't played on a field, but on *a pitch*. Oddly enough, in a sport where you can't use your hands, you never hear the word 'kick;' rather it's *strike, touch*, or *dribble*. And finally, if a player's 'caps' are mentioned, it's not an allusion to his hat collection. The number of caps a player has is the number of times he's made an international appearance for his country's team."

Emilie adds, "Two basic styles of play characterize the world game of soccer (though nuances exist on every team): the Latin style and the European style. The first is like flamenco—creative, colorful, flamboyant, individualistic, with an emphasis on dribbling and short passes. The other is like a waltz—disciplined, well-orchestrated, team-oriented.

Finally, pick a Western European team or Latin American team on your pool sheet. "Since the World Cup was born in 1930, only seven teams have won the quadrennial event: Brazil, West Germany, Italy, Uruguay, Argentina, England, and France!"

Whether you seek out the striker on the World Cup championship team or the top scorer on your daughter's team, you will be applying your knowledge of the game to the sport. By learning a few things about soccer, an SGIT can relate to the most-followed sport in the international arena and a highly popular sport among American children. Whether you're building relationships with international clients or a beloved child, a little knowledge of soccer can go a long way.

A SPORTS GODDESS TALKS
SAILING & THE
AMERICA'S CUP

A Sports Goddess knows:

The major international championship for sailing is—the America's Cup.

The America's Cup occurs—every few years. The winner determines the timing of the next championship series. It is almost always within the next five years.

The America's Cup is—a best-of-nine-races series.

The two competitors in the America's Cup series are known as—the defender and the challenger.

America's Cup yachts are—approximately 75 feet long. They usually sport three sails: a *mainsail*, a smaller *jib*, and a *spinnaker* (a balloonlike sail on the front).

Each yacht has—16 crew members plus a *17th man* who is a nonparticipant. Sometimes he is a corporate sponsor.

The "defender" in the America's Cup is—a yacht from the previous winner's country. Sometimes the host country runs a competition series known as *the Citizen's Cup* to determine the new defender.

The "challenger" in the America's Cup is—determined in a series of races prior to the America's Cup known as *the Louis Vuitton Cup*.

America's Cup Summary—It's a best-of-nine-races series. The course changes daily because of the wind. Each yacht must sail a series of *legs: downwind* (with the wind), *reaching* (perpendicular to the wind), and *upwind* or *windward* (into the wind). The fastest yacht wins the race.

TRADITIONALLY, VERY RICH people have sailed and competed in America's Cup races. Ted Turner, the media mogul, first came to prominence when he won the America's Cup in 1977. Alan Bond, an Australian real estate and mining tycoon, carried the Cup home in 1983. Bill Koch, an American oil heir, captured it in 1992. These days, it costs as much as $40 million to build, train, and organize an America's Cup challenger or defender boat. So syndicates are formed with private and corporate sponsorship to mount these challenges.

America's Cup races produce dramatic, easy-to-understand stories for the SGIT. There's industrial espionage (these boats possess state-of-the-art technical equipment), rumors of illegal equipment, and poor sportsmanship. Of course, national pride is at stake. So are the egos of some very wealthy individuals.

Secret #94.   Know that the America's Cup isn't always "America's Cup."

In 1851, the yacht *America* won the Cup in competition against boats from Great Britain. Thus, the cup was named after the boat and not the continent! However, it became America's Cup. For the next 132 years, the United States won it. And won it again. The cup was bolted down in a display at the New York Yacht Club in New York City. Sailing G & Gs thought it would never leave the island of Manhattan.

But it did.

In 1980, Dennis Conner's *Freedom* sailed into glory with its Cup victory. In 1983, Conner's *Liberty* lost his defense of the Cup to an Australian syndicate. Sailing G & Gs were furious. Humiliated. They had to unbolt the Cup from the New York Yacht Club. It traveled to Australia. Four years later, Conner traveled to Freemantle, Australia, and brought the Cup back to San Diego. However, in 1995, New Zealanders carried the Cup home. In February 2000, the United States will try to bring America's Cup back once again.

SPORTS GODDESS PROFILE: AMERICA'S CUP GODDESS

Dawn Riley

SG background: Riley is the first woman to head up an America's Cup syndicate, *America True*, a contender for the America's Cup challenger series in the fall of 1999.   *SG fun fact:* She enlisted NASA to help her with the design of *America True*.   *A few reasons she is a sailing goddess:* In 1989–1990, she sailed on the first all-female team in the nine-month Whitbread Round the World Race. In 1992, she was the only female crew member on *America3*, the winner of the America's Cup. In 1995, she was captain of the first nearly all-female crew in the defender series, the *Mighty Mary*. The *Mighty Mary* mounted a strong challenge but did not make the America's Cup final.

Julie Anderson's Bonus Secret—

"Knowing a little of the language of sailing can help you open up a lot of doors!"

Julie Anderson has woven her many talents through a series of diverse professions during her career. At the age of 10, she appeared in a Broadway show. During her teenage years, she excelled at both skiing and gymnastics. She taught skiing at Sugarbush, the famed Vermont resort, and raced in Chile. She also made the varsity gymnastics team at the University of Vermont.

After graduation, she balanced a high-profile career in sports television with an emerging one in film. She produced *Portraits in Black and White*, an Emmy-winning broadcast for ESPN on racism in sports. She edited a series of interviews with such prominent athletes as Charles Barkley and Jackie Joyner-Kersee concerning their personal encounters with racism. One year later, she received more awards for her HBO documentary on the late Arthur Ashe, the tennis player and civil rights activist. Julie built small, beautiful moments into this film. For example, the poet Maya Angelou read some of her work as a tribute to Ashe. Then Julie worked with Spike Lee on the film *Four Little Girls*, which was nominated for an Academy Award and produced for HBO's sports documentary unit, Real Sports. In 1999, a show which she produced on women and sports was screened at the White House. She is now director of documentaries for HBO.

In 1992, Julie produced features and reports on the America's Cup for ESPN. She advises SGITs "to learn the language of sailing. It can be a snobby sport—but knowing some of the key phrases and terms can open up doors."

SPORTS GODDESS POWER TALK: KNOW YOUR TILLER FROM YOUR RUDDER.

Port
Sailing definition: Port is the left-hand side of the boat.
If your boss says, "Go to the port side"—Move left.

Starboard
Sailing definition: Starboard is the right-hand side of the boat.
If your boss says, "Go starboard"—Move to the right.

Bow
Sailing definition: The bow is the front of the boat.

Stern
Sailing definition: The stern is back of the boat.

Aft
Sailing definition: Aft is at or near the stern.
If your boss says, "Go to the aft of the ship"—Move back.

Helmsman
Sailing definition: The helmsman is the individual who steers or has her hands on the wheel.
If your boss says, "You're the helmsman"—You're in charge.

Jibe
Sailing definition: To jibe is to turn the stern of the boat through the wind.
If your boss says, "Jibe ho!"—You're changing direction.

Tack
Sailing definition: To tack is to turn the bow of the boat through the wind.
If your boss says, "Change your tack here"—Change your direction.

Rudder
Sailing definition: The rudder is the blade at the back of the boat that directs its movement.

Tiller
Sailing definition: The tiller is the steering device for the rudder.
If your boss says, "Put your hands on the tiller"—You're steering the project!

You may never sail. You may never even watch a sailing competition or regatta. However, you may well use the language of sailing at some point. Most likely, you already have. Such words and phrases as *helmsman, hand on the tiller*, and *changing tack* can come in handy. As Sports Goddess Julie Anderson notes, knowing and using the language provides an entree into this exclusive sport. And if you do choose to follow the sport, you can enjoy the international, cosmopolitan ambience of the America's Cup with its blend of intense competition and never-ending intrigue.

15

A *SPORTS GODDESS BECOMES A*
SUPREME SPORTS GODDESS

CONGRATULATIONS! IF YOU have made it this far, you are no longer a Sports-Goddess-in-Training. You are a Sports Goddess.

Now the time has arrived. Read a sports magazine. Talk in a chat room. Watch more sports. Play!

Secret #95. **Subscribe to a sports magazine. Or at least read one frequently.**

Secret #1 told you to find out who was on the cover of *Sports Illustrated*. Secret #95 tells you to look inside.

Some sports magazines boast superb stylists and powerful prose. Some don't. Some sports scribes are considered among the finest writers of any genre. Some are not. An SGIT needs to know where to look! The following list includes some of the finest magazine writing around in any genre.

At first, don't try to read the entire magazine. Find articles of interest. Read about a player you have seen compete or a game you saw in highlights on *SportsCenter*. Focus and remember them. Return to that section each week. Then, eventually, add one or two more segments at a time. Soon you'll be reading it cover to cover.

Magazine	Comments	Prominent Writers
Sports Illustrated	The grand dame of the genre.	Everyone on the masthead! Seek out Frank Deford, Rick Reilly, and Gary Smith.
ESPN	Fun, feisty, and filled with information. Combines youthful spirit with tremendous depth of resources.	Tim Kurkijian, Tom Friend.
Condé Nast Women's Sports & Fitness	Geared toward women. Emphasizes participation and pro female sports.	Sally Jenkins, Gabrielle Reece.

SG TIP. At the beginning of each season, *Sports Illustrated* and *ESPN* publish special editions on each sport (e.g., college football preview, pro basketball preview, etc.). A Sports Goddess will use these crucial guides throughout the season.

Secret #96. Practice talking sports in a chat room on a web site.

Thus far, you have received 95 suggestions! You may be nervous about trying them on a boss, a brother, a boyfriend, a co-worker, or even your own child. There are no support groups out there to help women (at least not yet). However, sports web sites offer chat rooms. An SGIT can strut her stuff in them!

Sport	Chat Room	Comments
Any sport	CBS (*www.sportsline.com*) CNN/SI (*www.cnnsi.com*) ESPN (*www.espn.com*) FOX Sports (*www.foxsports.com*)	Four very popular web sites. All offer the chance to "chat" with top sportswriters, anchors, celebrity guests, and fellow fans.

Sport	Chat Room	Comments
Pro baseball	*www.majorleague baseball.com*	When you chat in any league's room you will talk with some die-hard fans of that sport. However, you also will meet neophytes.
Pro basketball	*www.nba.com*	
Pro football	*www.nfl.com*	
Pro hockey	*www.nhl.com*	

Let's say you have just watched the NCAA Championship Game on CBS. You have a few observations. You're unsure about how to phrase them. Zap to *www.sportsline.com*. Create a name for yourself. Write your observations. Read the feedback you receive. Adjust your position accordingly.

Secret #97.   Learn some history. Surf to ESPN's Classic Sports Network web site or cable channel.

Classic Sports Network caters to the SGIT. It airs many of the classic sports matchups from this century in their entirety. Thus, a Sports Goddess can make up for lost time. Now she can watch the last five minutes of NBA play-off games of the past as well as the present. She can see the all-stars introduced at baseball games from the 1970s. She can smile as she watches Edmonton Oilers teams from the 1980s sip from "the Cup." Douglas Warshaw, the executive producer of Classic Sports Network, offers this tip, "Just remember the classic sports paradox: The athletes keep getting bigger, stronger, and faster, but every male sports fan over the age of 25 believes that 'it used to be better.' And they're right!"

No matter what you watch on Classic Sports, you can talk about it. It airs only the classics. CSN appeals to the efficient

SGIT. It picks the good stuff for you. However, you may not get it on your cable system. If you don't, you still can glean highlights and reports of classic events from the web site (*www.classicsports.com*).

Secret #98.   Be savvy. Always sound like a Goddess.

I hope this book has connected you to the sports culture in this country. Perhaps you now understand a piece of jargon, a crucial rule, or the star status of a player. Ideally, you have developed a passion for a player or a team or a sport.

When I advise women on how to talk about sports, I always emphasize the importance of being savvy. **Do talk about what you know. Don't use lingo you don't understand. Do try to respond intelligently to queries about sports.** When in doubt, turn it around to the other person and ask, "What did *you* think of the game?"

No one should be forced to attend or watch a game against their will. No one should be made to talk about it, either. However, you can have fun with sports even if you do nothing more than change the subject or opt out of the game. For women who simply can't relate to an entire game, I often refer to my "BS" (Be Savvy) rule, originally named for Barry Sacks, an energetic sports executive.

Barry once pointed out to a Goddess that if she didn't want to go to a game with a dating interest, she should send someone in her place who would appreciate the opportunity. Someone who also could talk her up. A non-Goddess complains. A Goddess *sacrifices*. Barry says, "A true sports fan will always be moved by sacrifice."

I hope you will want to attend events, watch games, and share sports with others. However, if you don't, then use the BS rule! Don't say, "I can't imagine anything I would less like to do than go to that hockey game." Do say, "Is there someone who would appreciate it more?"

A few more ways to "BS" them:

A Sports Fan says, Come and watch this basketball game.

A Sports Goddess now knows to respond, Call me when there are five minutes left.

A Sports Fan says, Come and watch this hockey game.

A Sports Goddess now knows to respond, Who's in net?

A Sports Fan says, Come and watch this baseball game.

A Sports Goddess now knows to respond, Who's on the mound?

A Sports Fan says, Come and watch this football game.

A Sports Goddess now knows to respond, I'll catch the highlights later!

Secret #99.   Stop talking. Start playing!

I prefer to participate in sports than to discuss college or professional sports. I mostly participate with women from the office, but at times with some of the men. When interviewing people, I always look for athletes, particularly those who have played team sports. I am a woman. I think women who have played team sports adapt well in the workplace, which is still dominated by men.

—female fund manager

Personally, I enjoy participating in sports and don't have much interest in spectator sports. I believe that if one has enough time to watch, then one has time to play. Generally I prefer to associate with doers rather than watchers!

—male executive

Here is the final Sports Goddess Power Talk phrase: *in the zone*. When a Goddess achieves a special state of mind (i.e., "a zone") that allows her to perform at peak ability, she is *in the zone*.

You want to be *in the zone*.

Shelley Smith's Bonus Secret—

"Play!"

Throughout her career as a journalist and an author, Shelley Smith has challenged herself and others with her reportorial work. In 1988, she joined *Sports Illustrated* as a reporter for their Olympic unit. On the morning sprinter Ben Johnson was stripped of his gold medal because he tested positive for steroids, Shelley raced to Kimpo Airport in Seoul and jumped on a Korean Airlines flight with Johnson headed for New York. On the plane, she landed an exclusive interview with him and managed to ask tough yet thoughtful questions in an unusual situation. Over the next few years, Shelley wrote lengthy, expository features for *SI* on such complex individuals as former Colorado football coach Bill McCartney. She also penned short, searing columns on such issues as the present poverty of many former Negro League baseball players.

Today, Shelley reports for ESPN from every major venue in sports. She also continues to unearth powerful, provocative stories. In 1997, she documented the story of several NFL and NBA players who maintain their ties with the inner-city gangs of their youth. She co-authored the controversial book *Just Give Me the Damn Ball* with New York Jets wide receiver Keyshawn Johnson, considered one of the most talked-about sports books of the 1990s. She recently has finished another book, *Games Girls Play*, written with sports psychologist Caroline Silby. In it, the two authors examine the physical and psychological benefits of sports for young and adolescent girls. Since she is the mother of a teenage girl, Shelley relates personally to the topic.

"There weren't many opportunities for me to play sports, except for a little skiing and tennis, when I was growing up," Shelley says, "and frankly, being an athlete wasn't cool back then. Today I see a generation of young adolescent girls, like my own daughter, Dylann, who are deriving the incredible and vast benefits of participating in athletics. My daughter began a new school last fall, triple the size of her previous school. Where I would have been a shy, nervous, and scared-stiff seventh grader, Dylann walked into school that first day

> with a few butterflies, sure, but with tremendous confidence that she
> would adjust to the situation and make new friends. And she did. It
> also helped that she found she knew about a dozen girls through the
> various soccer and basketball teams on which she had been a teammate
> or an opponent. I wish I had her inner strength as a teenager.
> I wish I had played!"

My sister, Joanie, is a Sports Goddess. She doesn't watch much sports. She runs. A lot. She competes in 5K races. She shares her times, her training techniques, and her inspirational insights from her runs with her family, friends, and colleagues. While some would consider running a solitary sport, Joanie builds social, familial, and professional relationships through her participation.

Numerous studies have documented the many positive benefits of exercise. It lowers a woman's chances for heart disease and osteoporosis. It builds self-esteem. It lengthens lives.

The Women's Sports Foundation in East Meadow, NY, promotes the benefits of sports for women of all ages. You can visit its web site at *www.lifetimetv.com/WoSport/*. It points out the many opportunities available for girls and women in sports. Boys are channeled into football, basketball, baseball, or hockey. Girls and women have more options open to them and less societal pressure to play one or two. Donna Lopiano, the executive director of the Women's Sports Foundation, emphasizes the importance of connecting to the right sport and feeling passion for the activity. She says, "There are more than 100 sports out there for women to choose from—try a few and find the right one for you!"

Get in the zone.

Go for it, Goddesses!

AFTERWORD

WHEN I STARTED at ESPN, my daughter was five years old and just becoming aware of sports. For the first time in her life, her father had a job in sports. For the first time, she had a chance to play T-ball, and for the first time, she got to see live sporting events in person.

And now . . . 12 years later . . . Emily has enjoyed a variety of healthy, comfortable, and challenging sports experiences. She's hit a clutch 2–2, bases-loaded double in her otherwise all-boys team's last at bat to score three, she's boxed out in basketball, she's captain on her high school swimming team, and now she's on defense and in goal for field hockey, and she just finished her second crew season. Lots of cheering for the University of Connecticut's women's hoops, the Boston Red Sox at Fenway Park, treasured Whaler memories at The Mall, and, of course, cheering for her brother's ice hockey and Little League teams. (Of course, he's her biggest fan—after her mom and me.)

Wins, losses, joys, disappointments, emotional hugs, late-afternoon practices, early morning training, and always getting better. . . . A sports life that, so far, has been rich and rewarding and, most of all, fun.

I'm proud of Emily and everything she's accomplished in sports and the foundation she has in sports and how it's taught her the real-life meaning of those clichés—digging deep, coming back, putting on the game face, never giving up, 110 percent, and on and on. More important, Emily has a real understanding of how sports has increased the potential for achievement for the rest of her life.

It all sounds so simple, so obvious, and so natural. Why wouldn't she be doing all of these things?

Because it hasn't always been that way.

Because that's just not the way sports treated women, nor the way women viewed sports.

But now the sports world has changed . . . the way things have always changed in America: slowly, steadily, outlasting the opposition, overcoming the odds. The people made it happen. Female pioneers who went places women had never gone. Crusaders who fought on the front lines and behind the scenes. Gifted women athletes who, given the opportunity, performed spectacularly. Visionaries who saw what others couldn't, and helped make women's dreams into realities. And believers who followed and challenged. They were athletes and organizers and coaches and reporters and announcers and trainers and administrators and business managers and agents and promoters. To all of the women and men who have made the world of sports into a place of competition where women excel and enjoy, thanks.

Where do we go from here? With the dizzying technological advancements and the warpspeed with which trends explode and disappear, the future is as elusive as Marion Jones, the sprinter. So there's no time to revel in the present. As sports move into the 21st century, the leaders of tomorrow can't forget the lessons of the past. Some traditions stand above others and must remain a permanent page in the sports women's playbook:

Support your female colleagues. Beyond the public verbal support that comes so easily, today's women need to offer private encouragement and personal engagement in the problems and troubles of the women who will be tomorrow's leaders and zealots. In the 1960s, the baby boomers pledged that they would not ignore the next generation the way they had been ignored by their elders. In the 1990s, that pledge has been lost. That shouldn't happen again.

Find the next battleground for women. The next great challenge. The next most difficult confrontation. It could be a job, an issue, a cause. It might be so obvious on a grand scale or barely visible without scrutiny.

Keep the excitement going. From Babe to Billie Jean to Cynthia Cooper, there have been so many . . . star after star. . . . The star role must go on. If it's women's soccer in 1999, what will it be and who will it be in 2000? In this game, history is for the complacent.

Discover new allies to get out the message of women and sports. To this point in history, the alliances have been strategic master strokes. University athletic directors with sportscentric daughters. An ad agency with the passion for the power of words. Media mavericks with risk-taking fervor. The opportunities for women in sports have come, and will come, through smart alliances. Placing the right bets as we head toward the next century will be more challenging, more critical, and more complex.

And when everybody's got their brains together on all these heavy and stressful issues, hold on to the notion we seem to forget too much of the time—sports are fun!

John A. Walsh
Executive Editor
ESPN

APPENDIX: RESOURCES

MAGAZINES

Condé Nast Women's Sports & Fitness
  ESPN magazine
  Sports Illustrated

Note: Both *ESPN* and *Sports Illustrated* publish preview guides to upcoming sports seasons (e.g., college basketball, professional basketball).

NEWSPAPERS

USA Today's (*www.usatoday.com/sports/sfront.htm*) sports section covers all major national sports. A Sports Goddess should note the score summaries on the upper left-hand side of the front page.

The *New York Times* (*www.nytimes.com/sports*), the *Boston Globe www.bostonglobe.com/sports)* the *Chicago Sun Times* (*www. suntimes.com/sports*), and the *Los Angeles Times* (*www.latimes. com/sports*) all have excellent sports section.

Of course, a Sports Goddess should check the sports section of her own local paper.

TELEVISION

Check local listings. Times may have changed since this writing.

Cable Sports News Broadcast

  CNN airs *Sports Tonight* at 11 P.M. ET Monday through Sunday, 2 A.M. Monday through Sunday, 7:30 P.M. ET Saturday night, and 7 P.M. ET Sunday night.

  ESPN airs *SportsCenter* at 6:30 P.M. ET Monday through Friday, 11 P.M. ET Monday through Sunday, 2 A.M. ET Monday through Sunday, and at various times in the early evening on Saturdays and Sundays, depending on the sports season. It also re-airs the

2 A.M. ET version every hour on the hour from 6 A.M. to noon ET
Monday through Friday.

Fox Sports Net airs *Fox Sports News* on many cable systems
throughout the country. It mixes news programming with games.
It has regionalized its programming on these networks so that a
Sports Goddess can see games of interest. Check the web site
(*www.foxsports.com*) for listings in your area.

Sports News Networks

CNN/Sports Illustrated (CNN/SI) airs sports news 24 hours a
day. It can be found on most satellite dish systems and a relatively
small number of cable systems (most notably, Time Warner in New
York City).

ESPN News airs sports news 24 hours a day. It can be found on
most satellite dish systems and a relatively small number of cable
systems. However, you can see ESPN News updates at halftimes
of games on ESPN2.

Football Studio Shows

Football studio shows air before or after a game. A Sports God-
dess can learn a lot about the sport from these broadcasts. SG note:
The times of the pregame shows change during play-off season.
Once again, check local listings.

CBS's *NFL Today* airs at noon on Sundays. Sports God Jim Nantz
hosts. An SGIT should watch for Bonnie Bernstein's reports.

CNN Sports' *NFL Preview* airs at 10 A.M. ET on Sunday mornings. An SGIT should watch for CNN/Sports Illustrated's Peter
King. He knows a lot of inside stuff.

ESPN's *NFL Countdown* airs at 11 A.M. ET on Sunday mornings.
Sports God Chris Berman hosts the show. An SGIT also should look
for former NFL defensive great Tom Jackson and for reports from
Andrea Kremer.

FOX's *FOX NFL Sunday* airs at noon ET on Sundays. Sports God
James Brown hosts the show and former football great Terry Brad-
shaw volunteers commentary.

WEB SITES

Media
The following sites offer in-depth sports news and links to related sites.

CBS/Sportsline. *www.cbssportsline.com*
CNN/SI. *www.cnnsi.com*
ESPN. *www.espn.com*
FOX Sports. *www.foxsports.com*

Leagues/Additional Information
Horse racing. *www.drf.com* (daily racing form)
MLB. *www.majorleaguebaseball.com*
NASCAR *www.nascar.com*
NBA. *www.nba.com*
NFL. *www.nfl.com*
NHL. *www.nhl.com*
PGA. *www.pga.com*
Women's Sports Foundation. *www.lifetimetv.com/WoSport*

ESPN Sports Century
Find out what you missed over the past 100 years!

ACKNOWLEDGMENTS

FIRST AND FOREMOST, I wish to thank my undergraduate alma mater, Wellesley College, and its Center for Research on Women. For the past two years, I have sought refuge in an office on the top floor of Cheever House, the Center's beautiful home. Special thanks to Dr. Susan McGee Bailey, the Director of the Center, and to Laura Palmer Edwards, the Director of External Relations. I am grateful to my fellow Visiting Research Scholars, in particular the Thursday afternoon regulars, and most notably Dr. Suzanne Moranian, who tested my theories. In addition, thanks to the Wellesley Child Study Center, the University of Michigan, the Wellesley College Class of '01, the men and women alumni of Harvard Business School, and the patrons of the Crimson Grille sports bar who responded to my research surveys. Also, to professors David Upton and Stephen Greyser at the Harvard Business School, who shared insights at crucial times. Finally, I am indebted to my Wellesley "Sports Goddesses" who helped my research and tested each secret: Melissa Gilbert, Sara Grover, Lefty Keans, Rachel Mann, Kristina McBlain, and Morea Maguire.

I never could have written this book if I had not worked at ESPN. For six and a half years, John A. Walsh, the legendary Executive Editor, guided, inspired, and served as a mentor to me. I owe my career in sports and this book to him. At ESPN, I worked most closely on *Outside the Lines* and *Sunday SportsDay* with three of the finest sports reporters and human beings on the planet: Bob Ley, Chris Fowler, and Robin Roberts. Their critical support throughout this book and their friendship mean everything to me. Bob Eaton, Mary Ann Grabavoy, and Jimmy

Roberts encouraged me at the very beginning of this project. Bob Rauscher, Barry Sacks, and Howie Schwab offered suggestions. Jim Cohen, Vince Doria, Heather Faulkiner, Grace Gallo, Mary Jo Kinser, Jeremy Schaap, and Douglas Warshaw answered my many phone calls for help with unfailing humor. Steve Anderson, my former boss, gave me the confidence to write a book at the very beginning of the project, and to continue my career in sports during my time away from the industry. Chris Berman and Charley Steiner were Sports Gods to me at ESPN and during this project. Jeff Greenholtz proofread the final manuscript.

During an Olympic summer in Atlanta, I helped set up CNN/ Sports Illustrated for Jim Walton. Jim deserves his reputation as one of the most respected journalists *and* one of the finest gentlemen in sports television. Many would deem this an impossible feat. Jim makes it look easy. My conversations and interactions with Fred Hickman, Nick Charles, Inga Hammond, Jim Huber, Steve Robinson, and the rest of this kind and talented department enriched my life, my career, and this book. I also thank Robin Shallow of *Sports Illustrated* for her immediate and enthusiastic response to every request.

At CBS Sports, I thank Terry Ewert, Kelly Raferty, and Jim Nantz. At FOX Sports, I am appreciative of the time given to me by Scott "Axe" Ackerson and James "JB" Brown. At NBC Sports, I am grateful to Bob Costas for his insights into my research and for his patience in listening to one more Red Sox fan relive her experience of game 6 of the 1986 World Series. Sara Levinson of the NFL and Dan Shaughnessy of the *Boston Globe* met with me in the early stages of this project. At the Women's Sports Foundation, Donna Lopiano and Marjorie Snyder provided me with research and guidance. At IMG/TWI, I am grateful to my television agent, Irwin Weiner.

I would like to thank my family and friends who helped me throughout this journey, many of whom read portions or all of this book: Rhonda Abrams, Hilary Bernard, Bob Boxwell, Eileen Dowling, Larry Hamdan, Ellen Hartman, Heather Holley, Vicky Jacoby, Kyle Gibson and Mit Spears, Marianne Stack, Seth Ward, Matthew Longo and Margaret Winslow. My Harvard Business

School Section "I"-mates filled out my surveys, tested my suggestions, and shared "real life business/sports" situations with me. Most notably, Jay Mandelbaum allowed me to use his stories about his daughter, Sydney. My brother-in-law Chuck and my sister Patsy, the original Sports God and Goddess, called in their advice. My mother Joan, brother Bill, and sister Joanie lived with me, brought me food, took me out, and supported me throughout the final months of this book.

Once again, I am grateful to all the women and men who contributed "secrets" to this book. Finally, I thank the two people who believed in this book from the beginning: my editor, Sheila Curry, a true Sports Goddess; and my agent, Giles Anderson, a Sports-God-in-Training. They made it happen.

INDEX

Bold page numbers indicate tables.